Mom's Almanac

Edited by
ALICE WONG *and*
LENA TABORI

Designed by
TIMOTHY SHANER *and*
CHRISTOPHER MEASOM

welcome
BOOKS

NEW YORK · SAN FRANCISCO

Contents

Contents

Contents

Foreword

The best advice my pediatrician ever gave me was at my first child's one-month checkup. I remember still being physically battered from a hard delivery, sore from nursing, sleep deprived, and mentally and emotionally overwhelmed. I peppered the doctor with a million questions about my little one's weight and well-being, including sleeping, feeding, and even crying habits. "Just go for survival," she finally said. Seven years and three children later, that simple advice continues to be my touchstone. When life gets hectic and overwhelming, simply paring things down to the basics—the bare essentials—makes everything more manageable.

Of course, life with children is not just "going for survival." Much of the time, it is filled with wonder and laughter. Chi Chi, seven, and Sylvia, five, are so big now. I am so proud of their constant growth and achievements. I love having fun with them, whether it's playing a game of cards or reading a childhood classic at home, or picking strawberries, finding mummies at a museum, or riding on a carousel when we "step out." When you have children, seasons and holidays take on new significance. This past summer was the first one when both kids swam like fish, and so water games were huge. This fall, Sylvia stopped and listed the many colors she saw in the leaves (even pinks and purples), and Chi Chi patiently and persistently counted down to Halloween, months in advance. Now, we are anticipating the first sled ride and, of course, counting down to Christmas!

My youngest, Phoebe, is fifteen months, and she makes us laugh. She is just too cute for words, and both Chi Chi and Sylvia constantly wish that she would just stay a baby—chubby cheeks, baby talk, raspberries, and all. Whereas with my first two children I couldn't wait to see their next stage of growth, with Phoebe I watch every milestone with a bit of sadness. Children do grow so quickly; that's why preserving all those wonderful memories has become very important to me. I capture what I can by video, camera, journal, and mementos, but there is nothing I can do to capture the feel of a one-year-old's hug with her little arms clinging to my neck and her little body soft and melding into mine.

Mom's Almanac IS life with children. It is the bare essentials and information you need—how they grow, what they're ready for, safety, discipline.... It is feeding them and keeping them healthy. It is having fun, exploring the world, and celebrating. It is holding on to and recording precious moments. It is trying to give your children the best of everything. These are the chapters of *Mom's Almanac*. Dip into them. Use them. They will make your life with your children more manageable and fun, and fill it with wonderful memories to treasure.

—Alice Wong

Foreword

My daughters are grown, but I can remember the baby books I bought and the advice I sought as if it were yesterday. I had my children when I was young and felt that nothing I had learned at Sarah Lawrence College prepared me for what I needed to know. Now, there is this book—this adorable, knowledgeable book that my partner Alice is primarily responsible for; this book that loves and respects both children and their parents. The perfect mix of resources, recipes, crafts, activities, practical tips, and information, *Mom's Almanac* is the wise and loving friend I missed when Natasha and Katrina were little. In this book is the friend you can turn to for parenting advice on every subject from potty training to party games. Best of all, she is always available.

Brimming with commonsense health and nutrition information, she knows what safety tips to follow, what to keep in the diaper bag, and the foods basic to every family's pantry and refrigerator. Most important, she knows how to make healthy eating fun, so the little ones learn to love what is good for them. She is a chef and a wizard in the kitchen, whipping up good food almost as quick as you can order bad fast food. This friend knows how much sleep kids need and how to help them drift off. She has tips on discipline, advice about tantrums, and guidelines for dealing with allergies. She is not stymied by potty training or a messy room; she can organize all those toys, and she is a wizard on the subject of stain removal. She's a biologist who knows everything about bugs and butterflies; and a camper who can make tepees in the backyard and treat insect bites. She knows how rainbows are formed and how penguins stay warm. She is an information guru who keeps tabs on the best of everything: books, audios, magazines, music, games, soundtracks, movies, toys, crafts, board games, software and reference books, and even websites.

Mom's Almanac is more than a mom's best friend. Between its covers you'll find that cool older brother with bagloads of magic tricks, along with a great dad who has your kids' favorite car games and knock-knock jokes down cold. There's even a loving grandmother who helps little ones understand traditions and holidays, keeps a well-stocked dress-up chest (and, of course, decorates Easter eggs). This grandmother knows all the fairy tales, and (if you don't have your copy of *The Little Big Book for Moms*) she even tells you a few.

I hope this heavenly book makes your life just a little easier. I hope you trust it and I hope it fulfills your every expectation. Write us with your thoughts and suggestions. We are good listeners.

—Lena Tabori

chapter one

The Bare Essentials

Taking Care of Mom

The kitchen is a mess. Your boss keeps calling. The baby needs to be fed.... At no time in history have moms been expected to do so much with so little help. Until the late 1930s, most new mothers automatically depended on their relatives to take on household responsibilities. When there weren't relatives around, there were neighbors who were happy to pitch in. Most cultures around the world recognize that new mothers need to be taken care of just as much as their babies do. Don't feel guilty about taking care of yourself—it's the best thing you can do for your baby. The better you're cared for, the better you can care for others. Go easy on yourself. Don't worry about making mistakes. You're probably doing things better than you realize. What's important is that you're doing the best that you can. If, at the end of the day, you feel like you've gotten nothing done, remember that you're doing the most important job in the world—mothering your child.

- **SLEEP** When your baby naps, nap along with him. You need to catch up on the sleep you've been losing at night. If your children are older, you should be getting seven or eight hours of sleep.

- **STAY WELL-HYDRATED** If you're breastfeeding, drink at least eight to twelve glasses of water a day—otherwise six to eight glasses will do. Avoid drinks high in sugar and caffeine. They can get into your breast milk and potentially irritate your baby. Try to also avoid alcohol though having an occasional glass of wine or beer is okay.

- **EAT NUTRITIOUSLY** Choose your food wisely, especially if you are breastfeeding. Eat whole grains and cereals, fresh fruits and vegetables, and foods that provide plenty of protein, calcium, and iron. Check with your doctor or nutritionist to see if he recommends taking a vitamin or mineral supplement—but don't substitute supplements for nutritious food!

- **SAY "YES" TO HELP** Let your mother or mother-in-law stay with you for a week to help out. Let a neighbor pick up groceries. Let your friend cook dinner for you. Have your husband help out with chores and the children—and try not to be critical of him. If you're a single parent, team up with another parent and help each other out with cleaning, cooking, and childcare. If you can afford it, hire a baby nurse, or a college or high school student to help out around the house. Get together a roster of trustworthy babysitters before you actually need them.

- **SET LIMITS** Evaluate the number of activities and playdates your children have, and the running around you have to do. The more you're able to set limits, the easier your life can be.

- **DEPEND ON DAD** Let your husband or partner know specifically how he can help with chores or childcare tasks. Suggest that he be responsible for one of the baby's nighttime feedings or weekday morning breakfast and playground outings with older kids. If your baby is crying, let Daddy pick her up. If she continues to cry, hold off on coming to the rescue. Let her get used to Daddy and let Daddy figure out his own way to soothe his child.

- **GET MODERATE EXERCISE** Take brisk, twenty-minute walks with your baby or take an exercise class while Dad is watching the kids on the weekend.

- **PAMPER YOURSELF** Have someone take care of your children while you get a manicure, curl up with a good book, get a massage, soak in the tub, or get a haircut. The challenge: Resist the temptation to feel guilty.

- **SPEND TIME WITH FAMILY AND FRIENDS** Being a new mom or at-home mom can feel isolating, which is why it's important to stay connected to people who are close to you.

- **DON'T STRIVE FOR PERFECTION** The dirty dishes can wait. Try to let go of your idea of how things should be. Don't expect them to be the way they used to be. ***You're a mom now, and there's no turning back!***

Age by Age

Developments and Accomplishments

When you have children, you're in for the ride of your life. From booties to Little League uniforms to prom dresses, children grow at an incredible rate. Though each child is a unique individual, they usually go through predictable, universal growth patterns. At two he'll explore, at four she'll be afraid of the dark, at six he'll have mood swings, at eight she'll need lots of compliments. . . the list goes on.

As children go from phase to phase, you'll go right along with them, changing diapers, coaching soccer, chaperoning field trips, carpooling to karate, helping with homework, consoling tears, or feeding all the kids in the neighborhood. Just as you get used to one phase, another birthday comes up and your child will surprise you again. While you're scrambling to keep up with the ups and downs, curves and turns of childhood, remember that nothing lasts forever. Sit back and enjoy the rollercoaster of life. The adventure of childhood doesn't last forever.

BIRTH–3 MONTHS Newborns coo, kick, eat, sleep, cry, gurgle, burp, flap their arms, sleep more, and eat again, still too young for a schedule. They focus on faces and brightly colored objects and respond to sounds. Placing an infant on a safe, hard surface will make it easy to lift his head or roll when he's ready.

4–6 MONTHS Now he sits propped up, rolls over, holds his head up, grasps objects without using his thumb, looks for dropped toys, bears weight on his arms, and recognizes Mommy's voice. No wonder he laughs and babbles so much!

7–9 MONTHS "Mama." "Dada." Yes, that's an eight-month-old talking. Now she understands the word no, waves bye-bye, rolls a ball, drinks from a cup, picks up food, and passes an

object from one hand to another. This is the perfect time to play Pat-a-Cake and Peekaboo.

10–12 MONTHS When asked, "Where's Mommy?" this baby looks for her. He also responds to gestures and changes in tone, remembers simple events, identifies body parts, recognizes voices, explores, creeps, finds hidden objects, puts objects in containers, turns board book pages, and puts everything in his mouth. Listen closely—he will start to imitate words.

Up, Up the stairs

Nine months is a good time to teach your toddler to climb up and down stairs. Just to be safe, block the stairs with a gate when you're through with the lesson!

1 YEAR OLD When she's not busy walking, running, climbing, riding, kicking balls, or playing with push-pull toys, a one-year-old loves a good story. She knows her name, understands simple directions, develops friendships with familiar people, solves small problems, understands the passing of time, and can concentrate for five to ten minutes on block towers, scribbling, or simple shape or sorting puzzles. She loves to imitate you, and may say two-word sentences like "More juice!"

2 YEARS OLD Don't let him out of your sight! A two-year-old is always on the go—walking on the balance beam, bouncing on toys, climbing, bumping his head, pulling a wagon, or dashing out the door. He's becoming more independent, learning new words, gaining control of his hands, and

When to Seek Help

Some children develop faster and some slower than others. Usually there's nothing to worry about, but if your child seems to be lagging way behind other kids his age, seek professional help.

constantly asking "Why?" Sometimes he gets frustrated. Other times he has fun coloring, reciting nursery rhymes, doing puzzles, playing toy instruments, dancing, and pretending. By now he has some favorite picture books that he likes to hear over and over again. This toddler is proud of his achievements.

3 YEARS OLD With her love of learning and increasing attention span, she might be ready for preschool. It's a good time to show her how to be safe around water, fire, traffic, tools, and kitchen equipment.

She loves to be silly, tell others what to do, talk about things that happened, make up stories, make pillow forts, hear true stories, socialize, blow bubbles in the bath, choose her outfits, and draw simple shapes. Don't be surprised if she blurts out something you said in private.

4 YEARS OLD Get ready for a lot of bragging, grinning, wrestling, reading, doing jigsaw puzzles, and making up stories. Now he understands that pictures, numbers, words, and letters are symbols of real things. Ask him to draw his family, and you'll probably recognize yourself. Four-year-olds love to role play, dressing up as firemen, royalty, farmers, and more. How the world works is of major interest to him, and it's a great time to teach him a new word every day.

5 YEARS OLD Showing off is her specialty—"Look how far I can jump!" "Watch how fast I run!" "Look how fast I ride without train-

Baby's Firsts

With a new baby, it seems that every day is a first— the first laugh, the first full night's sleep, the first favorite toy. As your baby grows into a toddler, she'll be walking, talking, having play dates, or maybe even starting preschool. Here we have gathered some of the highlights to expect in the first months ahead. Keep in mind that the age ranges listed below are averages.

Smiles: 2 mos.
Holds head up: 3–4 mos.
Rolls over: 4–6 mos.
Sits up: 5–6 mos.
Eats solid food: 5–8 mos.
Grows teeth: 6–7 mos.
Crawls: 7–9 mos.
Stands: 7–9 mos.
Talks: 8–21 mos.
Cruises: 9–12 mos.
Remembers recent events: 9–12 mos.
Waves bye-bye: 9–12 mos.
Stacks blocks: 9–15 mos.
Walks: 9–18 mos.
Climbs up stairs: 12–15 mos.
Feeds self: 12–15 mos.
Rides on adult's shoulders: 12–15 mos.
Identifies pictures in books: 15–18 mos.
Rides four-wheeled toys: 15–18 mos.
Tries to climb out of crib: 15–18 mos.
Makes simple sentences: 15–24 mos.
Sorts shapes: 15–24 mos.
Understands language: 15–24 mos.
Makes friends: 16–24 mos.
Hums and sings: 18–24 mos.
Makes line drawings: 18–24 mos.
Does simple puzzles: 18–24 mos.
Does somersault: 18–24 mos.
Pedals first tricycle: 18–24 mos.
Pushes and pulls toys: 18–24 mos.
Runs: 18–24 mos.
Throws ball overhand: 18–24 mos.
Walks up stairs: 18–24 mos.

ing wheels!" "See how high I can climb!" She knows her name, address, phone number, and your office number. She listens to stories on tape and loves books. Whether she's playing card games or board games, she wants to be the best. She now has the ability to judge what she can and cannot do, and wants to do everything just right. This is a positive age, and she feels very secure with her family.

6 YEARS OLD This is the year of contradictions. A six-year-old goes from outgoing to shy, sweet to angry, or happy to sad, all in a day. Unsure of who he is and how he fits in the world, he's often indecisive and has a fragile ego. It's a good time to include him in a family softball game—he's ready to learn the rules and be on a team. This is when boy/girl stereotypes begin to make their appearance.

7 YEARS OLD Seven-year-olds tend to be quiet, serious, and withdrawn. She pulls away from her parents and towards her friends. These are friends she wants to think like, act like, dress like, and talk like. At times she feels like the world is against her, but can often be cheered up by a good knock-knock joke.

8 YEARS OLD "Who am I?" he wonders, trying on new roles every day. Eight-year-olds conform to peers of the same sex and enjoy playing with babies, pets, and dolls. Boys play with man dolls and action figures, while girls play with girl dolls. Girls are interested in nurturing the weak. Boys are interested in protecting them from a distance. Curious about the outside world, eight-year-olds want to find ways to meet its challenges. They need lots of compliments and attention— especially from Mom.

9 YEARS OLD Having a best friend is important to a nine-year-old as she gains self-confidence. Though she often has bursts of emotion and impatience, she tries to give the impression of being calm and controlled. Starting a club is right up her alley, and she's very selective in which activities she chooses to participate. She likes organized play with definite rules, has a great sense of humor, and is up on the latest styles and fads.

10–14 YEARS OLD Pre-teens are growing mentally, physically, emotionally, and morally at their own speed, and don't yet feel comfortable with the changes. By now, most of them focus intensely on activities, whether it's soccer, horseback riding, or computer games. Friendships are extremely important to them. Ten-year-olds enjoy organized activities, show concern and sensitivity to others, need constant reminders regarding routine responsibilities, and still enjoy being with their parents. But by eleven they're more self-centered, argumentative, moody, and sensitive, challenging rules and restrictions. Both sexes are interested in friends, styles, clothing, and the opposite sex. Twelve-year-olds understand they're no longer children and become more secure with themselves. Their group of friends is constantly expanding, and their growing interest in the opposite sex makes them restless and prone to daydreaming. A twelve-year-old either loves something or hates it— there's no such thing as a middle ground. Boys' voices begin to change. By thirteen, most pre-teens want little to do with their parents or other grown-ups. They're often critical, withdrawn, lonely, and unfriendly, and are uncomfortable in their changing bodies. Eating, talking, and listening to music make them happy. Fourteen-year-olds, basking in their new teenage status, begin to enjoy their life away from home— especially extracurricular activities and socializing with their friends.

Obviously we can only offer a quick glimpse into each age here. A series I highly recommend is *Your One-Year-Old* up to *Your Ten- to Fourteen-Year-Old* by Louise Bates Ames and the Gesell Institute of Human Development. These books offer valuable insights and advice for your child at every age. I discovered this series when my children were one, five, and seven years old, and was astonished by the accuracy of much of the text. Just the birthday party schedule and list of activities geared specifically to the abilities and interests of the age group discussed in each book are worth reading.

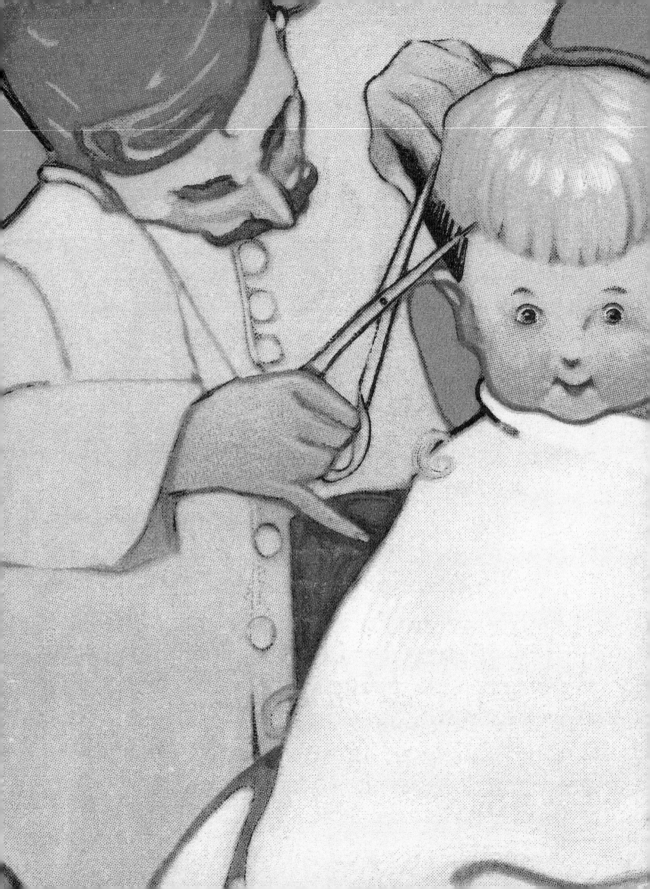

How They Grow

When new parents send out a baby announcement, they make sure to include pounds, ounces, and inches. That's because everyone is curious about the baby's size—and this is only the beginning. From birth to adolescence, a child's weight, height, and rate of growth are annually recorded at the doctor's office to be compared to other children of the same age and sex. Parents are always hoping their child's height and weight are considered "normal." During their first year, babies grow an average of ten inches and triple their weight. After that, their growth slows down. From age two to adolescence, children grow around $2^1/_2$ inches a year at an inconsistent pace. Children can go months without growing much and then experience a growth spurt. Believe it or not, they grow fastest in the spring! The most major growth spurt comes when boys and girls reach puberty—girls between eight and thirteen, boys between ten and fifteen.

The Basics to Growing Up Healthy

- Adequate sleep—need an average of ten to twelve hours a night (*See sleep chart on page 37*)
- Proper nutrition—a balanced diet full of essential vitamins and minerals (*See page 73*)
- Adequate exercise—at least thirty minutes a day

TOOTH TIME At birth, twenty primary teeth are waiting to break through the baby's gums. This can begin as early as six months. Teeth are susceptible to decay or cavities as soon as they appear, so use a soft-bristled infant toothbrush and water to wipe them clean after feedings. Never put a baby to bed with a bottle containing milk, juice, or any sugary liquid—this can cause a dental condition known as baby-bottle tooth decay or bottle rot. Most parents start taking their children to the dentist between the ages of one and two.

Children start to lose baby teeth between ages six and seven,

THE TOOTH FAIRY She has the largest tooth collection in the world, a talent for not setting off burglar alarms, and more fans than Santa Claus! Children know her as the tooth fairy—but she's really a mythic figure represented by you. Your job is this: When your child loses a tooth, have her leave it under her pillow. Then, when you're sure she's sleeping, replace the tooth with some coins. In the morning she'll be thrilled with the money and curious about her visitor. Be creative. Leave a sprinkle of glitter under the pillow along with the coins!

girls generally earlier than boys. Losing the first tooth—usually a lower front one—is exciting to some children, upsetting to others. Reassure upset children that a new adult tooth will grow in the open space. If the tooth is wiggly, it's ready to come out. Some children like to pull it out, others like to wait until it comes out on its own.

HOW THEY GROW: TEETH Baby teeth generally start appearing at 6 months and appear in the following order: **A** central incisors (6–12 months); **B** lateral incisors (9–16 months); **C** canines (16–23 months); **D** first molars (13–19 months); **D** second molars (23–33 months). At around age 6, the primary teeth are shed and replaced with permanent teeth in an approximate order: **A** central incisors (6–7 years); **B** lateral incisors (7–8 years); **C** canines (9–12 years); **D** first molars replaced by first premolars (9–11 years); **E** second molars replaced by second premolars (10–12 years). Three additional sets of teeth will erupt as part of your child's permanent set: **F** first molars (6–7 years); **G** second molars (11–13 years); **H** wisdom teeth (17–21 years).

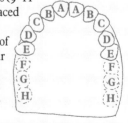

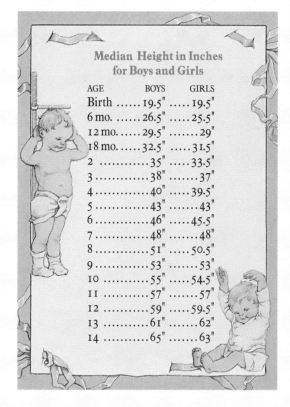

AGE	BOYS	GIRLS
Median Height in Inches for Boys and Girls		
Birth	19.5"	19.5"
6 mo.	26.5"	25.5"
12 mo.	29.5"	29"
18 mo.	32.5"	31.5"
2	35"	33.5"
3	38"	37"
4	40"	39.5"
5	43"	43"
6	46"	45.5"
7	48"	48"
8	51"	50.5"
9	53"	53"
10	55"	54.5"
11	57"	57"
12	59"	59.5"
13	61"	62"
14	65"	63"

AGE	BOYS	GIRLS
Median Weight in Pounds for Boys and Girls		
Birth	8	7.5
6 mo.	17.5	15.5
12 mo.	23	21
18 mo.	26	24
2	28	26
3	30	31
4	35	36
5	40	40
6	44	44
7	50	52
8	56	56
9	62	64
10	70	72
11	76	82
12	88	92
13	100	102
14	110	108

These charts are based on the Stature for Age and Weight for Age charts compiled by the Centers for Disease Control and Prevention (CDC).

TOO SHORT, TOO TALL Many children are insecure about their height—namely short boys and tall girls. Help your child feel good about himself. If shortness is his issue, encourage activities that don't focus on height or weight—soccer or baseball, chess or Scrabble. If she slouches to hide her height, introduce her to someone older who celebrates her own tallness and inspires her to stand proud. Tell your child that everyone has insecurities—especially the kids at school who do the most teasing. Once your child gains self-confidence, she may be inspired to help another child with a similar hang-up.

FAMILY GROWTH CHART Make or buy a growth chart to hang on a wall. Mark your child's or children's height on every birthday or New Year's Day. This keepsake will be fun to look back on for years to come.

WHEN YOUR CHILD IS OVERWEIGHT Children who are overweight know they are overweight. They see it in the mirror, they see it in their clothing sizes, and they see it in the eyes of the kids who tease them. These overweight children don't need crash diets—they need support, acceptance, and encouragement from their parents. Only then will they be able to raise their self-esteem and choose to become healthy.

To avoid hurting or embarrassing your sensitive child, focus on creating a healthier lifestyle rather than focusing on his extra weight. Shop for healthier foods for the whole family. Suggest and plan outdoor activities. Before you know it, your child will be losing weight. If he doesn't, seek professional help.

Family Exercise Ideas

- *Family Field Day:* Have relay races and three-legged races. Play softball and tag. Biking, hiking, or skating might be fun, too.
- *Hike 'n' Talk:* Set aside one day a week or month to hike with the family. Talking and walking are a perfect match.

Are They Ready?

Pets, Sports, and Everything Else

Moms have been saying *"Children grow up so fast!"* for centuries. *The first steps a toddler takes are his first steps away from Mommy, who excitedly cheers him on. Sure, she'll miss his days of infanthood, but with so many milestones to look forward to, who has time for nostalgia? Living in the moment is the only way to soak up the precious days of childhood. Before you know it, the child you used to hire a Saturday night babysitter for is ready to become a babysitter herself. The child you taught to ride a bike is ready to drive a car. Facing new challenges, learning new skills, and becoming more independent are important parts of a child's personal and social development. When your child shows signs of readiness for new activities, experiences, or privileges, it's your job, as a mom, to encourage her to do the best she can, teach her what she needs to know, and make sure she understands how to be safe.*

BED / BUNK BED Regular bed, age two; bunk bed, age six. When children are making the adjustment from a crib to a regular bed, they may do some wandering at night. Have a safety gate across any staircases if your child's room is on the second floor or above.

BICYCLE By ages four to six, your child will have developed necessary motor skills, like balancing, pushing, and steering, needed to ride a bike. Try teaching your child with training wheels at first, and gradually raise the height of the wheels so that she learns to balance on her own. Children under ten should not ride on the road.

BOARD GAMES Ages three and up, depending upon the game. Your three-year-old is ready to play bingo, Candyland, Hi Ho Cherry-O, Boggle Junior Letters, and other games that require taking turns. Your four-year-old is ready to play Uncle Wiggly, checkers, and Chutes and Ladders; your five-year-old is ready to play Scrabble Junior, Clue Junior, and Trouble; your six-year-old is ready to play Mastermind for Kids, Parcheesi, Sorry!, Twister, and Operation; your seven-year-old is ready for Pictionary, Jr., and checkers; your eight-year-old is ready for Scrabble, Stratego, Clue, Boggle, Yahtzee, Concentration, Rummikub, chess, Chinese checkers, and Jenga; your nine-year-old is ready to play Mastermind and Monopoly; your ten-year-old is ready to play Risk; your twelve-year-old is ready to play Pictionary, Trivial Pursuit, and Taboo.

CHEMISTRY SET Ages four to eight, depending on the kit. All kits are designed by educators, scientists, or toy manufacturers, with specific age groups in mind. Keep in mind the child's age and emotional maturity, the amount of supervision that will be available when the kit is being used, and the availability of replacements for kit contents. Adult supervision is a matter of safety rather than explaining instructions.

Pets

Children aren't really ready to take full responsibility for a pet until they are about nine years old, so until this age, you may say that a pet belongs to your child, but it will really be a family pet. Up to about age three, children will not be able to help care for the family pet, but may still enjoy pulling tails or stroking ears. Kids age three and older can help with pet care by filling food bowls and gently petting animals under supervision. Once your child is six and older, she can help clean cages or change water in a fishbowl. Five- and six-year-olds begin to express increasing interest in a pet's well-being, and will spend more time with the pet. You might want to start with a small, low-maintenance pet, such as a goldfish or hamster, and work your way up to a dog or cat.

DOGS Dogs are, of course, "man's best friend." The right dog will be your child's loyal friend for its entire life. Choose a dog breed known to be good with children—golden retrievers, pugs, or shih tzus are good choices. Be aware that puppies are almost as much work as babies!

CATS Felines make great pets for young children. They spend much of their time sleeping, so they don't need much care. It is probably best not to mix a kitten and a very young toddler, as kittens are both fragile and a little wild.

BIRDS Parakeets, cockatiels, and lovebirds can learn their own names and respond when your child calls them. It is best not to get larger exotic birds, such as parrots, as they may bite children. It is important to be very gentle with birds, so do not let a child under six handle them. Remember that birds like cockatiels and even small parrots are extremely emotionally dependent, and that canaries and budgies are better choices for busy families.

FISH Fish, of course, cannot be pet, but they are lots of fun to watch, and can teach your child about underwater life. Fresh-water fish are the easiest to care for. Tetras, guppies, and goldfish make good pets, as they are hardy and interesting to look at.

RODENTS Rodents are a perfect substitute for a cat or dog if you do not have room for a larger animal. Guinea pigs make great pets for children. They are cuddly and quite active and take up little space. Gerbils are social animals, so it is best to have more than one (pairs of same-sex siblings are recommended). Exercise wheels and clear plastic tunnels can be added to gerbil cages—your child will love to watch their antics. Hamsters are similar to gerbils, but are furrier and nocturnal. They, too, need an exercise wheel, and will often "run" all night long (make sure that wheel doesn't squeak)!

RABBITS Rabbits, while not rodents, can be good first pets, although not all of them like to be pet and will mostly resist being held. A pet rabbit can help a child learn how to care for a larger animal. Some rabbits can learn to use a litter box.

REPTILES Reptiles are very interesting to look at and learn about, but you will have to feed them other animals, so make sure that your child is ready to deal with this concept. Turtles are actually not generally recommended for young children, as they are quite sedentary and tend to carry the salmonella virus, so are not ideal for handling.

CHORES See page 60.

FLYING ALONE Age seven to eight. Flight attendants certainly watch over children traveling alone, but they can't be expected to do everything for a child. A lot depends on the maturity of your child. He should be able to take care of his own bathroom needs, cut up his own food, read and understand a simple itinerary, memorize his address and phone number, and make change with money—this ability shows a necessary level of cognitive functioning. He should also be well-behaved and able to control his temper and impulses. Each airline has its own rules and guidelines on "unaccompanied minors" and the ages this applies to.

GETTING AN ALLOWANCE Age five to six. Giving an allowance is the best way to teach a child financial responsibility—they can learn how to budget and negotiate. You might want to start with fifty cents for each year of the child's age. Here's something to try: Have your child divide the allowance among three jars. The money in Jar 1 can be spent on whatever the child desires; the money in Jar 2 is saved for a more expensive item; and the money in Jar 3 is reserved for long-term savings, such as a college fund. Once a month, pay interest into Jar 3 to show your child that money can make money. Habits learned early on will form the basis for a lifetime. Avoid linking allowances with grades or chores—unless the chore is a special one, like cleaning out the garage. When your child asks for a raise, use this as an opportunity to teach economic values and the art of negotiation. The sounder your own financial judgment, the better your kids' will

be. Seven- to ten-year-olds should not have to use their allowance to pay for school lunches and other necessities.

JOKES About age five. This is a perfect time to bring home a joke or riddle book. Five-year-olds have a good sense of humor and enjoy sharing jokes with adults. They're smart enough to understand simple puns, word plays, and jokes about characters they're familiar with.

MUSIC LESSONS Age three to eight, depending on the instrument. Your child needs to be able to recognize, identify, and remember objects. The recorder, a common first instrument, can be played as soon as your child's fingers are big enough to cover the holes. The piano can be played as soon as your child can reach the keys and press them down. The guitar and other stringed instruments, which often come in small sizes, are often started around age eight, depending on the size and stretch of your child's hands. Wind and brass instruments, not including the recorder, should not be played until your child's second set of teeth have come in, due to pressure put on teeth when played. Your child also needs to be big enough to hold and blow these instruments. Formal singing lessons are usually not recommended for children until they are in their teens, when their voices have become more developed.

READING About ages five to six. Children under five should never be pushed to read. If a child is not ready, pushing her will have a negative effect on her self-confidence. Most schools begin teaching reading in first grade and finish in third grade. Some children learn quicker than others. If your child is having a hard time learning or is behind the rest of the class, consider hiring a tutor to help.

ROLLER SKATING About age four. Choose skates that fasten over your child's shoes, can be expanded as your child's feet grow, have adjustable straps to secure the skate to the shoe, and have a lock to keep wheels from rolling backward when your child is learning. Encourage your child to walk on grass or carpet first to get the feel for the skates. Make sure your child wears protective gear: wrist guards, knee and elbow pads, and a helmet.

Sports/Athletics

While it can be lots of fun to spend time in a park with your kids tossing or kicking a ball, kids also can learn valuable lessons by participating in organized activities. For some, playing team sports will bring rewards, release pent-up energy, and develop physical and mental strength. Others find fulfillment in more solitary pursuits like tennis, karate, dance, or gymnastics. The age at which your children start playing sports is entirely up to you (and them). Here are some simple guidelines on minimum ages and what to expect from particular sports.

BASEBALL/SOFTBALL A child should have little or no trouble hitting a ball off a tee at age six, so this is a good age to begin practicing for baseball by playing tee-ball. Children of seven or eight will probably be ready to play baseball without a tee, but observe your child playing a game and make sure that she or he is really ready to give the game the concentration it requires.

> REMEMBER: Always bring sunscreen and put it on yourself as well as your child. You can get just as burned standing around watching a Little League game as your little pitcher can playing in it.

BASKETBALL Developmentally, most kids are not ready to really play the game of basketball until they are about nine years old. Before that, however, they may enjoy bouncing a ball around the court and tossing it at a low basket.

DANCING It is never too early to start dancing, and most infants will bounce along happily to music before they can even walk. Dancing around the house to music is an excellent way to help children develop both a sense of balance and a sense of fun. Formal dance lessons may begin around age six or seven, starting with modern ballet, jazz, tap, or perhaps ethnic dance if classes are available. Remember: Boys like to dance, too!

FOOTBALL Children as young as six may enjoy a simplified version of football—catching a ball and running down a field—but it is not until about age ten that they are ready to begin dealing with the complexities of the game. Many contend that children's bones are not developed enough till at least age 13, and that they should play only touch or soft tackle till then.

GYMNASTICS Most children enjoy tumbling from an early age and can safely take classes at the preschool level on the mat. Off-the-floor equipment use and more demanding routines should wait until a child is at least seven years old.

HORSEBACK RIDING Children as young as five may start riding. Your child may benefit most from classes that include grooming as well as riding, as this will teach them valuable lessons about responsibility and caring for animals.

SOCCER This sport is increasingly popular with both girls and boys, and is one of the safest sports for young children to play. Most experts agree that children are able to kick a ball around at age six, so they can begin to play soccer then. Because the ability to track a ball with the eye develops a bit later, though, goalies should be seven or older.

SKATEBOARD, SCOOTER, AND IN-LINE SKATING

Age seven to eight, supervised until age ten. Each type of equipment requires good balance, body strength, and coordination. Children must have good judgment, respect for cars, respect for safety, and control of the equipment. They need to practice gliding, turning, stopping, avoiding obstacles, and riding in a straight line until they can remain in control and prevent falls. They must wear protective gear, never travel too fast to stop, keep to the right and pass on the left, give way to pedestrians, stay on flat surfaces other than the road until the skills are mastered, and avoid wet or sandy surfaces. Adults are needed to monitor the child's skills while they develop, and to reinforce safety rules. Keep in mind that half of all injuries from "wheeled" activities among children under age fifteen occur between ages ten and fourteen.

SLEEP-AWAY CAMP

About age eight. Before sending a child to sleep-away camp, make sure she's spent time away from you, whether it's spending a night at a friend's house or going on an overnight field trip. You may be excited about sending your child to camp, but it's how your child feels that matters most. If she shows absolutely no interest at all, don't send her. If she shows an interest, talk with her about the benefits of going to camp. If you went to camp, share your own experiences. Let your child see slides or pictures of the camp. If there are other children in your town who are going to the same camp, organize a get-together so they know each other before they go.

SLEEPOVER

Age six to eight. Check for these signs that your child is ready: he asks to sleep over at a friend's house, he can spend four hours or more with a friend without crying or missing you, he gets ready for bed on his own, or he has successfully slept over at a grandparent's or relative's house. Still be ready for that late-night phone call from your child asking to come home, just in case.

STAYING HOME ALONE

About age twelve, fifteen and older if supervising younger siblings. Make sure your child feels comfortable, confident, safe, and willing to stay alone. Be confident that he consistently follows your rules, does not panic when confronted with unexpected events, has good judgment and problem-solving skills, and is truthful with you. He must understand the importance of safety and know basic safety procedures. If you know and trust your neighbors, be sure to leave their numbers. Leave the number of where you can be reached as well. Before you leave, role play "What-if?" scenarios with your child so he can practice decision-making and have the opportunity to discuss options and ask questions. If you won't be able to call and "check in," ask another adult to do this for you. If you live in an unsafe neighborhood, don't leave your child alone.

SWIMMING LESSONS

Age four. Before this age, children lack the cognitive ability to realize when they are in trouble in the water, but this doesn't mean that you should keep your kids out of the pool altogether. Sign up for water safety and swim readiness classes to get your little one used to splashing around. While swimming together, keep your baby in your arms at all times. As your toddler becomes more confident in the water, be sure to emphasize safety rules, like no running around the pool or never getting in the water alone.

Safety First

One of the biggest challenges as a mom is keeping children safe. It's important to understand the dangers your children will face, prepare ahead, supervise them carefully, and teach them well. Most injuries can be prevented. If you get rid of a poisonous household plant, your toddler can't pick off a leaf and chew on it. Make sure your eight-year-old wears a helmet, and she won't hurt her head if she falls off her scooter or bike. If your older child walks to school, know his exact route and encourage him to walk with friends. Only hire child-care providers and babysitters with excellent references. Learn CPR. Babyproof your house. Check car seats. The list goes on. You may not be able to prevent every bump, bruise, or scratch, but you will be able to keep your child safe in many ways.

Babyproofing 101

Even before babies begin to crawl, small hands can grab coins from countertops, hair clips from hair, and other choking hazards from almost anywhere. The best solution is to keep such objects—including toys with tiny parts—not just out of reach, but out of sight.

Once your child begins to crawl and to explore the world around him or her, you have to face the possibility of bumps, bruises, and other, more dangerous, accidents. Preventing such incidents is a matter of outthinking your child *before* an accident occurs.

At first you will only have to deal with a small area—the child's room, and perhaps an enclosed play space in the living area. But as baby grows, your child will want to explore beyond the boundaries that you've set. That means assessing your entire house for safety hazards.

No matter how extensively you babyproof your home, however, there's no substitute for constant supervision. Having your child under your eye is the best way to ensure your child's safety.

Secure ALL freestanding items to walls! My children have a large dresser that is so solid and heavy, I can hardly push it. I thought there was no way any of the kids could tip it over. When Sylvia was about three, she had all of the top two rows of drawers pulled out fully in search of something to wear. The weight of all those opened full drawers caused the dresser to start tipping over. My husband walked into the room just in time, preventing a horrible accident.

Bathroom: When it's not bathtime, keep this room off-limits. Know that small children can drown in less than an inch of water. Bathtubs, buckets, toilets, spas, hot tubs, and other containers of water are all hazards. Keep bathroom doors shut, keep toilet seats down and latched, and never leave water in the bathtub. Bathroom cabinets often contain medicines and cleaning products that can be poisonous. Make sure these cabinets have safety latches. Also, always check the water temperature before placing a child in the bath.

Baby's room: Your child should not be able to tip any of his or her furniture over. Make sure shelves and other freestanding items are securely fastened to the walls.

Kitchen: Like the bathroom, kitchen cabinets can contain poisonous cleaning products as well as foods that are not otherwise harmful but may present a choking hazard. Invest in safety latches for cabinets, or move such items to cabinets out of your child's reach. Another kitchen danger, however, is the stove. Turn pot handles away from the stove's edge so that curious hands can't pull hot pots and pans down on top of little bodies. Never allow your child to be in the kitchen unattended.

Electrical outlets: Place covers on all electric receptacles not in use.

Gates: Gates can allow your child a measure of freedom and you a measure of worry-free living. Gates can be used to create an enclosed play area, or to keep your children within (or from entering) rooms around the house. It's a good idea to put safety gates at the top and bottom of any staircases in your home.

Corner cushions: Child safety products now include cushioning specifically designed for furniture's sharp edges. These cushions can prevent both minor bumps and bruises and more serious injuries during that time when toddlers are particularly unsteady on their feet.

Preventing Accidents

Drowning: Never leave your child unattended in or near water. This includes the bathroom, of course, but also make sure that backyard kiddie pools are strictly supervised (or emptied when not in use) and that swimming pools are surrounded by a sturdy, high fence with a self-closing, self-latching gate.

Choking: See page 87.

Strangulation: Cords to window blinds or shades, even electrical cords, can be hazardous. Make sure such cords are out of reach and out of sight. Also, avoid high chairs, strollers, etc., that only have waist belts. A child can slip down and the belt can end up around his neck, causing strangulation. Always choose and use products with

> For a more complete list of babyproofing tips, check a childcare manual, or visit *parents.com/health/childproofing/index.jsp* and *childsafetyexperts.com/baby/babyproofing.shtml*

First Aid

When an accident happens or illness strikes, keep stress to a minimum by having a well-stocked first-aid kit on hand. Don't forget to keep your Emergency Numbers List handy (*see page 35*) and make sure to read the section on Choking Hazards (*see page 87*). A kit should include the following:

- First-aid manual
- Children's-strength acetaminophen (*Tylenol*) and children's-strength ibuprofen (*Advil, Nuprin*)
- Band-Aids, sterile gauze, and first-aid tape
- Tweezers and scissors
- Antibiotic ointment, for cuts and scrapes

- Antacid
- Topical antihistamine (anti-itch lotion), such as calamine
- Pedialyte, for dehydration and diarrhea
- Antiseptic wipes
- Alcohol wipes
- Disposable instant cold packs
- Thermometer

Make a second kit that can travel with you on outings and family vacations. It should be supplemented with adult-strength pain relievers for your own use, as well as a flashlight, a blanket, sunburn relief such as Solarcaine or aloe vera gel, and an elastic bandage. Store the first-aid kit under the front seat, not in the glove compartment, since heat can render medications less effective.

either a shoulder harness or crotch straps. Also, never put an item, such as a pacifier, on a cord around the child's neck.

Suffocation: Don't place soft toys and bedding inside your infant's crib. Count on snuggly clothes to keep your child warm, but if a blanket is required, anchor it under the foot of the mattress, and only draw it halfway up your child's chest. Lay your baby on his back to prevent sudden infant death syndrome (SIDS).

Scalds and burns: Set your water heater to 120°F (49°C) so that tap water won't cause your child a third-degree burn. Hot tap water 120°F or under, however, can still cause pain or scalds, so don't let your child play with faucets.

Don't drink hot liquids, such as tea or coffee, while holding your child. Don't hold your child while cooking at the stove, either, and make sure that pot handles are turned away from the stove's edge. Always unplug household irons, coffee makers, waffle irons, and electric frying pans immediately after use.

Take care with fireplaces and wood-burning stoves. Block your child's access to them with safety gates. Do not leave young children unattended in a room if a fireplace or stove is in use.

Walkers: Don't use them. Even when you supervise your child,

serious falls can happen too quickly to prevent. Choose play centers that remain stationary.

Falls: Don't leave your baby unattended on couches or beds. Move furniture away from windows, and make sure that window latches have safety bars or child-proof latches. When changing your baby always keep a hand on their body.

Poisoning: Household cleaners and over-the-counter or prescription drugs aren't the only materials that should be placed in locked or inaccessible cabinets. Make sure that household plants aren't poisonous.

Child carriers and strollers: Always place them on level surfaces, and, with strollers, engage the safety brakes. Don't leave your child unattended.

Fire: Install smoke and carbon monoxide detectors, and make sure their batteries are fully charged. Install a fire extinguisher near the stove (but out of your child's reach).

Sports-related injuries: When your child is old enough to participate in sports including bicycling, skiing, inline-skating, and skateboarding, invest in a helmet and other protective gear such as knee pads and wrist guards.

Sitting Pretty

All states require that infants and toddlers ride in car safety seats. Some states now require safety seats for children up to age six. Statistics show that safety seats do prevent injuries and save lives. They must be appropriate for the age and weight of your child, however, and they must be installed correctly. Go to *consumerreports.org* for the most up-to-date recommendations on child safety seats.

Children under the age of six should never ride in the front passenger seat. If an accident should occur, the airbag could inflate and inadvertently suffocate your child.

Tips on buckling in:

- Your baby must ride in a rear-facing car seat until he weighs twenty pounds and is at least twelve months old.
- The straps should be snug enough that you can fit only one finger between strap and chest.
- The clip should be at armpit level.
- The seat should be tilted at the proper angle and should move less than an inch when you push it in any direction.

Have car seats inspected! Car crashes are the number-one killer of kids. Eighty percent of kids riding in safety seats are at risk because they are not buckled in correctly. Go to *seatcheck.org* or call 1-800-SEAT-CHECK to find your nearest child safety seat inspection station.

Be Prepared

Getting Out the Door

You're most likely all too familiar with the dreadful scene—you're away from the house and there are no more diapers in the diaper bag. Or, you forgot to pack a snack and the kids' tummies are rumbling. Take a page from the Boy Scouts' book and vow to "Be Prepared." Assembling a comprehensive tote bag for outings with the kids is an art form that you too can master.

WHAT'S IN THAT DIAPER BAG?

Diapers ❧ Changing pad ❧ Baby wipes Bottled water ❧ Diaper cream ❧ Ziploc bags (*for dirty diapers, wet clothes, and other messes*) ❧ Change of clothes ❧ Sweater or jacket (*for drops in temperature*) ❧ Hat (for protection from exposure to sun or cold) ❧ Feeding supplies (*bottles, formula, sterilized water, cereal, crackers in lidded plastic containers*) Ice packs (to keep liquids, such as expressed breast milk, cool) ❧ Bibs ❧ Two clean pacifiers ❧ Favorite small toy or two ❧ Books ❧ Teething toys ❧ Tissues ❧ Cloth diaper or burp rag (*to clean up spit-ups, spills, etc.*) ❧ Sunscreen ❧ Baby Tylenol ❧ Antihistamine for babies such as Benadryl (*in case of a bee-sting reaction*) ❧ Moisture stick/Petroleum jelly ❧ Extra blanket ❧ First-aid kit (*see page 30*)

GENERAL TOTING TIPS

- You don't need to travel around town with the kitchen sink. Keep your bag down to the essentials.
- Place a name tag on or in your tote bag.
- Don't trust the weather report. Bring everything you need in case of a sudden change in weather (a sweater, sunscreen, a hat, gloves, a blanket, etc.).
- Replenish contents upon returning home each time so you're ready to go at a moment's notice.
- A good rule of thumb when calculating the number of diapers you'll need is one per hour you are away from home, plus two for emergencies.
- Never underestimate the magic of the multipurpose baby wipe!
- A fresh change of clothes should always include socks and shoes.

I love those soft vinyl lunch bags for children. I can stuff a lot into them and still feel I'm traveling light. I have multiple ones: in the stroller, in the car, at my in-laws. I have diaper and change of clothes ones, and distractions ones. My "main bag" contains the barest essentials: three to four diapers, baby wipes, ointment, onesie, bib, spoon, Ziploc bag of Cheerios, a board book, a few bandages, my trusty baby carrier that folds up smaller than a diaper, and a sunhat during the summer. On my way out, I might throw in a bottle of juice and a jar of baby food. Sometimes, I can even fit my cell phone, keys, and wallet, and that's all I carry. This bag goes everywhere with baby. My "distractions bag" contains several board books, some plastic toy figures, a notebook, and two pens for my older children. This comes with the main bag when we go to a restaurant.

Tips for Long Distance Travel

- Less is definitely more. Though your days of traveling light are long gone, it's good to plan carefully and only take what you absolutely need.
- If you are traveling overseas, don't forget to pack your family's health documents. Many countries require proof of immunizations before entry.
- When packing meals for a long journey, think about foods that are easy on the tummy, like bread, bananas, crackers, and yogurt.
- Chamomile tea can help settle queasy tummies. Prepare some ahead in a bottle, sippy-cup, or thermos.
- Don't forget those things you use often but don't travel in your diaper bag, such as your baby monitor, baby hairbrush, bottle/food warmer, and nail clippers. (You may also consider bringing your toddler's potty.)
- A portable crib and stroller can both help to provide safe spots for your wee one while away from home.
- Moisturizing lotion, lots of beverages, low-salt snacks and a pillow can help alleviate some of the dehydration and fatigue experienced with air travel.

TOTE BAGS FOR OLDER KIDDOS

Diaper bags aren't just for babies. Toddlers need many of the same items in a baby's diaper bag. Even big kids require some gear while away from home. Snacks, drinks, and portable distractions are the biggest considerations, but even potty-trained children can still require a fresh change of clothes—and the accompanying plastic bags for dirty or wet clothes—on occasion (e.g. muddy soccer games). First-aid kits are also a good idea to have on hand with kids of any age—and adults for that matter.

SNACKS ON THE RUN

It's good to have a spillproof cup (for toddlers), thermos, or bottled water along on any excursion. Napkins, paper cups, and plastic spoons and forks also come in handy. And, you're never too old to find a good use for a baby

wipe. Some great snack suggestions for eating on the go are, apples, bananas, hard-boiled eggs, peanut butter and crackers, string cheese, dry cereal, juice or soymilk boxes, and muffins.

PORTABLE DISTRACTIONS

Books ❧ Crayons and drawing pad ❧ Stuffed animals ❧ Favorite small toys ❧ Action figures ❧ Audiotapes and cassette player

TRUNK ESSENTIALS

Here are some items to have in your trunk so you and the kids will be ready for anything: Stroller ❧ Diapers ❧ Wipes ❧ Diaper cream ❧ Changing pad ❧ Washcloths ❧ Burp rags ❧ Change of clothes ❧ Sweater ❧ Hat ❧ Portable highchair ❧ A few toys or books ❧ Blankie ❧ Sunscreen ❧ First-aid kit ❧ Blanket for impromptu picnic or beach outing ❧ Nonperishable drinks and snacks

JUST FOR MOM

Lip balm with SPF ❧ Hand cream ❧ Bottle of water ❧ Tylenol ❧ Nutritious snack (*granola bar, apple, etc.*) ❧ Change of clothes ❧ Disposable camera ❧ Reading material ❧

Crib Notes Childcare

As in Peter Pan, we should all have Nana the nanny dog at our disposal for our precious darlings! Leaving your wee ones with a caregiver—especially one that's new to your family—is rarely easy. Having a checklist of points to cover and an information sheet for your child's caregiver can help put your mind at ease and ensure everything will run smoothly while you are away.

Childcare Checklist

Use this checklist to help you think about what's important to communicate to a caregiver.

❏ Provide the caregiver with an up-to-date information sheet (*see sidebar*).

❏ Decide if and when you'd like the caregiver to check in with you.

❏ If you don't want your phone answered by the caregiver, decide how you will get in contact with them in case of emergency or to notify the caregiver if you will be late.

❏ Leave a house key for the caregiver. Give instructions for what to do in case of a lock-out. Walk through alarm systems.

❏ Show the caregiver where the heat and/or air-conditioning controls are, and how to make adjustments if necessary.

❏ Discuss ahead of time if anyone will be dropping by the house for any reason. Give details about who is coming and when they're expected.

❏ If you have pets, talk to the caregiver about what you expect from them regarding care (walks, feedings, pooper-scooper patrol, etc.).

❏ Let the caregiver know if there are any chores, homework, instrument practice hours, or anything else to be completed by your child in your absence.

❏ Discuss your child's schedule with the caregiver, and give any instructions regarding food preparation, bottle feedings, bedtime routine, etc.

❏ Give the caregiver all necessary information relating to fire escape plans including location of extinguishers and fire exits, and where to meet once everyone is out of the house.

❏ Lay out the house rules for the caregiver both in reference to what your children are allowed/not allowed to do (such as ride bikes with helmets only, limit television to one hour, etc.) and what is expected of the caregiver (such as no telephone use, no friends over, etc.).

❏ Be very straightforward about your rules concerning disciplining your children. This will help to provide consistency for your child and avoid major misunderstandings.

❏ Let the caregiver know if you'd like them to take notes on your baby's eating and sleeping schedule, feedback about your toddler's behavior, etc.

Information Sheet

The information sheet should act as a quick reference guide for the caregiver with frequently used and emergency phone numbers and any special instructions regarding the children's care. Even if you've reviewed most of these things with the caregiver prior to your departure, it's a good idea to have it in writing so they can refer back to it.

General

Parent's Names, Our Phone Number, Our Address, Closest Intersection, Children's Names and Ages

Where You'll Be

Address, Phone number, Cell phone, Pager, Time expected home

Special Instructions

Mealtime, Snacks, Allergies, Bedtime/Naps, Pet care, Medications (what and when), Fire plan meeting place

Places to Call in Case of Emergency

Emergency: 911, Relative, Neighbor, Hospital, Police, Fire, Poison Control, Pediatrician, Family doctor, Dentist, Other doctors

Other Important Numbers

Day care and school, Carpool, Grandparents

Lullaby, and Good Night Sleep

It's the end of they day, and everyone's tired. And if it's one of those truly rotten days where everything seems to have gone wrong, bedtime can become a battle. Arm yourself against just such incidents by starting with (and sticking firmly to) a bedtime routine. No two children's routines will be exactly the same, and as a child grows older, some elements may be replaced or discarded. But the idea of the routine—your child knowing that bedtime is coming at 7 p.m. or 8 p.m., rain or shine—is the key.

Restless Nights

For days when your child just can't settle down, try softly stroking their face from forehead down the nose to the chin. Your child's eyes will reflexively close as you repeat this motion.

Countdown to Bedtime

1 *Dinner.* There needs to be adequate time between dinner and bedtime, which means dinner needs to be served at a set time.

2 *Props.* Make sure the stage is set before bedtime so that you aren't sent scurrying to find a favorite blanket, toy, or book. Kids may try to push bedtime back in this manner.

3 *Preparation.* A jump into jammies, a trip to the bathroom (which expands to include teeth brushing once babyteeth start emerging) should all happen before the official bedtime. These tasks also serve to remind children that bedtime is approaching.

4 *Bath.* For babies, a warm bath can help soothe them into sleep. As children leave babyhood—and the sticky messes of toddlerhood—daily baths can be skipped.

5 *Choices.* It sounds great in theory to ask for your child's assistance in deciding which book to read or what music to listen to. Unfortunately, this can lead to

prolonged negotiations (i.e., a way for your child to push his or her bedtime back). It's easiest to announce, "Tonight we're reading to/listening to *X*." Of course, it's okay to be flexible when your child has learned to make decisions quickly.

6 *Options.* Your child will let you know what they prefer as their final interaction with you before you leave their room for the night. Some like being read to, and, when older, may want to read to you. Others like to talk about what happened that day. If dad has been away at work, this may be a great way for him to catch up on what he's missed. Listening to music, or singing together, is also very comforting and soothing, particularly for babies and young children.

7 *Lights out.* If your child demands a nightlight, turn it on before you turn out any lamps or overhead lighting. Tell your child good night and then, after a hug and a kiss, turn and leave the room.

But Mom!

It's not uncommon for children to suddenly remember something they have to tell you five minutes after the lights go out. And then five minutes after that, they need a drink of water. And five minutes after that, they insist they can't possibly fall asleep. Nip this behavior in the bud, or "bedtime" can extend into a seeming eternity. And it's hard to break the habit once it's gotten a good hold.

How Much Sleep?

Logging the proper amount of sleep is very important. Studies have shown that a lack of sleep can negatively affect IQ, and may contribute to such problems as Attention Deficit Disorder (ADD) later in life. Studies conducted by the Sleep Medicine and Research Center (St. Louis, MO) suggest the following sleep durations for children. Some children may need more sleep and some slightly less. Some children nap until age five.

AGE	TOTAL SLEEP TIME	NAPS
1	14 hours	1-2 naps
2	11 to 12 hours	1-2 naps
3	12 to 12.5 hours	none
4	11.5 to 12 hours	none
5	11 hours	none
6	10.75 to 11 hours	none
7	10.5 to 11 hours	none
8	10.25 to 10.75 hours	none
9	10 to 10.33 hours	none
10 to 16	9.75 to 10 hours	none
17 to adult	9.75 hours	none

Sleep, Baby, Sleep

There is no right or wrong way to put your baby to sleep—go with what feels right to you. You or your partner can give him a massage, sing a lullaby, play soft music, snuggle in a rocking chair, or read a book. After soothing your baby, don't be afraid to put him down alone. You'll give him the opportunity to learn self-soothing skills to help him fall asleep and stay asleep on his own. Some moms prefer to break the association between feeding and sleep as soon as possible. This can be done by feeding your baby early in the evening and putting him in his crib while he's still awake. If he cries when you leave the room, give him five minutes to calm down. If he continues to cry, go into the bedroom and reassure him. Continue to check on him every five to ten minutes, and repeat the process each night until he learns to fall asleep on his own. If letting your baby "cry it out" doesn't feel right to you,

Things That Go "Bump"

To calm sincere nighttime fears, agree to sit quietly in the dark in a chair in the corner—or lie on the floor, if that's comfortable for you—for ten or fifteen minutes. Don't agree to requests for more stories or conversation. Greet attempts to interact with you with a soothing "Shhh, it's time for sleep." Try not to stay until your child is asleep. Your child will expect you to be there if he or she awakes in the middle of the night, or you will find yourself in their room every evening, waiting until they fall asleep. It's better to leave and respond to their calls than to begin the habit of waiting until they fall asleep.

try something less harsh. Your baby will learn to sleep if you put him to bed as soon as he shows signs of tiredness, use a consistent soothing style, and create a calm, peaceful environment that allows sleep to overtake him. When your baby learns to fall asleep on his own will most likely be determined by the approach you choose, but once he does, you'll be rewarded with restful nights for yourself and the rest of your family.

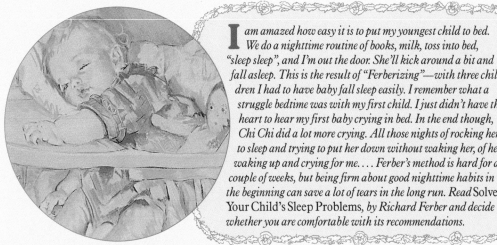

I am amazed how easy it is to put my youngest child to bed. We do a nighttime routine of books, milk, toss into bed, "sleep sleep", and I'm out the door. She'll kick around a bit and fall asleep. This is the result of "Ferberizing"—with three children I had to have baby fall sleep easily. I remember what a struggle bedtime was with my first child. I just didn't have the heart to hear my first baby crying in bed. In the end though, Chi Chi did a lot more crying. All those nights of rocking her to sleep and trying to put her down without waking her, of her waking up and crying for me. . . . Ferber's method is hard for a couple of weeks, but being firm about good nighttime habits in the beginning can save a lot of tears in the long run. Read Solve Your Child's Sleep Problems, *by Richard Ferber and decide whether you are comfortable with its recommendations.*

Nap Time

As paradoxical as it sounds, the more tired your child is, the harder she may find it to fall asleep at night. For babies and toddlers, a regular nap schedule is big part of what it takes to have a happy, rested child (and a rested and happy you). Make sure the naptime preparations—perhaps a bath followed by a diaper change and then a song—always occur in the same order. A predictable routine helps prepare your child for sleep.

Keep to the same nap schedule. And if the plan is to lay your child down at 3 p.m., make sure any props—a favorite stuffed animal, cuddly blanket, sleepy music—are ready by 2:30 or so. That way, naps won't be delayed by a demand for a lost item. Be aware that sunlight streaming through a window can signal your child's brain that it's time to be alert. A dimly lit room will help put your child "in the mood" for sleep.

Even if your child insists they aren't sleepy, encourage them to lie down, close their eyes, and "rest." Have your child nap in bed. That way you can use the time to catch up on chores or indulge in a little quiet time of your own, without fear of disturbing the little sleeper.

Calming Caresses

Is your baby restless, colicky, cranky? Try integrating massage into your child's daily routine or bedtime ritual. A soothing massage can calm both you and your child, convince a reluctant toddler to get into bed, and may provide health benefits far beyond just encouraging a healthy night's rest. For massage tips and techniques, try the following websites: *parents.com* and *makewayforbaby.com/massages.htm* .

Partners in Parenthood

Nowhere is the need for a united front more necessary than when it comes to bedtime. It's the end of the day, and everyone's a little tired. The last thing you want is for your child's bedtime to cause strain between you and your spouse. Make sure that you both share the same expectations of the routine, and that you each support the other's authority when in the child's presence. Any discussion of bedtime, or other disciplinary issues, should take place between you and your spouse in private.

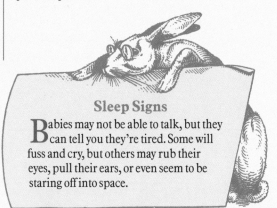

Sleep Signs

Babies may not be able to talk, but they can tell you they're tired. Some will fuss and cry, but others may rub their eyes, pull their ears, or even seem to be staring off into space.

Lullaby

Now, far o'er the tree-tops,
Soft winds are blowing,
Swaying every nodding flower,
Deep into dreamless sleep:
With you, oh pretty ones,
Little Star-eyes are closing,
Hide them fast, oh little ones,
Mother Earth, too, is dozing.

Discipline Molding Behavior

In the old days, discipline was another word for punishment. Today, discipline is more about having a good relationship with your child, teaching him to feel good about doing the right thing, and modeling desired behavior. Children have an innate desire to please others—it's up to us to show them how. Create a set of house tasks to show your children what is expected of them. What may start out seeming like a chore—making a bed every morning or throwing dirty clothes in the hamper after taking them off—will eventually become quite natural as they get older. They'll realize that a few minutes of work will earn them a neat room they enjoy spending time in.

Put yourself in a young child's shoes—so many rules and so many things to remember! It's not easy to live up to mom's expectations if she has too many. Decide what is important to you and be consistently firm about those things. Things that you can live with can be worked on later. My children know that naps and bedtime are sacred, but heaven knows their table manners can be greatly improved.

Different children need to be disciplined in different ways. Some just need little reminders. Some may need to be punished or grounded. Disciplining a difficult child can bring out the worst in a parent. The challenge is being able to separate your own anger and frustration from the child's so you can act like the adult you want your child to become. This isn't easy when a child is constantly pressing your buttons. Understanding your child's feelings and reactions will lead you to a greater understanding of yourself.

TIPS ON POSITIVE DISCIPLINE

- *Praise and reward your child for good behavior.* The more you do this, the more good behavior you'll see. Change incentives often to keep a high level of motivation.
- *Make sure a punishment fits the crime.* If your child scribbles on the wall, take away his crayons.
- *Allow your child to learn from her mistakes.* If she wants to wear high-heeled princess shoes to school, let her learn on her own how uncomfortable they are. (Send a comfortable pair of shoes along—just in case.)

- *Encourage your child to talk about her feelings—especially when she's upset.* Offer suggestions on how to resolve the situation.

- *Say what you mean.* Mean what you say. Be consistent.
- *Use humor if the situation feels right.* If two children are fighting over a stuffed dog, walk in with a leash and say it's time for the dog's walk. If your child won't throw his socks in the hamper, pretend you're the socks begging to be washed.
- *Love your child regardless of his behavior.* Treat him with respect and he'll treat you and others with respect. Maintain a foundation of love, trust, and respect.

DISCIPLINE NO-NO'S

- *Don't withhold love.* This can threaten a child's self-esteem and cause future problems.
- *Don't be too rigid.* If your child is afraid of you, he might start misbehaving when you're not around.
- *Don't yell at children from another room.* Face to face works best.
- *Don't use emotional blackmail.* Children shouldn't have to behave just to keep a parent happy.
- *Don't act before you think.* It can humiliate and frighten children and teach poor coping methods.
- *Don't get caught up in "winning."* Sometimes children are right. Sometimes a compromise is best.
- *Don't use foul language.* If you do, your child will too.
- *Don't scold a child for an accident.* Accidents happen.
- *Don't act like a child.* That's your child's job.
- *Don't respond to your child's anger with your own anger.*

TALKING BACK When your child talks back, stop the conversation promptly and exit the room. If your child follows you, sternly say you will not tolerate disrespect. When you're calm, tell your child that for every time she back talks, she will lose another quarter from her allowance or gain another household chore.

TEASING If a child being teased by another child is okay with it, let it go. If he's not, comfort the child being teased. Give him tips on how to protect himself. Announce to both children that it's rude and unkind to tease.

BITING When your child bites another child, comfort and apologize to the child who was bitten, wash the wound, and state clearly to your own child that biting is not okay—it hurts. Explain that there are ways to express anger that won't hurt anyone—talk about it, pound pillows, growl like a lion. Your child will learn more from the experience if you stay calm and firm. Be confident that your child has the ability to make positive changes.

SWEARING Children repeat what they hear, even if they don't know what it means. If your child swears without knowing what it means, explain that the word is not one children use. Suggest replacing it with "jelly," "crayon," or "somersault." If he does know what the swear word means, say, "That language is disrespectful and unacceptable." If he continues

Disciplining a toddler is considerably different from disciplining an older child. You can't expect a toddler to learn a lesson the first time it's taught. Toddlers have short attention spans, can't always control their impulses, and often have trouble grasping concepts. They do, however, understand the word "no", so it's not too early to instill an understanding of what's right and wrong. A toddler is ready to learn "please," "thank you," and "I'm sorry." Act as his model and, eventually, your self-centered child will transform into a caring, respectful adult.

swearing, fine him a quarter of his allowance each time it happens. If your child directs the swearing at you, take away a special privilege.

TAKING TIME-OUT

Every toddler, child, teenager, and adult could use a "time-out" now and then. "Time-out" is a strategy that does two things: it makes a quick break in undesirable behavior, and it allows a person to cool down quietly after an emotional outburst and reflect on what happened. Choose a place in your house for "time-outs" to take place. If you're not home, a park bench, the car, or another unexciting location will do. Keep time-out brief—thirty seconds to a minute for toddlers, five to ten minutes for everyone else. "Time-out" should not be used as a punishment, but rather to help shape behavior.

Tantrums

*O*ne of the greatest challenges as a parent is learning how to handle your toddler's temper tantrums. Tantrums are a normal childhood reaction to anger and frustration and usually occur between ages two and four. While they often make a parent angry and frustrated enough to have a temper tantrum of her own, it's important that she doesn't. This is the time for the parent to be firm. If a parent doesn't take control, tantrums will happen again and again. All children need—and on some level want—parents to set limits, create structure, and act with consistency. They understand these qualities as expressions of love and concern. The earlier children learn that choices have consequences, the better prepared they'll be for the real world.

WAYS TO AVOID A TANTRUM

- When your child becomes angry, validate his feelings and encourage him to talk about it.
- When your child become frustrated by not being able to communicate verbally, be patient and try to sense what he wants.
- If your child wants something you don't want her to have, include a "yes" with your "no." ("You can't have a cookie now, but you can have one after dinner.")
- Offer choices and ask questions so your child will feel in control of the situation. ("If you waste time now, there won't be time for a bedtime story. What would you like to do?")
- When you sense a tantrum brewing, distract your child with an activity, book, song, or game.
- Ease your child into new situations. Get to the dentist early so there's time to play calmly in the waiting room. Prepare her in advance for what to expect when she goes to school.
- Avoid situations that allow your child to become overtired, hungry, and over stimulated.

WAYS TO CALM A CHILD DOWN FROM A TANTRUM

- Call a "time-out" so your child has time to cool down. If you need a "time-out" too, take one. (*See page 41*)
- Be sensitive to the situation. If your child doesn't want you to touch her, don't.
- If your child can't regain control by himself, help him. Comfort him with a hug, offer him a glass of water or give him a special blanket.

EXPLODING BY THE RULES Giving children a constructive way to throw a tantrum is safer for everyone. Choose a room—not a bedroom—in your house where all tantrums are to take place. Without an audience, tantrum loses momentum. Set rules. "No hitting or punching"—unless it's a pillow.

WHEN TO IGNORE TANTRUMS When a tantrum occurs because the child doesn't get her way, ignore it. Don't ignore tantrums when the child lacks the verbal skills to express herself or when the child totally loses control and falls apart emotionally.

WHEN TO GET OUTSIDE HELP If your child has frequent, intense tantrums, or if you're constantly losing your temper with her, talk with your pediatrician, a counselor, or a family therapist for a fresh perspective with some successful coping methods.

Swimming in Advice

A Parenting Primer

No doubt about it—parenting advice abounds. From stacks of childcare manuals to "pearls of wisdom" from Great-Aunt Ruby, today's parents are drowning in advice, oftentimes unsolicited. Complete strangers have no qualms about stopping you on the street to tell you to button your little one's coat—often reaching in the stroller to do it themselves. Grandparents love to get in their two cents' worth about how you should raise your child, supplying, "When you were that age..." anecdotes. Self-proclaimed childcare experts have published enough literature to make your head spin. But who has time to sort through the dizzying amount of information? Here is a briefing of ten notable parenting experts of the twentieth century.

I find it useful to have two basic books in the house. I like The American Academy of Pediatrics Caring for Your Baby and Young Child: Birth to Age 5 *by Steven P. Shelov, et al. and the* What To Expect *series by Heidi E. Murkoff, Arlene Eisenberg, et al. Of the many child parenting books I've perused, I've found a few that suited me and contributed to my mothering skills. When I had my first baby, I frequently referred to Burton L. White's* The First Three Years of Life *and* How to Raise a Happy, Unspoiled Child. *Seven years later with my third baby, I still follow and agree with a lot of his recommendations.* Your One-Year Old, *and the rest of the year-by-year series by Louise Bates Ames is a recent discovery. The book on seven-year-olds made me more understanding towards my daughter's recent "woe-is-me" attitude. As each slim volume is insightful rather than instructional, this is a good series to borrow from the library rather than purchase.*

Ten Experts Agree (Or Do They?)

- **G. STANLEY HALL** (1844-1924): Nurture, nurture, and nurture some more! Hall, the first American psychologist, proposed that good behavior in children is brought about by nurturing them in a manner appropriate to their age and stage of development.

- **L. EMMETT HOLT** (1855-1924): Avoid sentimentality! Holt, one of the early presidents of the American Pediatric Society and a contemporary of Hall, wrote the popular tome *The Care and Feeding of Children* (1917), which spells out a very strict dietary plan and urges parents to avoid spoiling their children through sentimental parenting.

- **JOHN BROADUS WATSON** (1878-1958) Stimulus-response. Watson is the father of the Behavioral School of Psychology. He believed that all living creatures operate under the system of stimulus-response, and it was by using that system that behaviorists systemized the raising of children. Watson believed that the basic emotions in infants are love, rage, and fear. He developed ways to use these emotions to teach children to exhibit good behaviors and eradicate bad ones.

■ ARNOLD GESELL (1880-1961): Milestones. Gesell was the first psychologist to chart child development through assigning age-appropriate milestones. See *Your One-Year Old*, and the rest of the year-by-year Gesell Institute series by Louise Bates Ames.

■ MELANIE KLEIN (1882-1960): Object-Relations. Klein embraced Freud's theories and held that the mother/child relationship is the learning template for all future relationships.

■ JEAN PIAGET (1896-1980): Development stages of children. The inventor of the intellectual and moral development stages of children, Piaget's research is responsible for why we believe, for example, that children don't begin to understand abstract math notions and concepts like "justice" until around age 12.

■ BENJAMIN SPOCK (1903-1998): Maternal confidence. Spock's book, with record sales rivaled only by the Bible, *The Common Sense Book of Baby and Child Care* (1946) was revolutionary for its time. In his book, Spock pushes for parents to rely on their own instincts and common sense over conflicting advice from parenting experts.

■ BRUNO BETTELHEIM (1903-1990): No "formula." Bettelheim was a fierce critic of Spock. He believed that there is no "formula" for raising children. His work focused primarily on the treatment of autistic children. He committed suicide in 1990, and was posthumously accused of brutalizing a number of his patients.

■ T. BERRY BRAZELTON (b. 1918): The first child expert trained both in pediatrics and psychology, Brazelton advocates, as did Spock, nurturing and listening to children.

In his work with Boston's Children's Hospital, Brazelton developed a universally used system for measuring neonatal development called the Brazelton Index. See his *Toddlers and Parents* and *Touchpoints*.

■ PENELOPE LEACH (b. 1937): Love your children. One of the world's most prominent (and popular) child psychologists, Leach, like Brazelton, is one of Spock's successors advocating loving, compassionate parenting techniques. See *Your Baby and Your Child* and *Your Growing Child*.

For more in-depth information about these experts, see Ann Hulbert's book, *Raising America: Experts, Parents, and a Century of Advice About Children.*

Beware of Parenting Paranoia

The overabundance of child-rearing advice weighs heavy on today's parents. We often feel that we are doing our children a great disservice if we don't educate ourselves about the latest in parenting theories. Parents lacking confidence in their own abilities reach for their parenting books to confirm their instincts and make the smallest of decisions. This inclination toward relying on books instead of common sense and parenting instincts leads to confusion as not all "experts" agree, and it creates nervous parents and nervous children. It is important to find a balance between referring to solid sources and following our own instincts as parents. (After all, who knows your child better than you?)

Before you dive into one more book on how to be the perfect parent, consider the following parenting acumen:

■ Common sense and parental instincts are your most valuable tools.

■ Look for local resources like area websites and local newspapers as resources for activities, education, support groups, and doctors.

■ Some parents find Internet chat groups can be a helpful resource for putting your mind at ease about non-medical concerns.

■ Having a trustworthy, highly qualified pediatrician is essential. Don't be shy about using them as your primary resource for health- and development-related concerns.

Statistics

- 10% of children up to age five wet during the night
- Up to 10% of children ages six to eight wet the bed
- 5% of children wet the bed until age ten
- A small percentage of children wet the bed until they go through puberty.
- Bed-wetting is hereditary. If a child wets the bed, chances are one of his parents did too.

Potty Training

When it comes to potty training, *your toddler calls the shots. No matter how much you beg and plead, he'll only do it when he's good and ready. The average age for potty training is two-and-a-half, with girls slightly ahead of boys. Some toddlers learn to use the potty with almost no help, but the majority need our help and encouragement. A casual, pressure-free approach works best. If you feel your child is physically and emotionally ready—yet he's not showing the slightest bit of interest—try buying him some fun, colorful undies or tempt him with a musical potty available at* tinkletoonz.com. *Accidents are part of the potty training package. Carry around a change of underwear, pants, and socks, just in case. When your child has an accident, be laid-back about it. Treat it as you'd treat his shoes on the wrong feet, a missed button on her shirt, or a dab of ketchup on his chin. Tell her not to worry—soon she won't have accidents at all.*

Signs of Readiness

- A dry diaper for a few hours at a time.
- Letting you know he has to go or is going.
- Interest in being clean and dry.
- Able to understand and follow simple instructions.
- Understanding the association between dry pants and using the potty.
- Having the ability to undress himself.
- A curiosity about the potty and the desire to be trained.

Good Timing

- Summer is the ideal time to potty train. Your child can run around naked, and you'll have less laundry.
- While training, dress your child in pants with an elastic waistband.
- Place potties in as many rooms as possible.

Bad Timing

It's best not to start potty training when:
- There's a new baby in the family.
- You've just moved to a new neighborhood.
- Your toddler has switched pre-schools, day-care centers, or babysitters.
- You or your spouse has just started working again.

Great Potty Books, Activity and Gift Sets

Toilet Training in Less Than a Day, by Nathan H. Azrin and Richard M. Foxx ■ *The American Academy of Pediatrics Guide to Toilet Training* ■ *Mommy! I Have to Go Potty!: A Parent's Guide to Toilet Training,* by Jan Faull ■ *Once Upon a Potty—Boy (Girl),* by Alona Frankel ■ *Everyone Poops,* by Taro Gomi ■ *My Big Boy (Girl) Potty,* by Joanna Cole ■ *My Potty Reward Stickers for Girls (Boys):* 126 Girl/Boy Stickers and Chart to Motivate Toilet Training ■ *Once Upon A Potty His (Her)/* Gift Package/Doll, Book, Potty, Music Video, by Alona Frankel

Staying Dry Through the Night

If your child is a bed-wetter, don't be too concerned. Ten percent of children wet the bed until age five. Your child's bladder and nervous system may not be fully developed yet, preventing your child from being able to wake up from a deep sleep when his bladder is full, or he could have an especially small bladder.

Whatever the reason, explain it to your child. Assure her that it isn't her fault and it will eventually go away. If other children tease her, suggest she respond with, "Sometimes I wet the bed, but I'll grow out of it." Trust that your child will stay dry when her body has matured to the point where she can hold in her urine all night, or wake during the night and walk to the bathroom. Be patient, and know that dry days are ahead.

Constant Companions Siblings

"Jack scribbled on my homework!" "Chloe ate my gummy bears!" Sound familiar? Sibling spats are quite normal, but if it's too hard on your nerves, there are things you can do to encourage good feelings between your kids. Be a role model—when kids see their parents fight, they fight. Do your best to get along with your spouse and friends. When a conflict comes up, be sure to fight fair and resolve things in the end. Praise kids for working it out themselves. Make sure there's a place for each child to have peace and quiet when needed. Stress the importance of family time by scheduling weekly meetings. Talk about the importance of defending and protecting each other outside the home—chances are your kids already know this instinctively. If siblings are constantly hurting each other, it might be wise to make an appointment with a licensed child psychologist.

Ten Teachings of Sibling Rivalry

1. How to negotiate
2. How to share
3. How to control aggressive impulses
4. How to solve problems verbally
5. How to air feelings
6. How to maintain a long-term relationship
7. How to be a good friend
8. How to value someone else's perspective
9. How to compromise
10. How to love, care for, and get along with others

Tips for Mom-in-the-Middle

- **Set Rules.** If your kids insist on fighting, make sure they fight fair. Come up with a set of rules. "No cursing," "no physical violence," and "no name-calling" are good ones to start with. You might want to assign a special place in the house for conflicts.
- **Ignore Simple Arguments.** Let kids work these out themselves.
- **Don't Take Sides.** Your kids are already competing for your attention, so if you choose a side one of them is going to be even more upset. Also, never judge a dispute you didn't see.
- **Give a Two-Minute Warning Before You Intervene.** This gives kids the chance to decide how they want to end the argument.
- **Separate Siblings.** Have each kid go to a quiet place in the house to come up with a way to resolve their conflict and prevent it from happening again. Have them share their ideas with each other.
- **Hear Them Out.** It's only fair to listen to each side of an argument.
- **Stay Calm.** Hopefully your kids will pick up on your energy.
- **Teach Problem Solving.** Come up with creative ideas for solving an argument. Eventually your kids will be able to do this on their own.

Make Each Kid Feel Special

- Give each kid a turn at being "Kid of the Day," and let him make all major decisions, including what's for dinner, what movie to watch, and what music to listen to.
- Set up teamwork activities. Whether it's playing a game or cleaning the house, team cooperation encourages camaraderie as they work toward a common goal.
- Celebrate the unique qualities and differences of each child.
- Be careful not to lock your kids into the stereotypes of birth order. Think of ways for each child to experience their siblings' privileges and responsibilities that go with being the oldest, middle, or youngest child.
- Don't compare your kids with each other. It will only encourage sibling rivalry (the competition between brothers and sisters for their parents' love and attention.)
- Spend one-on-one time with each child as often as possible. Be enthusiastic about his hobbies and interests. Avoid mentioning her siblings during this time.

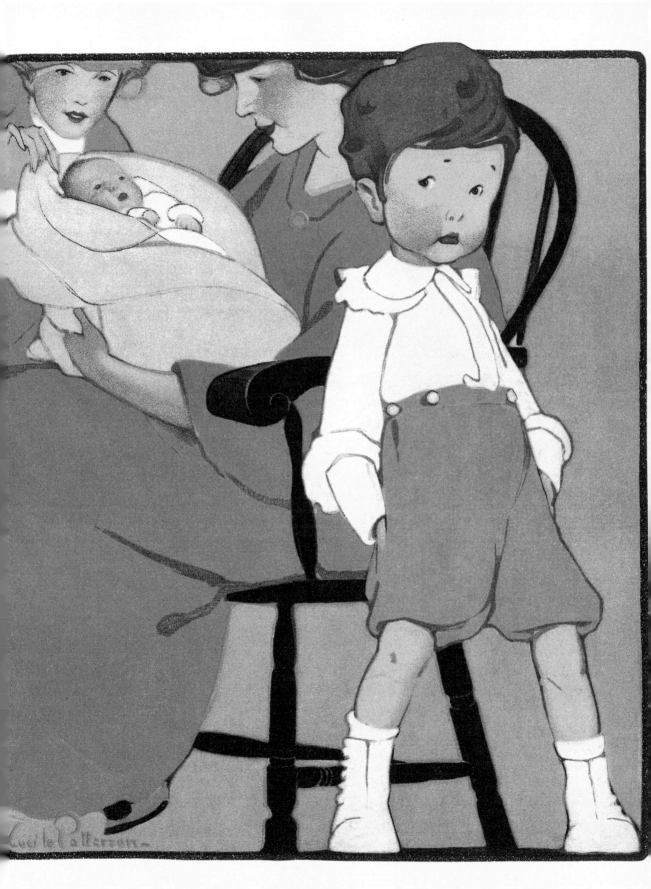

■ ***Start young.*** If your eight-month-old child bites or swats an older sibling, tell her no and show her how to caress the boo-boo with her hands. I think this is important for both children. Your baby will understand at some point and your older child is reassured you are watching out for him, not just the baby. The goal is for your children to love and care for each other. Letting a younger child get away with unloving actions, even if it doesn't really hurt, only creates bad feelings.

■ ***Reinforce good feelings.*** Sylvia was four when her baby sister was born. When the baby started toddling, she walked towards and grabbed Sylvia's legs one day. "Why did Phoebe walk to me?" "Because she loves you, Sylvia." Her face simply lit up and I immediately noticed a more caring attitude from Sylvia to her little sister. ■ ***Treat young and older children equally.*** Parents tend to expect more of their older children. They tell them to take care of the little ones or for them to be "old enough" not to fight. Rather than instructing just the older child, instruct all your children to take care of each other. I was interested to hear my oldest child's reaction once. "I don't need Sylvia to do that for me." It occurred to me that while I was trying to teach my middle child to give, I needed to teach my older child to receive.■ ***Let them be best friends.*** While they have separate playdates from time to time, my children spend a lot of their free time together. My threats of "If you are annoying each other, don't play together today," are only effective when they don't have other playmates to turn to. They usually get so bored alone, they are chums within the half hour.

■ ***A firm NO on bad feelings.*** There are things that are simply not allowed in our home. No physical violence, obviously, but they are also not allowed to say hurtful things. "You are annoying me," and "I don't want to play with you now," is appropriate, but "I hate you," is not. Teach your child phrases he or she can use to express their anger, but not create bad feelings.

Twinkle, Twinkle, Sibling Stars

Ask each child to imagine herself as a star shining down from the sky. Have her notice how much space there is in the sky for each start to glitter on its own—with its unique talents, interests, and personality. Notice together how much space there is for billions of other stars to shine—including her brothers and sisters. Allow her to see that there may not be room for billions of stars in your home, but there's certainly room for her and her brothers and sisters to shine on their own. This is a great way to overcome jealousy.

Picture Books About New Siblings

I'm a Big Sister (Brother) Now, by Joanna Cole ■ *The Baby Sister*, by Tomie DePaola ■ *Max's New Suit*, by Rosemary Wells ■ *Arthur's Baby*, by Marc Brown ■ *A Baby Sister for Frances*, by Russell Hoban

Doctor, Doctor

Sniffles, fevers, bumps, scrapes, rashes...the list goes on. When you have a child, it's always something. That's why it's important to have a pediatrician or family doctor you can trust—someone who has good credentials, maintains a healing philosophy similar to your own, and respects your instincts as a mother. Make a list of the qualities you're looking for. Would you prefer a doctor who is easygoing or businesslike? One who suggests natural remedies before prescribed medicine? A man or a woman? Get recommendations from friends, neighbors, the La Leche League, or the local chapter of the American Medical Association, and start your search a couple months before you give birth.

Make it a habit to arrive early at the doctor's office for your young child's check-ups. The waiting room is usually filled with books or toys. Let your child have time to play so they don't associate a doctor's office with only shots and pain.

Questions for the Receptionist

- What are the doctor's credentials?
- Is he or she affiliated with a teaching hospital or certified by the American Board of Pediatrics?
- What insurance do they take?
- How much will you have to pay for a checkup?
- How is billing handled?
- Is it a group practice?
- How long does it take to get an appointment?
- How long will you be expected to wait at an appointment?
- How are emergencies dealt with?
- Does the doctor make house calls?

UP-TO-DATE The best pediatricians are often affiliated with teaching hospitals and certified—or about to be certified—by the American Board of Pediatrics. These doctors keep up with the latest medical advances.

CALL THE DOCTOR WHEN YOUR CHILD... gets injured ■ can't move a particular body part ■ refuses to eat for longer than a day ■ coughs or wheezes persistently ■ has ear pain or ear drainage ■ has jaundice—skin or whites of eyes turn yellow ■ has a long-lasting cough or cold that gets worse with fever ■ has green vomit ■ has a seizure ■ has profuse bleeding ■ has a head injury with loss of consciousness or vomiting

■ has bloody urine or diarrhea ■ has a sudden lack of energy or other behavioral change ■ has a high fever—or any fever in the case of an infant ■ vomits or has diarrhea for several hours ■ shows signs of dehydration—dry mouth, lips, and skin; decreased urination, no tears, weight loss ■ has recurrent nosebleeds ■ extreme sleepiness ■ stiff neck

VACCINATION CONTROVERSY Vaccinations are recommended for all kids in the United States. They should not harm kids, but some parents have claimed that they do. There are risks associated with all vaccines, and it's important that your doctor tell you what these risks are. For some vaccines, like tetanus, the risks associated with the disease are greater than the risks associated with the shot. But today there are vaccines against some common childhood illnesses like chickenpox. While these vaccines provide temporary immunity, getting the actual illnesses provides permanent immunity. *Remember:* vaccination schedules are only recommended. If you'd like to wait until your infant is older, have more space between shots, or avoid some of the vaccines, you can. For more information, visit *909shot.com*.

TIP
Prepare a list of questions and issues ahead of time to talk about with the doctor.

Recommended Immunization Schedule

VACCINE	AGE
Hepatitis B (HepB): 3 shots	Birth; 1–4 mos.; 6–18 mos.
Diphtheria, Tetanus, Pertussis (DtaP): 5 shots	2 mos.; 4 mos.; 6 mos.; 15–18 mos.; 4–6 yrs.
Haemophilus influenzae Type B (Hib): 4 shots	2 mos.; 4 mos.; 6 mos.; 12–15 mos.
Inactivated Polio (IPV): 4 shots	2 mos.; 4 mos.; 6–18 mos.; 4–6 years
Measles, Mumps, Rubella (MMR): 2 shots	12–15 mos.; 4–6 years
Varicella (chicken pox): 1 shot	12–18 mos.
Pneumococcal conjugate (PCV): 4 shots	2 mos.; 4 mos.; 6 mos.; 12–15 mos.
Diphtheria and Tetanus (Td): 1 shot	11–18 years
Hepatitis A (series)*	24 mos.–18 years
Influenza (yearly)*	6 mos.–18 years
Pneumococcal polysaccharide (PPV): 1 shot*	24 mos.–18 years

*Vaccines recommended for high-risk groups. Check with your local health authority to see if you or your child falls into these groups.

FEVERS A temperature of more than 100.4°F is considered fever. Call the doctor for all fevers, unless it's in an older child or due to an upper respiratory infection or a cold and lasts less than three to five days.

OVERUSE OF ANTIBIOTICS Beware of doctors who prescribe antibiotics for just about everything. Kids can fight off most childhood illnesses better without antibiotics. The routine use of antibiotics can be harmful to kids. They may get better quickly at first, but they are likely to become sick more often with longer, more stubborn infections caused by more resistant organisms. Antibiotics should not be used for a sore throat (unless it's tested as strep), bronchitis, the common cold, a sinus infection (unless it exceeds two weeks), and some ear infections, which often respond well to natural remedies.

HOMEOPATHIC REMEDIES FOR CHILDREN

Many of the most common childhood ailments can be quickly and effectively treated at home with homeopathic remedies. Homeopathy is a medical approach that respects the wisdom of the body, stimulates the body's own immune and defense system to initiate healing, and individualizes medicines according to a person's physical, emotional, and mental makeup. For more information try *Nature's Pharmacy for Children*, by Lendon H. Smith, M.D., Lynne Paige Walker, and Ellen Hodgson Brown and *Homeopathy A-Z*, by Dana Ullman, M. D. Or visit *homeopathic.com*.

RESOURCES When do you simply give your child some pain reliever and send them to bed instead of calling your doctor for an appointment or rushing to the emergency room? The following books and websites provide exhaustive advice as well as helpful and calming suggestions.

- *Healthy Child, Whole Child.* Stuart Ditchek and Russell H. Greenfield.
- *Mayo Clinic Family Health Book: The Ultimate Home Medical Reference*, Mayo Clinic.
- *Taking Care of Your Child*, Robert H. Pantell, et al.
- *Your Child's Health: The Parent's Guide to Symptoms, Emergencies, Common Illnesses, Behavior and School Problems*, Barton D. Schmitt.
- *AAP.org*—the American Association of Pediatrics' website. Child healthcare information, including information about Medicaid coverage.

- *Kidshealth.org*—medical information for children, from infants through teens. Site has separate areas for kids, teens, and adults, containing age-appropriate information.
- *WebMD.com*—a comprehensive health site for the entire family.

Mommy, I'm Scared Fears

Whether it's spiders, strangers, or monsters in the closet, the world can be scary to children. Fears usually show up between ages two and six, and can stem from anything—dreams, overheard conversations, stories, shadows, TV, actual events, seeing other kids get scared, or active imaginations. What the fear is varies from child to child and will, most often, disappear in early childhood.

Fears change as children get older. Toddlers tend to be afraid of separation from their parents, loud noises, strangers, falling, the dark, animals, insects, and using the potty. Pre-schoolers tend to be afraid of animals, insects, imaginary figures, ghosts, getting lost, loss of a parent, and bedtime. School-age children are often afraid of new situations, social rejection, war, burglars, physical injury, health, school performance, thunderstorms, natural disasters, and death.

Fear is not a bad thing—it can keep a child out of harm's way. The completely fearless toddler will most likely get into hazardous situations. Helping your child overcome fears not only eases his anxieties, but also teaches him to depend on you for support. This can result in the child feeling safe in his present life and in the future.

FEAR OF THE DARK There's no need to keep a child in the dark alone. Get a nightlight. Keep a flashlight next to her bed. Stay in the room after "lights out" and talk about how different things look. Illuminate shadows with the flashlight to show her nothing has changed. If she wakes up in the middle of the night, comfort her in her own room. Leave the door open when you leave. Assure her you'll be nearby. If she wants to sleep with the lights on, let her. The need for light will eventually disappear.

FEAR OF HOUSEHOLD ITEMS Fear of a household item is quite common. Have a family member demonstrate how the item works while you hold your child at a distance. Show him that a bath toy is too big to go down the drain—so he is too. Show her that a doll is too big to be sucked into the vacuum cleaner—so she is too. Show him how to be safe around blenders, fans, and food processors.

FEAR OF THUNDERSTORMS Here a simple, rational explanation works best. Explain that thunderstorms develop when warm, wet air from below meets cool, dry air from above. This meeting of hot and cold creates so much energy, it turns into lightning.

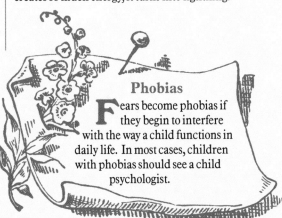

Phobias

Fears become phobias if they begin to interfere with the way a child functions in daily life. In most cases, children with phobias should see a child psychologist.

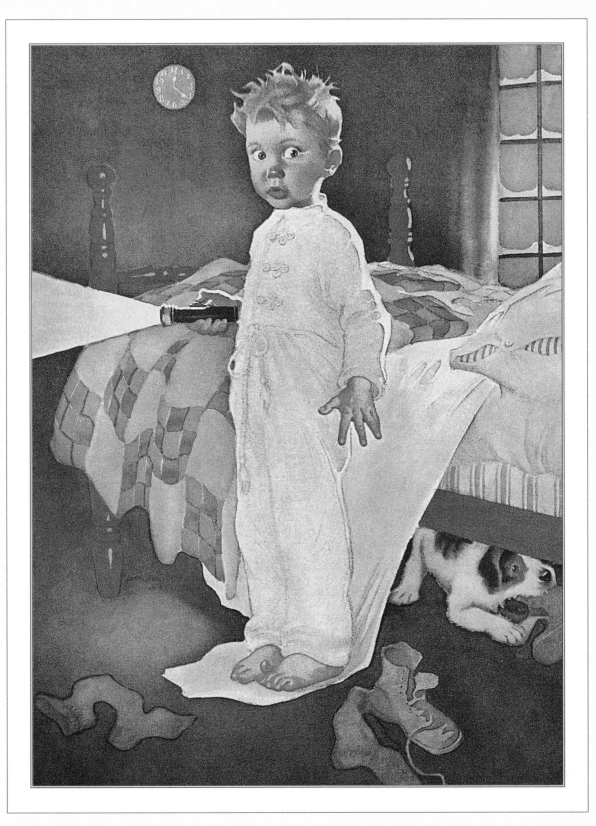

The lightning heats the air so much that it expands and explodes into thunder—a sharp crack when it's near, a low rumble when it's far. Tell your child she can protect herself by going inside when she hears thunder. On her way in, she should stay away from metal, water, and tall trees.

FEAR OF NEW SITUATIONS Not knowing what to expect from the first day of school, or the first day with a new babysitter, can be scary to a child. Role playing is a great way to ease his fears. Guide him through a fictional version of the upcoming situation over and over until he begins to feel comfortable.

FEAR OF NATURAL DISASTERS When she asks questions, avoid giving superficial answers. Go to the library and take out books on the subject so she can indirectly, and safely, experience it from beginning to end. If he's worried about surviving a fire, start having family fire drills. If she's afraid of a flood and you don't live near water, tell her this. If he's afraid of an earthquake and you do live near a fault line, go over the steps you and your community have taken to protect yourselves in an emergency. If you're actually experiencing a natural disaster, stay as calm as possible so she'll stay calm.

FEAR OF DEATH No matter how well we protect our children, sooner or later someone in their life will die. The best way to ease a child's fear of death is by encouraging her to talk about it. Listen closely, be sensitive, and offer honest, simple, age-appropriate explanations. If it's a young child, you may want to explain that when people die they do not breathe, talk, think, feel or eat anymore. If it's an older child, you may want to explain that different people believe different things—and that's okay. Talk about the natural cycle of life, which is actually quite beautiful in concept. If your child is afraid of losing a parent, which is very common, you may want to say that neither parent is expecting to die any time soon. If your child knows someone who died, encourage her to reminisce about the good times, assure her that death isn't contagious and wasn't her fault, and let her know that though the person is physically gone he or she will continue to love her and live in her heart.

FEAR OF IMAGINARY CREATURES The more vivid a child's imagination, the more "scary" characters he can create. Teach him the difference between real and imaginary. Play a game where he has to pick out what's real (a penguin) and what's pretend (an ogre). Use your own imagination. You can spray "magic" water under the bed to make a troll disappear, or send

Tips on Handling Your Child's Fears

- Respect your child's feelings and fears. Let her know it's all right to be afraid.
- Explain that everyone has fears. Take the time to talk about her fears.
- Share your own childhood fears—just don't dwell on them.
- Reassure him that you or another trusted adult will keep him safe.
- Never force a child to confront his fears head-on. Support him as he slowly learns to master his fears, and allow them to go away naturally.
- If you're also scared by a present situation, try to control your own fears and stay calm.
- Remind her of fears she had in the past that she successfully overcame.
- Identify the sources of fear, whether it's TV, a story, or something else. If possible, avoid his future exposure to it. If it's something he over-

heard you say, talk to him about it in a reassuring way, and be more careful about what you say in front of him.
- Reassure and comfort him with hugs, soft music, a low-key story or video, a warm bath, a cuddly teddy bear, or a blanket. Humor works too—just don't laugh at the fear.

P.EBNER

a closet monster to a hotel while your child's in the tub. Encourage your child to make a sign reading: NO GOBLINS ALLOWED, that she can hang on her door. Before bed, search the closet and under the bed, assuring your child that they're gone.

FEAR OF DOGS There are plenty of great dog characters in books and on video. Get them for your child. Take her to a pet store where she can safely watch playful puppies. Pay a short visit to a house with a small dog. Then pay a longer visit to a house with a large dog. If you see a dog at the playground, act calm and cool to show your child he's safe. Never force a child to pet an animal. Let him do it when he's ready and ask the owner first. Show her how to feed a dog—and before you know it she'll be asking you for a puppy.

FEAR OF VIOLENT SITUATIONS If your child is afraid you'll be burglarized, murdered, or victims of a car crash, allow him to talk through his feelings. If she heard it on the news, explain how the news often sensationalizes events. If he overheard a conversation, talk about what was said. If she has questions, give her honest answers without becoming too graphic. Point out the precautions you've taken to keep your family safe. Talk about how well-equipped your local police and fire departments are to handle emergencies. If a violent

crime has happened to someone your child knows, or if you live in a potentially dangerous area, be more sensitive to your child's fears. They have a valid source.

FEAR OF STRANGERS Ironically, more children are harmed by someone they know and trust than by strangers. Teach your child to judge situations instead of people. Teach him to trust his feelings, to say no, and to avoid any adult asking for help or directions. If your child has a plan for self-protection, she'll be less afraid. More information on child safety can be found at your local library and at the National Center for Missing and Exploited Children (NCMEC at missingkids.org)

FEAR OF NIGHTMARES As a child's imagination becomes more complex, so do her nightmares. When she awakens from a nightmare, the scary creatures in her dream are still very real to her. Turn on the light, comfort her, and let her know she's safe. Encourage her to talk about the dream. Let her know it wasn't real— it was make-believe just like Cinderella and Pinocchio. Explain that everyone has bad dreams once in a while. Before leaving the room, check for scary visitors with a flashlight. Let her sleep with the light on if she wants to. The next morning, encourage her once again to talk about the dream. Be sure to tell her she's safe over and over so she won't be afraid to go to sleep.

A home should reflect the people who live there. This doesn't mean a home with children—the kings and queens of making messes—has to be cluttered. No matter how many toys, books, stuffed animals, school flyers, or pieces of sports equipment, clothing, collections, and artwork children accumulate, there are ways to keep the house neat and organized. First, everything in the house must have a place: toys, blocks, art supplies, school items, clothes, treasures, and miscellaneous items. A home that appeals to a child's internal sense of order will encour-

Keeping House

age habits of organization in his future. With a bit of planning, thought, and enthusiasm you can create the ideal home for your family—one that's functional and fun to live in.

*T*oys have a habit of getting everywhere. It can be quite an exercise to constantly pick them up and take them back into the children's rooms. Assign spaces in frequently used areas of your apartment or house—a basket by the stairs, a kitchen cabinet, or a drawer in the living room. Simply toss the toys into their spaces as you walk by. Teach your children to do the same.

ARTWORK GALLERY Turn a wall into an art gallery to display your children's artwork. It's more spacious than a refrigerator and more fun, too. With inexpensive frames, each picture will look like a masterpiece. Or secure a cord across a wall and use clothespins to hang an ever-changing display of art.

START A TOY LIBRARY Between their birthday presents, holiday gifts, and souvenirs, young children often become overwhelmed with their toys. Starting a toy library is the perfect solution. Let your child select a group of toys to keep out

and store the rest in large, plastic bins. After a month, bring those toys back to the library and take out another group. Having a toy library prevents kids from getting tired of the same old toys.

CLUTTERLESS CLOSET IDEAS

■ Keep clothing in a wardrobe with an adjustable hanging rail that can be raised as your children grow taller.

■ For younger children, remove closet doors, lower clothing rods, and buy child-sized hangers. Keep a container on the floor for toys, dolls, and stuffed animals.

■ Keep in-season clothing in the closet. Store off-season clothing in large, plastic, labeled bins in the basement or attic. Donate clothes the child doesn't need or wear to charity.

■ Since babies don't need much hanging space, install a versatile storage unit with adjustable shelves, drawers, and rods to create a functional storage place from floor to ceiling. Things will be easy to find and to put away.

■ Top shelves of closets are great places for older children

and teenagers to store their belongings in clear plastic shoeboxes with labels.

CREATIVE STORAGE

■ Get colorful or clear storage cubes to hold toys, blocks, videos, puzzles, and CDs, and label them. Young children need to be able to see the contents without opening every cube in search for something. Several can be stacked together.

- Get storage boxes that can double as seats with pillows or a drawing surfaces for budding artists. (Get one that doesn't close completely to prevent fingers from getting pinched.)
- Use rolling bins or drawers that fit neatly under a bed; look for flat plastic lidded boxes that are low enough to place under the bed frame, or choose a bed with built-in drawers.
- If a child's room lacks space to keep things, look up. You can install display shelving about a foot down from the ceiling. Use it to show off collections and trophies.
- Set up a desk for homework, art projects, and a computer if your child has one. Make sure it has lots of drawers to organize pencils, pens, scissors, rulers, paper, tape, and markers.
- Keep art supplies in a portable box with separate containers labeled *crayons, markers*, and *paintbrushes*. This way they can be used in any room or out on the porch.
- Get a filing cabinet so the child can organize schoolwork, report cards, pictures, cards, awards and certificates, stories, mementos, and other stuff. File folders and drawers should be labeled.
- Stow bathtub toys in a large colander or hanging net.
- Store books in a child-sized bookcase so your child can take out and put back books.
  - Give your child a space for small personal knickknacks and treasured items, from fabulous gum wrappers to pebbles. It can be a drawer or simply a nylon bag that hangs on a bedpost.

Information Area

Set aside an area in which to keep information and schedules. A wall in the kitchen near a phone is a good location. The following items are useful:

■ *Information Sheet*. See page 35. ■ *A large, wall calendar with spacious day slots.* Whenever someone makes a plan, whether it's a bake sale, doctor's appointment, practice schedule, or school play, it must be recorded on the calendar. Record times, dates, places, and phone numbers. You might want to assign each family member who is old enough to write a different-colored marker and keep them in a special container. When a child brings home a flyer for an event she wants to attend, it must be recorded. When you receive a birthday invitation, decide if you're going to go. If you are, record the info and RSVP immediately. ■ *A corkboard or magnetic board.* For school notices, invitations, phone lists, grocery lists, and other information you want to find again! ■ *A blackboard or dry-erase board* To jot down reminders and messages to other family members. ■ *Writing instruments secured with strings.* Save yourself from forgetting to write things down because you don't have a pencil handy at the right moment.

COMING & GOING ROUTINE

"I can't find my homework!" "Did you see my keys?" "Who took my sunglasses?" Getting ready to go out can be very chaotic—especially if you have a large family. Establish a "coming & going" routine by assigning each family member a special place for important stuff. It could be a hanging set of baskets—the low basket for the shortest kid and the highest for an adult. It could be color-coded plates—one per person. It could be backpacks that hang on each person's chair or on adjacent hooks. It could be low-hung pegs where you can hang jackets and keys. What's important is that each family member always knows where to put things when they enter the house and where to find them when they leave.

CLEAN-UP TIME
Hold a family clean-up time. Toddlers can put loose toys into bins. They can also be taught to fold their clothes (not perfectly) and sort them into drawers. Older kids can wipe up spills, fold and sort laundry, dry dishes, and dust, among other things. Encourage kids to keep their own rooms clean by making their beds in the morning, putting stuff away, and tossing their dirty clothes in a hamper as soon as they take them off. Having daily clean-ups will prevent the buildup of messes.

DEALING WITH AN OVERWHELMINGLY MESSY ROOM

- Help your child sort clothes, toys, school supplies, and other belongings into labeled bins.
- Initiate a daily clean-up time to prevent the mess from recurring.
- Let her have one messy drawer, shelf, or corner where she can toss things temporarily.
- If you're feeling generous, clean up the room yourself when your child is out. Showing her how beautiful the room could be might inspire her to keep it that way.

Dividing the Work Chores

Asking your child to do chores has to do with much more than your acquiring a source of free labor. Your child learns valuable lessons about responsibility, accountability, and how to work with others from performing chores. Pitching in around the house also helps your child understand his relationship to his environment and teaches him that good things often come about through hard work. These are wonderful lessons that will last a lifetime, and if you work side by side, chores can help strengthen family ties.

ROTATE CHORES Make a "chore wheel" using a piece of stiff paper with a pointer in the middle. Divide the wheel into different sections, with a different chore in each. At the beginning of each week, gather the family together and spin the wheel to decide which chore each person will do for the week. It is important for your child to see that every one has to pitch in and that no one gets special treatment.

Hint: Make the chore wheel like a game show—choose a theme song for spinning the wheel and let

General Tips on Assigning Chores

- Make sure chores are age-appropriate.
- Remember that small children should not use cleaning products without supervision.
- Children can start doing chores at age five or six, but until eight or nine will need to be reminded frequently.
- Give fair warning. If you are asking your child for help, don't demand it immediately, but say, "In five minutes I'd like you to help me…"
- Make it sound important. You can make a chore more appealing by making it sound impressive. Instead of saying, "You have to sweep the floor," you can say something like, "You are officially in charge of sweeping, and will be our floor monitor this week."
- Practice what you preach. If you ask your child to do a chore, make sure that you are also working at the same time.
- Make it fun. Put on some lively music for chore time and let your child see that you can dance while you dust.

each "contestant" spin the wheel to select a chore. Make a drum roll with chopsticks on a countertop as the wheel spins. Applaud each time a chore is selected.

GIVE YOUR CHILD A CLEANING KIT You can help interest your child in chores by giving him his own cleaning tools. Cleaning kit items might include: bucket ▪ broom (child size) ▪ dustpan ▪ cloth rags scrubbing sponge ▪ bottle of homemade glass cleaner: *one part white vinegar to three parts water* ▪ rubber gloves

GIVE DAILY AND WEEKLY CHORES Make your child responsible for certain chores every day and others every week. This teaches him that there are different levels of responsibility. A good daily chore to start with is making the bed, as this is a very quick and easy one to learn. A good weekly chore is sorting laundry, either separating colors from whites or making piles of clean laundry for each family member.

PROVIDE ON-THE-JOB TRAINING Make an illustrated instruction sheet for each chore and walk your child through it. For instance, if you are asking your child to be in charge of setting the table for dinner, give him a "cheat sheet" taped inside the china cabinet. Draw a picture of what the table should look like, clearly indicating which side is right and which is left. Do the chore together a few times until he gets the hang of it. Once he has it down, say something like, "Well, I can see you're a real expert table-setter now, so I'm going to leave you to work your magic alone."

WORK TOGETHER You can make chore time into chat time if you work alongside your child. You might give her the task of picking things up off the living-room floor while you start with the dusting, for instance, and you can talk or tell stories as you go along. It is important for your child to see work as a potentially social experience that can make chores much more pleasant to perform. Your child will get a sense of self-importance if you recruit her to work with you.

SAY PLEASE AND THANK YOU This is an excellent time to teach children about valuing other people's time and contributions.

COMPLIMENT YOUR CHILD'S WORK Make sure to let your child know that you appreciate what

he's done. Be specific about what you like. Say something like, "You really got every last dust bunny out from under the bed, didn't you?" Even if it's not entirely true, it will spur your child on to do a more thorough job next time in order to be worthy of the praise. In the meantime, compliments let him know that you recognize his efforts.

REWARD GOOD JOBS WITH GOOD TIMES Many experts think that it is a bad idea to link chores to allowance money. Children should learn to do chores because they are part of the family, not because it will make them rich. So, reward your child for a job well done by going somewhere fun, like a movie or the zoo. Alternatively, you might simply promise your child a nice "coffee break" when the two of you have finished work. Sit down together with a glass of juice and put your feet up. Say, "We've done a lot of good work today. Let's take a break now."

Wardrobe Basics

Shopping for a child can be challenging. You must consider what he likes, what size he wears, and what size it makes sense to buy if you're shopping for another season. If you have a toddler, getting shoes with Velcro® rather than laces makes more sense. If you have school-age children, it's important to get clothes they feel comfortable and confident wearing. Don't buy clothes too far ahead of time—an unexpected growth spurt can turn new clothes into hand-me-downs before your child has worn them. Don't spend too much money on everyday clothes. Everyday spills and messes can quickly ruin shirts. It's wiser to invest in good outerwear that lasts and can be handed down.

Year-Round Wardrobe Staples

Underwear ■ Pajamas ■ Short-sleeved shirts ■ Long-sleeved shirts Gym shorts ■ Socks (athletic and dress) ■ Sneakers ■ Shoes (dress) ■ Bathing suit ■ Sweatpants ■ Sweatshirts ■ Sweaters ■ Jeans Pants ■ Dresses ■ Skirts

Extras for Spring

Light jacket ■ Raincoat ■ Rubber boots/galoshes ■ Rain hat ■ Baseball cap

Extras for Summer

Shorts ■ Sleeveless shirts ■ Sundresses ■ Sandals ■ Flip-flops

Extras for Fall

Fleece jacket ■ Tights ■ Warm wool and cotton sweaters

Extras for Winter

Snow suit ■ Snow boots ■ Mittens/gloves ■ Scarves ■ Warm winter jacket ■ Turtlenecks ■ Hat ■ Flannel pajamas ■ Wool or thermal socks ■ Silk, merino wool, or polypropylene long underwear

Dressing Baby

Your newborn will grow quickly, so don't invest too much money in newborn clothing. Choose clothing that your child can grow into. And since you'll be changing your baby many, many times a day in the first few weeks of his or her life, choose clothing that's easy to remove. Here's a suggested list of clothing, and the amounts you'll need when you're starting out. Wash the items before they're worn to remove harsh chemicals and to give them a soft, snuggly feel.

One-piece outfits	4 to 7	"Onesies" are body-suit-like garments that snap along the inseams of the legs.
One-piece pajamas	4 to 7	The baglike bottoms of these garments are sometimes fastened with snaps or drawstrings. The drawstrings make nighttime changes easier.
Undershirts	4 to 7	Soft cotton shirts with snaps at the neck will fit well and protect tender newborn skin.
Sweater or jacket	1	Avoid pullover garments for your newborn; instead choose items that button or snap.
Socks	4 to 7 pairs	Keep your baby's feet warm with soft socks or booties.
Cap	1 to 3	Winter babies will need a soft, warm hat, and summer babies something with a wide brim to protect their skin from the sun.

Shoe Sizes

The best recommendation is always to bring your child with you when purchasing shoes for them. Use the chart below or visit *iftheshoefitsetc.com/chart.html* for a foot-measuring guide when shopping for shoes by catalog or online.

Inches	U.S	European
3	0	
3 1/3	I	
3 2/3	2	17, 18
4	3	18, 19
4 1/3	4	19
4 2/3	5	20
5	6	21, 22
5 1/3	7	23
5 2/3	8	24, 25

Inches	U.S	European
6	9	26
6 1/3	10	27, 28
6 2/3	11	28, 29
7	12	30
7 1/3	13	31
7 2/3	I	32
8	2	33, 34
8 1/3	3	35
8 2/3	4	36

THAT'S ABOUT THE SIZE OF IT Clothing sizes for babies and toddlers can vary wildly from brand to brand. Look for brands that don't just give a size by age such as "three months." Brands that use measurements, such as weight and length, will help you find clothes that fit.

General Guidelines for Clothing Sizes

BABIES

AGE/SIZE	WEIGHT (LBS.)	LENGTH (IN.)
Newborn	up to 7	up to 17"
3 months	7–12	17–23"
3–6 months	12–17	23–27"
6–12 months	17–22	27–29"
12–18 months	22–27	29–31"
18–24 months	27–30	31–33"

GIRLS

SIZE	AGE	HEIGHT	WAIST
3/XS	3	36–39"	20–21"
4/XS	4	39–42"	20.5–21.5"
5/S	5	42–45"	21–22"
6/S	6	45–49"	22–22.5"
7/M	7	49–53"	22.5–23"
8/M	8	53–55"	23–23.5"
10/L	9–10	55–57"	24–24.5"
12/XL	11–12	57–60"	25–25.5"
14/XXL	13	60–62"	25.5–26"
16/XXL	14	62–65"	26.5–27"

BOYS

SIZE	AGE	HEIGHT	WAIST
3/XS	3	36–39"	20–21"
4/XS	4	39–42"	21–22"
5/S	5	42–45"	22–22.5"
6/S	6	45–49"	22.5–23"
7/M	7	49–53"	23–23.5"
8/M	8	53–55"	23.5–24"
10/L	9–10	55–57"	24.5–25"
12/XL	11–12	57–60"	25.5–26"
14/XXL	13	60–62"	26.5–27"
16/XXL	14	62–65"	27.5–28"

Extended sizes: Don't be too concerned if your child doesn't fit perfectly into these sizes—kids come in all shapes and sizes, and stores are starting to catch on! Many retailers are making extended sizes for children, from extra slim to plus and husky sizes. Be sure to ask at the store if your child needs these options.

STORING CLOTHES Instead of scrunching every item of your kids' clothing into their closets, store the items that aren't in season. Get one or two large, plastic storage bins for each child and label them with the child's name, the type of clothing, and the season or age they are for. (*Jane, Sweaters and Turtlenecks, Winter '05 or 3 years old*) When filling the bins with clothes, be sure to include clothes outgrown by one sibling in a younger sibling's bin. Clothes like T-shirts, underwear, and gym shorts never need to be stored. If you have a few clothes to give away but want to wait until you have more, store them in another bin labeled GIVEAWAYS. Store the bins in a basement or attic. When the season changes, have a "switchover day" so each child can take the new season's clothes out of his bins and pack the old season's clothes into the bins. Don't forget to change the labels each time.

Doing laundry for a houseful of kids isn't an easy task. One way to keep track of what clothes belong to whom is to mark the inside tags with permanent marker. Use one mark for the eldest child, two marks for the second child, three for the third, and so on. Whenever an article of clothing gets passed on as a hand-me-down, add a new mark. You will still have a heavy laundry load, but sorting will be a breeze.

Grassy Pants & Berry Shirts

*L*aundry is a never-ending job with kids in the house. Each load is fraught with stains that would even make your grandmother shriek. Grass, ketchup, chocolate ... and those are just on little Jessie's soccer jersey. But don't lose hope. The answers to how to remove any stain imaginable (well ... almost) are finally revealed.

Stain Removal

Around-the-House Cheaper Remedies

baking soda; club soda; 1 part rubbing alcohol & 2 parts water solution; window cleaner

Fabric Stains

BLOOD If the blood has dried, brush away excess so stain won't spread when dissolved. Flush stained area with cold water right away. Then sprinkle the stain with meat tenderizer and cool water. Let stand for twenty minutes, then rinse and wash garment as directed. If it is a stubborn stain, flush with vinegar or hydrogen peroxide (if the fabric can stand it). This will remove the color.

CHOCOLATE Before applying stain remover, scrape off as much chocolate as possible. Start with a full-strength detergent. If the stain won't budge, switch to an equal parts vinegar and water solution, blotting the stain with a clean cloth. If you need to pull in the big guns to get the job done, try lighter fluid or bleach heavily diluted with water. After treating the stain, launder as directed.

COFFEE or TEA Flush with stain remover or lemon juice (remember to test on an inconspicuous area of the fabric first). Wash fabric in cold water and dry in the sun.

CRAYON (melted) Place a stack of paper towels on the stain. Spray WD-40 on the backside of the fabric. Flip the towels to the backside and spray directly onto the stain. Next, apply liberal amounts of dishwashing liquid to the stain, replacing towels with clean ones as they absorb the stain. Wash garment in hot water and rinse in warm. Repeat process if stain remains.

Dry only after the stain is removed. Note: Clear your dryer of any residual wax by wiping the drum with a WD-40 sprayed cloth. Run a load of clean rags through the drying cycle to pick up any loose wax.

FRUIT JUICE Flush with stain remover (the alcohol/water mixture is best for dark fruit juices). For white fabrics, lemon works well as a natural bleach. After treating the stain, wash as directed.

GRASS Liquid detergent or slightly diluted hydrogen peroxide or bleach (if fabric can take it).

Rules of Gum (Er ... Thumb)

*T*he cardinal rule of stain removal is to treat the stain immediately. Not tomorrow. Not five minutes from now. Immediately! For most stains (and most washable fabrics) it's best to rinse the area in cool water, wetting as little of the fabric as possible. Cool water should be used for all but grease stains, as hot water can set a stain.

Always test your stain remover on an inconspicuous portion of the fabric (e.g., a hem) for color change. If no change occurs, add a small amount of the remover to the back of your fabric to avoid spreading the stain deeper. Dab at the fabric from the outermost portion inward, and rinse well. AVOID SCRUBBING STAINS, as scrubbing will only cause the stain to spread.

Repeat this process until the stain is gone. As soon as possible, launder the garment according to the manufacturer's instructions. Air-dry it, in the sun if possible, so you can fully assess the dry fabric for any stain residue. Never put a stained item in the dryer, even if you think you've probably gotten it out, as heat can set the stain.

GREASE Launder in a generous amount of regular detergent and hot water, and rinse. Try club soda on more delicate fabrics. For grease on textured fabrics, apply cornstarch and let sit overnight to absorb.

GUM or **WAX** Use ice to freeze soiled area, or throw garment in the freezer for a time. Break gum or wax from fabric and treat any residual stain with full-strength detergent. An alternate method for removing wax is to sprinkle area with cornstarch. Place a paper towel over the

Top (Commercially Available) Stain Removers
Goop, Lestoil , Out! , Oxyclean Spot Shot , Totally Toddler-Nursery Stain & Odor Remover & Prewash, Whink

stain and heat with a moderately warm iron. Wax should come away with the paper towel. Then wash as above. *Note:* Clear your dryer of any residual wax by wiping the drum with a WD-40 sprayed cloth. Run a load of clean rags through the drying cycle to pick up any loose wax.

MUD Let dry, then brush excess dirt off. Pretreat the fabric with stain remover and wash.

LIPSTICK Use petroleum jelly, soda water or hairspray to pretreat the garment if you can't throw in the wash right away. Toothpaste also works.

MUSTARD Flush stain with a household ammonia and water mixture. Then wash with dishwashing detergent.

RED WINE Dab with club soda or sprinkle with salt and let sit for fifteen minutes. Wash in cold water.

SOFT DRINKS Soften stain with petroleum jelly prior to applying your stain remover. Launder as directed.

SOY SAUCE Use dishwashing detergent and water to start. Flush with hydrogen peroxide if stain is really set.

TOMATO SAUCE Using a toothbrush, brush dry dishwasher detergent into stain. Launder, then dry in the sun.

URINE If the stain is stubborn, try a vinegar and water solution. Your last resort could be a diluted hydrogen peroxide wash, but beware: This mixture can act as bleach, fading colors on some clothing.

VOMIT Sponge stain with one part ammonia in six parts warm water. Rinse well. If the stain covers a large area, dampen the stain and sprinkle with pepsin powder. Leave for thirty minutes and then rinse.

Other Stains

MILK SPOTS ON FURNITURE Apply vinegar and water solution with a clean cloth. Dry thoroughly.

INK/CRAYON ON WALLS Spray hairspray directly on ink stains. Wipe clean with a dry cloth. Crayon can be removed using a damp cloth and baking soda, dishwashing detergent, or Goop. Baby wipes also work amazingly well.

Out, Out Darn Spot

For ballpoint, if the stain is still wet, sprinkle with salt and sponge with water. Then apply dishwashing detergent and a few drops of vinegar. If the stain has dried, apply hairspray directly to the stain and dab with a clean cloth. Flush with water and wash. For felt tip, flush with an alcohol/water solution. Then wash with dishwashing detergent.

chapter two
Feeding Time

General Nutrition   What You Need

Our culture does not make it easy to raise a healthy child. The media is constantly bombarding children with ads for candy and sugary snacks. Fast food restaurants offer salty, fatty foods that appeal to taste buds and are served with toys. Teaching your child to eat nutritiously may be a long, challenging process, but it's well worth it. Children need to eat a variety of foods, including protein, carbohydrates, fruits, and vegetables—it's essential to their growth. Be a role model. If children see their parents buying and enjoying nutritious food, they are more likely to do so themselves. Create a pleasant, unhurried environment around the breakfast, lunch, and dinner table. Keep a variety of easily accessible nutritious snacks—a raw vegetable tray or fresh fruit salad on a low refrigerator shelf or raisins, whole-grain crackers and pretzels, and rice cakes in a low cupboard. Show your child how to recognize foods that support growth and those that don't. Explain that different foods help them grow in different ways. "If you eat yogurt, you'll have strong, healthy bones and teeth." Teach older children how to read and interpret nutrition labels. Keep a pitcher of water—the most vital drink of all—where children can reach it. Be patient—learning to eat healthy doesn't happen overnight.

The Five Essentials

All essential nutrients needed by you and your growing children can be found in a varied, well-balanced diet.

- CARBOHYDRATES are the body's primary source of energy. Complex carbohydrates are energy-rich foods, including whole-grain cereals, breads, pastas, and rice. These foods retain vitamins, minerals, and fiber, unlike their refined counterparts, such as white bread or most store-bought cookies.
- PROTEIN is needed for growth and repair of our body tissues. Our bodies don't store protein naturally, so it's important to eat foods containing protein every day. While animal proteins provide all the amino acids the body needs, other protein sources need to be combined with other foods to provide complete protein. Serve whole grains with legumes or beans for complete protein.
- FATS are especially important for the littlest ones in your family—they're essential for children's growth. Babies up to age one need as much as 50 percent of their energy intake from fat. Children between two and five need up to 35 percent.
- VITAMINS keep us healthy. Heat destroys water-soluble vitamins, such as B and C, so it's best to avoid overcooking vegetables or fruit that are high in these vitamins. Fat-soluble vitamins A, D, E, and K stay stored in the body and can be harmful in large doses.
  - *Vitamin A:* Good for eyesight, growth, appetite, making red blood cells, and taste. *Sources:* Carrots, red peppers, tomatoes, sweet potatoes, mangoes, apricots, corn, liver, fish liver oil, eggs, green leafy vegetables, and milk products.
  - *B Complex Vitamins:* Good for nervous system, digestion, growth, muscles, heart, skin, nails, hair, and eyesight. *Sources:* liver, yeast, rice, peanuts, pork, chicken, milk, cheese, green leafy vegetables, tofu, sardines, eggs, whole-grain cereals, avocados, bananas, and dried beans.
  - *Vitamin C:* Good for growth, the immune system, protection from bacteria and viruses, tissue repair, cell lifespan, lowering cholesterol, and aiding in iron absorption. *Sources:* kiwi fruit, citrus fruits, strawberries, dark green leafy vegetables, peppers, and potatoes.
  - *Vitamin D:* Good for strong bones and teeth and absorbing calcium and phosphorous. *Sources:* sunlight, cod-liver oil, salmon, sardines, tuna, herring, milk products, cheese, and eggs.

◆ *Vitamin E:* Good for fighting poisons, healthy cell structure, and maintenance of red blood cells. *Sources:* nuts, avocados, soybeans, vegetable oils, broccoli, spinach, whole-grain products, and eggs.

◆ *Vitamin K:* Good for normal blood clotting and regulation of calcium levels in the blood. *Sources:* spinach, kale, collards, broccoli, soybean oil, olive oil, and canola oil.

■ MINERALS help proteins, fats, and carbohydrates produce energy. They work with vitamins to maintain metabolism, prevent disease, and continue healthy body processes.

◆ *Calcium:* Good for healthy teeth, bones, nerves, muscles, and heart tissue. *Sources:* milk, yogurt, cheese, leafy vegetables, tofu, nuts, sardines, and sesame seeds.

◆ *Zinc:* Good for growth, immune system, and protein and fatty acid metabolism. *Sources:* red meat, shellfish, sunflower seeds, and peanuts.

◆ *Iron:* Good for carrying oxygen from the lungs to all body cells and mental and physical development. *Sources:* liver, red meat, oily fish, legumes, green leafy vegetables, dried apricots, and raisins.

What's a Serving?

The portion sizes listed below under the five major food groups are recommended for anyone over age four. Younger children need smaller portions, but the number of servings needed is the same. Serving sizes for the Milk group remain the same for children ages two and up.

■ *Milk, Yogurt, and Cheese (2 servings daily)* 1 cup of milk or yogurt, 1 1/2 ounces of natural cheese, 2 ounces of processed cheese

■ *Meat, Poultry, Fish, Dry Beans, Eggs, and Nuts (2 servings daily; 1- to-3 year-olds' daily amount should equal 3 1/2 ounces; 4- to-5-year-olds' daily amount should equal 5 ounces)* 2-3 ounces of cooked, lean meat, poultry, or fish, 1 cup tofu, 1/2 cup of cooked dry beans count as 1 ounce of lean meat; 1 egg or 2 tablespoons of peanut butter count as 1 ounce of lean meat

■ *Vegetables (3 servings daily)* 1 cup of raw, leafy vegetables, 1/2 cup of other vegetables, cooked or chopped raw, 3/4 cup of vegetable juice

■ *Fruit (2 servings daily)* 1 piece of fruit or melon wedge, 1/2 cup of chopped, cooked, or canned fruit, 3/4 cup of fruit juice

■ *Bread, Cereal, Rice, and Pasta (6 servings daily)* 1 slice of bread, 1 ounce of ready-to-eat cereal 1/2 cup of cooked cereal, rice, or pasta

Food Guide Pyramid

The Food Guide Pyramid shows how to make nutritious food choices for your family's daily diet. Children should follow the lowest number of servings listed next to the pyramid—the higher servings are for adults. There are five major food groups: Grains, Vegetables, Fruits, Milk, and Meat. Each of these food groups provides a variety of nutrients that children need to grow, to be active, and to be healthy.

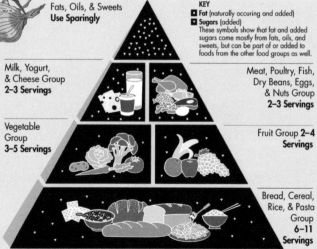

Fats, Oils, & Sweets
Use Sparingly

KEY
■ Fat (naturally occuring and added)
▼ Sugars (added)
These symbols show that fat and added sugars come mostly from fats, oils, and sweets, but can be part of or added to foods from the other food groups as well.

Milk, Yogurt, & Cheese Group
2–3 Servings

Meat, Poultry, Fish, Dry Beans, Eggs, & Nuts Group
2–3 Servings

Vegetable Group
3–5 Servings

Fruit Group **2–4 Servings**

Bread, Cereal, Rice, & Pasta Group
6–11 Servings

SOURCE: U.S. Department of Agriculture/U.S. Department of Health and Human Services

Food Basics   What's Good For You

As a mom, you are in charge of your child's health—at least when it comes to nutrition. You have control over what type of food you keep in your kitchen. You decide whether to buy whole foods, organic foods, or processed foods. You know about good nutrition, or if you don't, you have the ability to learn. Your child does not have the knowledge and understanding you do. Children often go for candy, ice cream, and other sugary snacks, which provide instant gratification. Prohibiting your child from having any junk food can be tricky, but there are ways to compromise. Become familiar with reading and understanding food labels—some junk foods are better than others. Keep some naturally sweet snack foods in your kitchen. Explain to your child that you want her to eat well because you care about her so she won't feel deprived. If your child wants a candy bar or sugary drink that you don't want her to have, don't be afraid to say no. Remind yourself that when it comes to nutrition, Mom knows best.

You can reduce the amount of salt in canned beans, vegetables, and tuna fish by draining the contents into a colander and rinsing under cool water.

Partially Hydrogenated Oil

You may want to think twice before buying another bag of goldfish, box of animal crackers, or box of cereal at your local supermarket. Read the labels and you'll find many contain partially hydrogenated fat, as do doughnuts, fast food French fries, microwave popcorn, soft-serve ice cream, graham crackers, granola bars, and commercially made baked goods. Partially hydrogenated fat is a vegetable fat that's been bombarded with hydrogen to make it solid at room temperature—a big advantage to processed-food makers. It solidifies liquid margarine to give it a longer shelf life. When a food contains partially hydrogenated fat, it contains trans-fat, an artificial fat manufactured to imitate naturally saturated fats. There is evidence that trans-fats predispose children to diabetes, obesity, and cancer, and stimulate insulin production.

Read labels. You may find certain brands do not use partially hydrogenated oil. Otherwise, shop at health food stores.

Cooking vegetables in water depletes the amount of vitamins B and C naturally found in the food. You can keep your veggies vitamin-rich by steaming or stir-frying. If your recipe calls for boiling vegetables, reuse the water in soups or gravy as a yummy way to recapture the lost vitamins.

Why Choose Organic?

Commercially grown produce is sprayed with legal amounts of toxic pesticides, which interfere with the way the body processes nutrients. Some farmers use sewage sludge to fertilize their crops. In addition to human waste, this can contain toxic chemicals, cleaners, and heavy metals. Another concern is the use of antibiotics. From 60 to 80 percent of all cattle, sheep, and poultry in the United States will receive antibiotics at some point. The commercial dairy business is dominated by huge farms where cows are machine-milked, confined to the barnyard, fed hay and grain grown in fields sprayed with pesticides, and routinely given antibiotics to combat diseases. Twenty to 30 percent of these cows are given hormones. Organic food is grown without synthetic fertilizers, pesticides, herbicides, hormones, or antibiotics, and reduces the risk of getting cancer or other diseases.

WHOLE FOODS The best way to get the most out of the food we eat is to include a wide variety of whole foods—grains, legumes, nuts, seeds, and fresh fruits and vegetables—in our diet. Natural foods are the best sources of vitamins, fiber, minerals, complex carbohydrates, fats, and nutrients necessary for healthy physical and mental function.

Be on the lookout for processed foods containing questionable additives, preservatives, chemicals, artificial ingredients, and unwanted sugar, sodium, or saturated fat. Many of these additives can result in adverse health.

REDUCE SUGAR Carbohydrates provide our bodies with their best source of fuel. Sugars are simple carbohydrates. When we eat sugar in its natural state, such as in fresh fruits, starches, or complex carbohydrates, it is diluted and coexists with fiber and other nutrients necessary for digestion and healthy brain function.

The problem with consuming refined sugars is that they give us energy without significant nutritional value. Table sugar, brown sugar, molasses, honey, and powdered sugar contain roughly between fifty and one hundred calories per tablespoon. We may think that eating empty calories is okay if we burn them off with physical activity, but in fact we are robbing our bodies of existing vitamins and minerals in order to digest these empty calories. Reducing sugar will significantly decrease your family's health risks related to obesity and malnutrition.

REDUCE SODIUM Sodium is an essential mineral for the body, necessary for healthy muscle and nerve function and for regulating the body's water balance. The typical American diet contains far more sodium than is necessary, which is generally less than a teaspoon per day. Be on the lookout for high-sodium foods, such as canned soups, cured meats, snack foods, pickled foods, processed cheeses, dehydrated mixes, and fast foods. Too much sodium can put the ones you love on an unhealthy path toward hypertension (high blood pressure), heart attack, stroke, and kidney disease.

HEALTHY FATS Fat is an essential source of energy. Fats are lipids, compounds that make up important components of cells, tissues, and organs. The body needs fats to make hormones and to absorb fat-soluble vitamins A, D, E, and K. Fats fall into two basic categories: saturated and unsaturated.

- ***Saturated fats*** are solid at room temperature. They are primarily found in animal and dairy products, although some vegetable products, such as coconut and palm oils, are also saturated fats. Once in the bloodstream, saturated fats become the forerunners of low-density lipoproteins (LDL) or "bad cholesterol," which can inhibit blood flow and contribute to heart disease and some forms of cancer.
- ***Unsaturated fats*** are liquid at room temperature. They include fish, vegetable, and nut oils that do not contribute to bad cholesterol, heart disease, or cancer. Limit your saturated fats to less than ten percent of your daily diet. Hydogenated fats should be avoided (*See page 76*).

Value of Variety Getting Creative

*E*ncouraging your family to experience a wide variety of tastes at mealtimes is the best way to ensure optimum nutrition and encourage healthy eating habits. When it comes to menu planning, be creative and have fun. Serve dishes with different textures: crunchy, chewy, smooth, crisp, or melt in your mouth. Some examples would be to add croutons to pureed soups, nuts to sautéed vegetables, or raisins to rice or couscous. Try to give your plates visual appeal by adding color. Contrasting colors do more than look good—they can stimulate the appetite! Red or yellow peppers add color and zest to stir-fry or salad. Pair foods with contrasting shapes. Cube, julienne, or slice vegetables to give them a completely different look from the last time you served them. Use cookie cutters to create fun shapes out of cheese, toast, sliced fruit, and veggies. Variety early in life prevents your little ones from developing loads of dislikes as they grow older.

Top 10 Ways for Mom to Get Kids to Eat Better

1 TAKE TIME TO INTRODUCE NEW FOODS Children's taste buds aren't always ready for new flavors or textures. Be patient if your son or daughter shows resistance to trying new foods. Introduce a new food again at a later date or sneak it into a dish that you know they already love. Of course revealing that a favorite relative, celebrity, or hero likes spinach can work wonders to get your tot to try it.

2 BREAK THAT FAST Breakfast is the most important meal of the day—make it count. You can prepare whole-grain waffles on the weekend and freeze them for the coming week. Pop them in the toaster oven in the mornings and top with fresh fruit, yogurt, and honey for a quick delicious and nutritious way to start the day.

3 PLAN AHEAD Keep your pantry packed with basic staples that make it easy to whip up nutritious meals. Think about variations on whole-grain pasta, bread, or rice; sautéed, steamed or fresh vegetables; and a protein source such as tofu, poultry, meat, fish, cheese, or beans. Casseroles, stews, and chili are also easy ways to serve a balanced meal in a single dish.

4 ENCOURAGE YOUNG COOKS As your children grow, encourage them to participate in preparing and creating meals. When kids can be creative in the kitchen, they'll naturally show more interest in what they're eating.

5 DRESS IT UP If your children aren't excited about fruits and vegetables, try creative sauces, hummus, and salsas. Blend plain yogurt with herbs or honey for dipping vegetables or fruit. Try salad dressings on raw veggies. Sprinkle a bit of sugar or cocoa powder on fresh fruit.

6 PACK A PICNIC If you know that you'll be spending a fair amount of time driving the kids to and from school and extracurricular activities, keep a cooler in the car to keep the munchies (and grumpies) at bay. Stock it with fresh-chopped veggies, pretzels, yogurt, juice boxes, water, apples, and bananas.

7 DON'T MAKE A FUSS Try to resist making comments on what or how much your children are eating. As long as you are doing your part to serve them balanced and nutritious meals, the rest is up to the kids. Telling them to eat their peas and carrots may end up creating resistance rather than compliance.

8 CREATE SIMPLE, FLEXIBLE MENUS. Don't get trapped into making separate meals for all the members of your family. Plan menus that you can serve family-style and allow your children to choose what they want to eat. Eventually, they may follow your example to sample everything.

9 HAVE A HEALTHY ATTITUDE. Your approach to diet, health, exercise, and lifestyle sets an example for your children. If you skip meals or make unbalanced choices, your kids may think that's okay for them, too. By listening to your body to tell you when you're full or hungry, your children will learn to do the same.

10 MAKE FOOD TIME A FUN TIME Get creative in the kitchen. You can turn a morning of pancakes into a smiley-face contest. Cut and arrange sandwiches to represent different animals. Make a meal of just mini foods or try serving "breakfast" for dinner. And take on ideas from your kids—your enthusiasm will be infectious.

My family is lucky enough to sit down regularly for dinner, and meals are a big part of our extended family. I believe my kids try more foods and have a more varied diet because they eat with adults frequently. Meals usually contain ingredients I know they like and new items for them to try. The rule for my five- and seven-year-olds is a taste. They can spit it out if they REALLY hate it. They can try again another day. Every so often, they add to the list of foods they like. I've also noticed eating with slightly older children helps. My children tend to try new foods when one of their older cousins is eating it.

Off the Beaten Path

You can easily turn an ordinary dish into a feast for the eyes and stomach by introducing a sense of humor or artistic playfulness.

- Cut bread into a fish shape and pile on tuna salad, with an olive for an eye.
- Use a heart-shaped cookie cutter to remove the center of a piece of bread. Put the bread in a pan, break an egg into the cut out shape, and fry.
- Turn mini-pizzas into clown faces with olives broccoli, and peppers.
- Build sailboats by hollowing out the centers of zucchini halves, filling with cottage cheese, and creating sails out of pepper triangles and carrot spears. (A crew of peas can sail the craft!)
- Let your kids pick one or two colors and serve a meal with only the chosen color(s).

A Perfect Pantry

When you don't have time to plan ahead for dinner or don't want to shop for food in inclement weather, a well-stocked pantry and refrigerator can be a godsend. Purchase extra dried and canned ingredients for your family's favorite meals. Then, when you're in a pinch, you can still whip up waffles and smoothies for breakfast, or jazz up plain pasta with an herb sauce.

Staples

Beans (chickpeas, lima, kidney, pinto, black) ❀ Breakfast cereals ❀ Bouillon cubes: chicken and beef ❀ Broth: chicken and beef ❀ Canned and instant soups (tomato, chicken noodle, vegetable) ❀ Canned fruit and fruit juices ❀ Dried fruits (raisins, cranberries, apricots, pineapple, mango) ❀ Grains (millet, kasha, couscous) ❀ Nuts (walnuts, almonds, cashews, hazelnuts, pine nuts) ❀ Oil (extra-virgin olive oil, canola, sesame, corn) ❀ Pasta varieties ❀ Popcorn ❀ Powdered nonfat milk for out-of-milk emergencies ❀ Rice ❀ Split peas ❀ Tomatoes (whole and crushed) ❀ Trail mix ❀ Tuna ❀ Vinegar (red, white, balsamic)

Baking Supplies

Baking powder ❀ Baking soda ❀ Breadcrumbs ❀ Cornstarch ❀ Dried fruits ❀ Evaporated milk ❀ Extracts (vanilla, almond, orange) ❀ Flours (whole-wheat flour, barley flour, buckwheat, cornmeal) ❀ Honey ❀ Molasses ❀ Powdered milk ❀ Rolled oats ❀ Salt ❀ Sugars (white, brown, confectioners') ❀ Wheat germ ❀ Yeast

Condiments

Butter ❀ Garlic ❀ Ginger ❀ Herbs ❀ Horseradish ❀ Jam or jelly ❀ Ketchup ❀ Maple syrup ❀ Mayonnaise ❀ Mustard ❀ Peanut butter ❀ Peppercorns ❀ Relishes ❀ Salsas ❀ Soy sauce ❀ Spices ❀ Tomato paste ❀ Tomato sauce ❀ Worcestershire sauce

In the Freezer

Bread ❀ Chicken breasts ❀ English muffins or tortillas ❀ Frozen fruits (berries and peeled bananas are good to toss into smoothies) ❀ Frozen juice bars ❀ Frozen juice concentrate ❀ Frozen vegetables (lima beans, peas, corn, spinach) ❀ Frozen waffles ❀ Ground beef or turkey ❀ Tortellini or ravioli (*See page 81 for freezing guidelines*)

In the Fridge

Apples ❀ Baby carrots ❀ Cheeses (string, mozzarella, parmesan, Swiss) ❀ Cream cheese ❀ Eggs ❀ Hummus ❀ Juice ❀ Milk ❀ Yogurt

Favorite Extras

Applesauce ❀ Bottled pasta sauce ❀ Brownie mixes ❀ Cake mixes ❀ Chocolate chips ❀ Cocoa/chocolate drink mix ❀ Fig bars ❀ Gelatin ❀ Hot cereals ❀ Macaroni and cheese ❀ Muffin mixes ❀ Munchies: pretzels, breadsticks, crackers ❀ Pancake mix ❀ Rice cakes

Food Safety & Storage

*W*hen it comes to eating right, making food choices is only half the battle. A few simple precautions in the kitchen when handling and preparing food can make all the difference between nutritious meal and unwanted food contamination. Just follow these simple guidelines for best results.

Prepping & Cooking

- Shop smart (buy freshest food possible, shop in well-maintained and clean stores).
- Clean your work surface before you start.
- Thaw frozen meat in the refrigerator.
- Scrub hands thoroughly before handling food.
- Rinse fish, meat, and poultry in cold water before cutting and cooking to reduce bacteria.
- Clean cutting board and knives with soap and water in between use. If possible, use a separate cutting board for vegetables and meats.
- Keep raw, fresh foods refrigerated until you are ready to cook them.
- Prepare thawed foods immediately.
- Never use a dish that hasn't been washed.
- Cook eggs and chicken thoroughly to kill salmonella bacteria. Whole chickens should be heated to 180°F; breasts to 170°F.
- Cook ground beef to an internal temperature of at least 160°F.

Storing

- Keep cold foods cold and hot foods hot. Bacteria thrive between 40°F and 140°F.
- Do not leave cooked food out at room temperature for more than two hours.
- Keep raw meat, poultry, and fish well wrapped in the refrigerator. Drippings can spread bacteria to other foods.
- Do not store leftover canned food in the original can. Check for bulges in cans and jar lids for evidence of bacterial growth.
- Cool hot food before freezing it and, when possible, refrigerate a few hours before freezing. Wrap foods in airtight freezer containers or bags. This prevents freezer burn, protects flavor, and minimizes dehydration.
- Be sure to date and label all foods stored in the freezer. Follow the rule, "first in, first out."

Freezing Guidelines

Maximum Freezing Time

Vegetables	up to 6 months
Fruits	up to 12 months
Meats	
Hamburger	up to 4 months
Hot dogs and lunch meats	up to 2 months
Bacon	up to 1 month
Sausage	up to 1 month
Ham	up to 2 months
Beef steaks and roasts	up to 12 months
Pork chops and roasts	up to 6 months
Lamb roasts	up to 9 months
Cooked meat dishes	up to 3 months
Poultry	
Chicken or turkey, whole	up to 12 months
Chicken or turkey, parts	up to 9 months
Fish	
Fresh fish	up to 3 months
Fatty fish, such as salmon	up to 2 months
Shellfish	up to 2 months
Cooked fish dishes	up to 3 months
Dairy	
Egg whites	up to 12 months
Butter	up to 6 months
Cream	up to 2 months
Milk	up to 1 month
Cheese	
Hard	up to 6 months
Processed	up to 4 months
Baked Goods, Breads	
Quick breads	up to 2 months
Yeast breads	up to 6 months
Yeast dough	up to 2 weeks
Cookie dough	up to 4 months
Unbaked pastry	up to 2 months
Baked pastry	up to 2 months

Breastfeeding

hoosing to breast-feed is a wonderful gift a mother can give her baby. Breast milk is uniquely designed to meet the complete nutritional needs of a baby and a toddler. It prepares their immune system to protect against illness, keeps them healthy, and promotes optimal growth and development. Colostrum, the first milk produced by the breasts, is so high in white blood cells and infection-fighting proteins that it can be considered your baby's first immunization. Breast-fed babies have a decreased likelihood of allergies, pay fewer visits to the doctor and dentist than formula-fed babies, and show the benefits of their diet long after breastfeeding has stopped. There are also numerous benefits for mom. The loving relationship a nursing mother establishes with her baby is emotionally fulfilling and enjoyable. Breastfeeding helps moms lose weight. For every day she nurses, a lactating woman uses an extra five hundred calories. Breastfeeding also hastens a mother's postpartum recovery, delays ovulation, and reduces her risk of ovarian cancer, pre-menopausal breast cancer, and post-menopausal hip fractures. Breastfeeding doesn't always start out smoothly. Having the baby latch on properly is key. Taking a breastfeeding class or meeting with a certified lactation consultant before giving birth to learn the proper positioning and latching-on techniques ahead of time can be very beneficial. Other helpful hints are breastfeeding as close to delivery as possible, rooming with the baby so you're there if she needs you, not restricting the length or frequency of feedings, and avoiding the use and frequency of artificial nipples.

Benefits of Breastfeeding a Toddler

- *Convenience.* You don't have to bring snacks and drinks everywhere you go, and it's the best way to put an energetic toddler to sleep.
- *Tantrum-taming.* Nurse a raging toddler for a few minutes and she'll transform into a calm, confident child. Soothing her like a baby once in a while can work wonders.
- *No need for "mommy substitutes."* You can lose a favorite blanket, stuffed animal, or doll, but you always know where your breasts are.

- *Good nutrition.* Some toddlers refuse to eat at times. If a toddler is still breastfeeding, you'll rest assured that he's getting nature's perfect food.
- *Helps speech development.* Breastfeeding aids in the development of teeth and jaws, which has a positive affect on speech.
- *Makes a smarter child.* That's what existing studies show! DHA, a fatty acid found in mother's milk, is linked with brain development. Breast-fed children tend to have higher IQs than bottle-fed children.

- *Fights dehydration.* When toddlers are sick, they often refuse to eat and drink. When the bottle-fed toddler is dehydrated, parents struggle to get oral rehydration products down, and sometimes resort to a hospital IV. Breast-fed babies rarely refuse to nurse.

Breastfeeding Support and Education
lalecheleague.org; 800-LA LECHE or look in your white pages under *La Leche League.*

- **Helps moms lose weight.** An extra five hundred calories is used per day when breastfeeding, helping the mother to get rid of the weight she didn't lose during the first year.
- **Delays menstruation.** It also delays PMS and other related troubles, and there is decreased exposure to estrogen, which may protect against cancer of the breast and reproductive organs.
- **Good for the planet.** There are no cups to wash, no bottles to sterilize, and no packaging for the landfill.

Breastfeeding and Work

- Inform your employer ahead of time that you'll be pumping milk at the office. If you don't have an office with a door, decide on a private place where you can do it.
- Buy a quiet double pump. Hospital-grade rentals are also available.
- If you work near your home, arrange to breast-feed your baby at home or have the childcare provider bring the baby to you at the office.
- Dress in comfortable clothes and

If you want to and can: try. If you don't want to or can't: don't. Breastfeeding is a personal choice. New motherhood is stressful enough without dealing with feelings of guilt or inadequacy for not breastfeeding as well. Your baby will do wonderfully with a loving mother and a formula your doctor recommends. I loved breastfeeding my babies, but the beginning it was hard: a lot of worries and tears, a bit of pain, and too little sleep. A visit to a lactation consultant with my first baby a week or two into breastfeeding was invaluable. (I think this is essential for new mothers.) I hated pumping at work; being away from baby for an evening out and not pumping carried the risk of mastitis (breast infection). Yet here I am with my last baby at fourteen months old, nursing away still because I cannot bear the thought of not nursing again.

a nursing bra to make pumping easy and convenient. Remember: Dark colors are better than light colors at hiding leak stains and nursing pads.
- Be prepared for leaking breasts. Keep a spare change of clothes at the office.
- Keep your breast pump, nursing pads, wipes, and milk bottles or bags in an organized bag.
- If there's no refrigerator in your office, bring a small cooler with ice packs to store the milk.
- Try to pump twice a day.
- Look at a photo of your baby while you pump. Your milk will automatically flow better.
- Drink at least six to eight glasses of water daily.

Foods to Avoid While Breastfeeding

Many babies have reactions to dairy products, caffeine-containing foods, grains and nuts, spicy foods, and gassy foods. If you suspect this is happening to your baby, consider removing the specific food from your diet for a while.

Breastfeeding Books

The Nursing Mother's Companion, by Kathleen Huggins ❀ *The Ultimate Breastfeeding Book of Answers: The Most Comprehensive Problem-Solution Guide to Breastfeeding from the Foremost Expert in North America,* by Jack Newman, M.D., and Teresa Newman ❀ *The Breastfeeding Book: Everything You Need to Know About Nursing Your Child from Birth Through Weaning,* by Martha Sears, R. N., William Sears, M. D.

What Research Says

- The World Health Organization recommends exclusive breastfeeding (no liquid or food other than breast-milk) for the first four to six months, and that children continue to be breast-fed at least until they are two.
- The American Academy of Pediatrics recommends exclusive breastfeeding for six months and continued breastfeeding for a minimum of one year, but offers no upper limit.

First Foods

Single-grain cereals are generally recommended as the first foods for babies. Rice is a great place to start, as it is a highly digestible food. The very first feeding should be one tablespoon of cereal to three tablespoons of liquid, such as expressed breast milk, formula, or water—hardly what you'd call "solid!" Many pediatricians suggest moving next to pureed vegetables (rather than fruits) in order that babies become accustomed to more subtle flavors. Thin the consistency of these foods with water as well. The foods should drip off the spoon when you tilt it to baby's mouth.

Plan to spend the first month working through this list of great firsts: Rice cereal, Millet cereal, Sweet potatoes, Avocados, Bananas

6 MONTHS Oatmeal, Barley cereal, Yogurt, Squash, Pears, Peaches, Mango, Papaya, Apricots, Nectarines, Plums, Prunes

7 MONTHS Multigrain cereals, Egg yolk, Tofu, Whole-milk cottage cheese, Asparagus, Carrots, Peas, White potatoes, Rice cakes

8 MONTHS Apple, Cantaloupe, Honeydew, Kiwi, Broccoli, Grapes, Cheese, Teething biscuits, Diluted juices: Apple, Pear, Grape

9 MONTHS Legumes (not peanuts), Pineapple, Spinach, Beets, Kale, Rutabaga, Turnips, Whole-grain pasta

12 MONTHS+ Grated carrot, Whole milk, Citrus fruits and juices, Tomatoes and tomato juice, Egg white, Honey

It's perfectly normal, and in fact desirable, for breast milk or formula to remain the core of your baby's diet for the first year (24-32 ounces daily).

Into the Mouths of Babes

Starting Solids

Have you caught your baby eyeing your food plate lately? Do you think it might be time for the much anticipated "first meal"? Well, always check with your child's pediatrician before beginning solids, but more than likely it will be around the half-year mark. (Some babies can begin solids around four months of age; however, delaying the start as long as possible will allow your baby's digestive system a chance to mature.) Some of the signs that your baby is ready to eat solid food are the fact that she sits without support, has good head and neck control, no longer thrusts her tongue forward, shows interest in food, and is no longer being satisfied by 32 ounces of breast milk or formula per day. Don't be surprised if it takes the rest of the first year for your baby to genuinely take to food.

Starting solids is hard work for your baby. As much as your little one fusses when denied a bite of your tuna-fish sandwich, his first bite of solid food might not bring a smile to his face. Try to be as encouraging as possible. Reassure him and talk to him about how proud you are and how "yummy" it must taste. Taste some yourself to provide security. And during the first few meals, watch carefully for cues that say your baby needs to stop. If the meals don't seem to get off the ground at first, wait a few days and try again. He'll appreciate your patience.

Homemade for Baby

We all know that homemade food is the most nutritious fare. This is infinitely truer for babies, when you consider that they must derive a slew of nutrients out of very few calories (approximately 50 calories a day per pound of weight). And though it may not be possible to feed your baby fresh, homemade food every day, you can come close. The trick is in the planning, preparation, and storage. Of course, no one wants to slave away in the kitchen for an hour, only to have the beets you steamed or the cereal you whipped up thrown all over the floor. Here are some tips to help make the food preparation easy enough so it won't matter if a little ends up on Junior's splash mat.

Making just enough pureed carrot to satisfy the tiny appetite of your seven-month-old can be time consuming. And, when you consider that you'll be doing the same thing for the next three nights à la the four-day trial period, it's enough to have you singing the hot-stove blues. What if there was a way to do it once for all four nights…no…for six months' worth of carrots for your little rabbit? Well, that's exactly what you can do with the food-cube method. (And while you're at it, you can cook the asparagus, peas, and white potatoes you'll be serving this month.) Suddenly that hour (or so) you are relegated to the kitchen, washing, steaming, straining, or pureeing the veggies, becomes entirely worthwhile.

Sticking with Month Seven as an example, here is what your "hour" in the kitchen might look like:

1. WASH THOSE VEGGIES (5-10 minutes): Before you start the washing, put some water in your steamer to boil so it will be waiting for you, instead of the other way around. Using a mild soap-and-water solution, gently wash the carrots, asparagus, and potatoes. Peas should only need a quick rinse if they are just shelled. Use a vegetable brush on the carrots and potatoes, but leave the skins on (unless the carrots are very mature and large), as that is where much of the nutrients lie. Do remove any spoiled spots and the eyes, sprouts, and any green areas on the potatoes. Break the tough ends from the bottoms of the asparagus stalks and discard them. Stand the stalks upright in a container of cool water.

2. STEAM THOSE VEGGIES (10 minutes): Add first the coarsely chopped carrots (10 minutes), then the sliced potatoes and shelled peas (8 minutes), and finally the asparagus (5 minutes).

3. PUREE THOSE VEGGIES (10-15 minutes): After your veggies are cooked, separate them out and puree each type in your blender or mini food processor. If you have more than one batch of a vegetable, don't waste time scraping every last bit out between batches. Just pile more food in and keep going.

4. FREEZE THOSE VEGGIES (10-15 minutes): After you have removed the portion of vegetables you will need for today's feeding(s), transfer each type of vegetable into ice-cube trays. For beginning eaters, it's a good idea to fill each cube slot only halfway. Later, your child will eat two or three full cubes at each meal. Cover the trays with plastic wrap to prevent freezer burn, and throw the trays in the freezer.

5. BAG THOSE VEGGIES Once your food cubes are frozen, usually after eight or so hours, you should transfer the cubes into plastic freezer bags. Mark each bag with the date you prepared the food, and the expiration date (see *Food Safety and Storage*).

Equipment for Feeding Baby

You don't need much in the way of special equipment to prepare homemade foods for babies. A fine-mesh sieve comes in handy for straining fruits and vegetables for beginning eaters. After your child becomes accustomed to gumming and swallowing foods, you can use a blender for pureeing fruits and vegetables. Alternatively, a mini food processor or hand mill—though not a necessity—that you use only for preparing your baby's food can reduce the risk of cross-contamination from other foods. You will also need ice-cube trays and freezer bags. (Make sure the storage bags you buy are specifically for freezing.)

In addition to these kitchen supplies, you will need a safe highchair, a plastic-coated bib, and a plastic-coated spoon for those tender gums.

Food Allergies

The chances that your child will have a food allergy of one kind or another is about one in twenty, one in ten for if you or your partner have food allergies—not insignificant probabilities when it's your wee one we're talking about. Immediate symptoms may include itchy/swollen throat, sneezing, and watery eyes. (In very rare instances, food can cause anaphylactic shock, in which a child's throat will swell to the point of obstructing breathing and a sharp decrease in blood pressure occurs.) Other symptoms may take up to a few days to surface, and they include skin rashes, stomach cramps, gas, bloating, and diarrhea. *A majority of food allergies are caused by the following foods:*

Dairy products (*1 year for cow's milk*) ❀ Citrus fruits (*8 months*) ❀ Egg whites (*1 year. . . yolks are fine at 9 months*) ❀ Peanuts (*18 months–3 years*) ❀ Soy products ❀ Shellfish ❀ Artificial additives ❀ Tree nuts (*walnuts, cashews, almonds, etc.*) ❀ Wheat (*8 months*)

Some less-common culprits:
Berries ❀ Chocolate
Cinnamon ❀ Mustard
❀ Peas ❀ Pork ❀ Sugar
❀ Tomatoes ❀ Yeast

Choking Hazards

According to the American Academy of Pediatrics, children under four years of age are at greatest risk of choking on certain foods. Since infants and young children do not yet grind or chew their food well, round, firm foods that they may attempt to swallow whole are of greatest concern. The following present potential choking hazards:

Hot dogs ❧ Marshmallows ❧ Ice cubes ❧ Dried fruit ❧ Pretzels ❧ Nuts and seeds ❧ Chunks of meat or cheese (especially string cheese) ❧ Pasty globs of bread (lower risk with whole-grain breads) ❧ Whole grapes ❧ Hard or sticky candy ❧ Popcorn ❧ Chunks of apple ❧ Peanut butter ❧ Chips ❧ Raw vegetables (especially peas, carrots, and celery) ❧ Whole cooked peas ❧ Whole cherries or olives (especially with pits) ❧ Raisins ❧ Chewing gum

Never leave an infant or young child unattended while eating. Provide small amounts of food so your child takes one bite at a time. Chop food into small pieces and peel and quarter fruits like grapes and blueberries. Also, insist that your children sit down (not run, walk, play, or lie down) while eating.

Starting Right **Breakfast**

Breakfast is considered the most important meal of the day. Some complex carbohydrates (bread, cereal, or fruit), some protein (milk, egg, beans, or leftover chicken), and a little fat (a bit of cream cheese or a slice of cheese) will give your kids a full tummy and keep them full of energy. The hot cereal chart will hopefully inspire you and your children to reach less often for a bowl of sugary cold cereal. The egg recipe gives you lots of options to jazz up scrambled eggs. The bean recipe is easy and nutritious. The waffles are a fun way to spend a weekend morning. Make extra to freeze for the weekday. Fruit shakes are also a breakfast staple for children (see page 93).

Hot Cereal

Old-fashioned hot cereal is comfort food that's hard to beat as a great breakfast standard. You can keep altering the texture and flavor by trying different grains and adding a variety of fruits and nuts. An easy way to avoid adding sugar at the table is by tossing in a quarter cup of raisins to the cereal while it's cooking—their flavor will sweeten the cereal and the raisins will become nice and plump for extra-chewy porridge goodness.

1. Bring water to a boil.
2. Add grain or cereal. (*If using milk, add grains to cold milk and bring to a boil together*).
3. Simmer partially covered for time indicated in chart above, or prepare as directed on package.

VARIATIONS Flavor with a teaspoon of vanilla extract, almond extract, cinnamon, or orange zest. ❀ Top it off with fresh fruit, such as peaches, apples, pears, berries, banana slices, cranberries, raisins, dates, applesauce, or dried fruit slices. ❀ Give it some crunch with walnuts, almond slices, sesame seeds, wheat germ, pecans, or chopped hazelnuts. ❀ Stir in a spoonful of honey, maple syrup, brown sugar, fruit syrup, marmalade, fruit spread or jam, or molasses.

GRAIN PREPARATION CHART				
GRAIN	CUPS OF GRAIN	CUPS OF WATER/MILK	MINUTES TO SIMMER	YIELD (IN CUPS)
barley, pearl	1	2–2$\frac{1}{2}$	15	3
brown rice	1	2	45	3
buckwheat groats (kasha)	1	2	15–20	2$\frac{1}{2}$
bulgar	1	2	15	2$\frac{1}{2}$
cream of wheat	$\frac{1}{2}$	2	$\frac{1}{2}$	2
grits (instant)	$\frac{3}{4}$	3	5–7	3
instant rice	1	1	5	2
millet	1	3	45	3
quick oats	1	2	1	2
rolled oats	1	2	15	2
white rice	1	2	20	3

Mom's Finer Diner Eggs

Scrambled eggs are a quick and versatile way to dish up a nutritious breakfast for the whole family. With a few choice ingredients, you can turn plain old scrambled eggs into a fancy feast à la Mom. Serve alone or on top of toasted bread, bagel, or English muffin for a yummy egg sandwich.

1 tablespoon butter
4 eggs, beaten
*4–6 tablespoons Mom's Finer Diner ingredients

1. Melt the butter in a frying pan over medium-low heat.
2. Pour eggs into pan and turn heat to low.
3. Add Mom's Finer Diner ingredients evenly over egg mixture.
4. Gently stir eggs with a spatula by lifting them up from the bottom as they thicken. Continue stirring until eggs are scrambled to desired level of moistness.

Yield: 2 to 4 servings

*MOM'S FINER DINER INGREDIENTS

Add one combination of the following: chopped tomato and minced fresh basil ❀ finely chopped ham and grated Swiss cheese ❀ cottage cheese and chopped fresh chives ❀ cream cheese, dill, and chopped lox ❀ crumbled bacon and grated cheddar cheese ❀ chopped spinach, chopped cherry tomatoes, grated pepper Jack cheese ❀ avocado, chopped cilantro, and salsa

For fluffier eggs, whisk in 1 to 2 tablespoons of milk. ❀ Eggs continue to dry and thicken quickly as you cook them. If your kids like them on the moist side, remove the eggs from heat a little before they've reached their desired texture. They'll continue to cook a bit after you've taken them out of the pan. ❀ Check the fridge for leftovers. Chicken, vegetables, and rice taste great stirred into eggs. ❀ Add leftovers from a Mexican-style meal and wrap up scrambled eggs in a heated tortilla for a scrumptious breakfast burrito.

Baked Beans on Whole-grain Toast

This simple dish goes great with eggs for breakfast, or as a quick hot lunch.

1 tablespoon butter
1/2 onion, chopped
1 can baked beans
1 tablespoon dark brown sugar
1 tablespoon soy sauce
Tabasco or chili pepper sauce (optional)
2 slices whole-grain toast

1. Melt the butter in a skillet and fry the chopped onion until golden brown.
2. Add the beans, sugar, and soy sauce and bring to a simmer.
3. Add chili pepper sauce to taste and stir well.
4. Spoon onto toast and serve immediately.

Yield: 2 servings

Whole Wheat Banana Nut Waffles

These waffles are a snap to throw together and pack a lot of nutritional goodness. Make a whole batch and freeze the rest for later in the week. They'll reheat to crispy perfection in the toaster oven in a few minutes and taste better than any store-bought frozen waffles.

2 egg yolks
2 cups milk
2 cups whole wheat flour
1 tablespoon baking powder
1/4 teaspoon salt
1/3 cup oil
2 bananas, mashed
1/2 cup walnuts, chopped
2 egg whites, stiffly beaten

1. Preheat waffle maker.
2. Put all ingredients except egg whites in large bowl. Whisk until moistened and batter is smooth.
3. Use spatula to gently fold in beaten egg whites.
4. Pour approximately 1/2 cup of batter onto waffle grids. Close waffle maker and bake until golden.

Yield: 8 round waffles or 16 square waffles

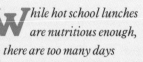

hile hot school lunches are nutritious enough, there are too many days when your child doesn't like what's being served. ("What do you mean all you had was a pickle!?" is my all too frequent response to my seven-year-old's daily lunch report.) If you pack their lunches, the biggest problem is boredom. Here are some ideas to add variety to too many peanut butter and jelly days.

Good Lunching

Quick 'n' Easy Quesadillas

These Mexican-style sandwiches can be spruced up with meat, veggies, herbs, or condiments for a fast and yummy lunch. You can also incorporate leftover ingredients from last night's dinner. These are best served hot, so save this recipe for a weekend treat.

2 flour or corn tortillas
2 tablespoons grated cheese

1. Preheat the oven to 450°F.
2. Place tortilla on a cookie sheet. Sprinkle cheese evenly on top and cover with second tortilla.
3. Cook for 7 to 8 minutes until edges are golden. Cut into quarters and serve hot.

Yield: 1 serving

Jazz it up: 2 tablespoons black or refried beans ❦ 1 to 2 tablespoons chopped spinach, cilantro, zucchini, peppers, tomatoes, or other favorite vegetable ❦ 2 tablespoons shredded chicken, ground beef, or turkey. ❦ Serve with sour cream, guacamole (*see page 93*), or salsa.

Mini Pizzas

Whether you're having lunch at home or brown-bagging it, these alternatives to "genuine" pizza really deliver. You can prepare a batch to freeze individually. You or your kids can grab a few to heat up in a toaster oven for a quick lunch or snack anytime. *Start with:* English muffins, sliced bagels, small baguette, pita, tortilla. *Spread on:* tomato or marinara sauce, pesto. *Add:* cheese. *Top it:* mushrooms, olives, peppers, zucchini, scallions, corn, tomato slices, basil leaves, spinach, broccoli, eggplant, artichoke hearts *Heat:* in the toaster oven or broiler until the cheese is melted.

Lunch-Sack Stuffers

Pickles ❦ Pretzels ❦ Bananas ❦ Apples ❦ Grapes ❦ Peeled oranges ❦ Baby carrots ❦ Cherry tomatoes ❦ Yogurt cups ❦ Pudding cups ❦ Applesauce ❦ Juice boxes ❦ Crackers with sliced cheese and salami ❦ String cheese ❦ Fortune cookies ❦ Popcorn ❦ Hard-boiled eggs ❦ Fig bars ❦ Edamame ❦ Peanuts in their shells ❦ Sunflower seeds ❦ Homemade cookies or brownies

Better Brown Bag Tips

Put juice boxes or water bottles in freezer the night before. You'll have a cold drink for lunch and an ice pack to keep the rest of your lunch cool ❦ Keep lettuce, tomatoes, and other "moist" foods wrapped separately. Build your sandwich at lunchtime and avoid soggy sammies! ❦ Pack travel-sized moist hand wipes for easy cleanup after you eat. ❦ Thermoses can be used for more than just juice—keep leftover spaghetti, chili, or soup warm for several hours, or pasta , potato , or fruit salads nice and cool. ❦ Save prepackaged condiments from take-out restaurants for bread-spreads or dipping sauces

Pinwheel Pleasures

These attractive mini-sandwiches are easy to make and ideal for lunch, snacks, or party hors d'oeuvre. Trim crusts off a slice of bread and flatten with a rolling pin. Top with a thin layer of filling, then roll up. Seal with a dab of butter or skewer with a toothpick. Cut into thin rounds.

MIX & MATCH *Try one of these suggestions or create your own combination:* Whole wheat bread with egg salad; Rye bread with peanut butter and jam; Sourdough bread with smoked salmon and cream cheese; Raisin bread with cottage cheese and mashed avocado; Sprouted wheat bread with tuna salad; White bread, hummus with alfalfa sprouts; Pumpernickel bread with spinach pate.

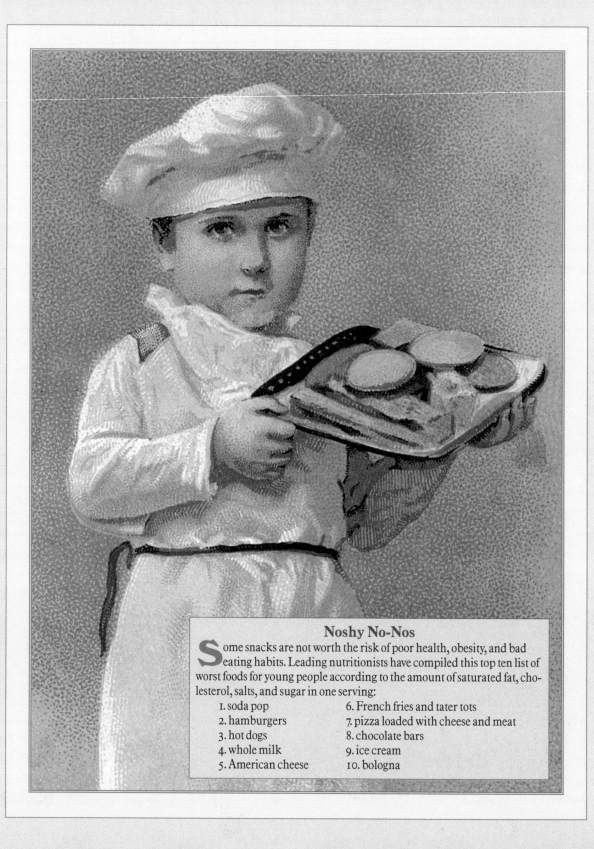

Noshy No-Nos

Some snacks are not worth the risk of poor health, obesity, and bad eating habits. Leading nutritionists have compiled this top ten list of worst foods for young people according to the amount of saturated fat, cholesterol, salts, and sugar in one serving:

1. soda pop
2. hamburgers
3. hot dogs
4. whole milk
5. American cheese
6. French fries and tater tots
7. pizza loaded with cheese and meat
8. chocolate bars
9. ice cream
10. bologna

I'm Hungry

Super Snacks

A fair percentage of your children's daily caloric needs will come from snacks. Children can't eat a lot at any one time, so they need to eat about every three hours. By keeping junk foods to a minimum, you can make these mini meals a nutritious part of their diet. Any food appropriate for a meal is good, in smaller portions, for a snack. Snacks that will keep your child full until lunch or dinner should have some protein, fat, and carbohydrate, the same as any nutritious meal. Plan on keeping a designated drawer, cupboard, or refrigerator shelf with mom-approved foods or ingredients for snacks.

My seven-year-old is always hungry. I try to avoid the constant "Can I have something to eat?" by serving her a mid-morning and mid-afternoon practically-mini-meal snack—hard-boiled eggs or soybeans, apple slices or berries, a cheese stick, a few pretzels, and some juice or milk. If she's satisfied, she is less likely to ask for something every half an hour or dig out my stash of potato chips. It's fine if she doesn't eat everything, but she knows that's it until lunch or dinner.

SNACK ATTACK When your kids have the tummy grumbles, try these quick and easy snack solutions: black beans ❋ bowl of cereal ❋ cheese slices and crackers ❋ cottage cheese and peaches ❋ dried fruit, nuts, and yogurt-covered raisins ❋ frozen grapes ❋ frozen yogurt ❋ fruit kabobs with yogurt dip ❋ fruit leather ❋ graham crackers ❋ granola bars ❋ hard-boiled eggs ❋ mini-burgers ❋ oatmeal cookies ❋ peanut butter and banana mini-wich ❋ pita, hummus, and cucumber slices ❋ rice cakes ❋ smoothies ❋ soybeans veggies and dip ❋ whole wheat bagel ❋ yogurt with blueberries

FREEZE IT! Give your children alternatives to ice cream with homemade frozen fruit. Skewer bananas, strawberries, pineapple, plums, peaches, berries, and watermelon wedges with Popsicle sticks or toothpicks, cover with plastic wrap, and freeze for at least four hours.

SO-SMOOTH SMOOTHIES Smoothies are a treat as a snack or for breakfast. Always keep some peeled and diced fruits handy in the freezer—let thaw for 5 minutes and throw into blender with 1 cup yogurt, milk, or soy milk. You can also pour freshly made smoothies into small paper cups and cover with plastic wrap. Insert Popsicle sticks through the plastic wrap and freeze for at least five hours. When you don't have time to whip up a smoothie for your child, you can simply whip out a smoothie pop!

Guacamole

This south of the border favorite goes well with virtually any Mexican-style dish, and is great as a dip for chips or veggies. What's more, it's really good for you! Avocados are an excellent cholesterol-free, sodium-free food that supplies more nutrients for fewer calories than any other fruit. They're nutrient-rich in potassium, folate, dietary fiber, Vitamin C, Vitamin E, riboflavin, and Vitamin B6.

> 2 to 3 ripe avocados
> 1 tomato, chopped
> 1 jalapeno pepper, seeded and chopped fine (optional)
> 1/4 cup red onions or scallions, chopped
> 1/4 cup fresh cilantro, minced
> 2 teaspoons lemon or lime juice
> salt to taste

In large bowl, mash avocados, and stir in remaining ingredients until blended. Serve immediately. (To prevent guacamole from turning brown, stir in a splash of milk.)

Makes about 3 cups.

Keep your refrigerator stocked with a variety of sliced vegetables, baby carrots, and grape or cherry tomatoes in a sealed airtight container. Serve with hummus or plain yogurt mixed with salad dressing seasonings for a fast midday bite.

Get Those Veggies!

Children need three to five servings of vegetables a day. Get them familiar with the taste of vegetables when they are young. Steamed broccoli or fork-smashed peas with a sprinkle of Parmesan cheese are good for little ones. Work to expand your children's tastes at the dinner table. Make simple vegetable dishes the adults in the family will enjoy, and one day your children will follow their lead. Older kids can help with picking ingredients for salads and for skewering. Hopefully their involvement in the preparation will encourage them to try and like more things. The Fajita and One-Dish Stir Fry recipes on page 96 and 98 are also delicious ways to serve vegetables.

Four Fabulous Veggie Sides

These are my fabulous vegetables side dishes. They are all elegant and delicious enough for company— I've had guests gaze heavenward after a taste of the sugar snaps—but so easy I've made each regularly for years. Since each can be set aside until ready to toss and can be served at room temperature, they allow me to concentrate on the main dish. When my children were younger, I would toss their portion with less dressing. Over the years, they've gotten more and more used to the seasonings, even the minced coriander and shallots. I prefer using rice vinegar in my dressings—it is less sharp than wine and balsamic vinegars. For my one-year-old, I let a portion of the vegetables cook much longer and add only a drop or two of the dressing.

*G*etting your kids to eat their vegetables can be difficult. My only advice is to keep at it. Steamed broccoli is almost a constant in my household. The kids have had it since they could eat solids. When they are young, I always serve a small portion of the vegetables they normally eat (peas or broccoli). I think sometimes they are so completely bored by the familiar, they are happy to try the other vegetables on the table. Another rule at my table is that they are not allowed to backtrack. The point is to add to the list of things the kids will eat, not subtract from it. If my children decide they don't like something they liked yesterday, they still have to eat at least one bite. I would serve that vegetable again soon so the taste does not become foreign.

SUGAR SNAPS WITH SESAME HONEY DRESSING

1 pound sugar snaps or snow peas, washed and stems removed
2 tablespoons orange juice
2 tablespoons rice or wine vinegar
1 teaspoon honey
$1/2$ teaspoon soy
2 tablespoons peanut oil
1 teaspoon sesame oil
2 scallions, sliced (optional)
$1/2$ teaspoon peeled, grated ginger (optional)
2 teaspoons sesame seeds, toasted (optional)

1. Blanch sugar snaps for 3 minutes, test for consistency. Remove when cooked but crisp. Immediately soak vegetables in separate pot of cold water to prevent further cooking. Drain. Wrap in paper towel and put in refrigerator until ready to serve.
2. Whisk all the ingredients except for the sesame seeds in a serving bowl. Toss sugar snaps in dressing, sprinkle with sesame seeds, and serve.

CILANTRO BEANS

1 pound green beans or haricot verts, wash and trimmed
4 teaspoons cider vinegar
2 tablespoons olive oil
1 tablespoon cilantro, minced
1 tablespoon sesame seeds, toasted (optional)

1. Prepare beans. See step 1 of Sugar Snaps recipe above.
2. Whisk vinegar and oil in a serving bowl. Add rest of ingredients. Toss beans in dressing and serve.

ASPARAGUS WITH MUSTARD DRESSING

1 pound asparagus, washed well and trimmed
4 tablespoons olive oil
2 tablespoons rice vinegar
   or 1 1/2 tablespoons balsamic vinegar
2 tablespoon Dijon mustard
1 clove garlic, minced
2 tablespoons minced parsley (optional)

1. Steam asparagus for 4 minutes for thin stalks, 8 minutes for thick stalks. (For thick stalks, use a vegetable peeler to scrape off the tough outer skin from middle to end of each stalk before steaming.) Immediately soak vegetables in separate pot of cold water to prevent further cooking. Drain, wrap in paper towel, and put in refrigerator until ready to serve.
2. In a small bowl, whisk together oil, vinegar, and mustard until well blended. Add garlic and parsley and mix.
3. Arrange asparagus on a plate and drizzle dressing over top.

CAULIFLOWER WITH SOY DRESSING

1 pound cauliflower florets, washed
2 tablespoons rice or wine vinegar
1 tablespoon olive oil
1 tablespoon sesame oil
2 teaspoons soy sauce
2 scallions, sliced (optional)

1. Steam cauliflower 8 to 10 minutes, until tender.
2. While cauliflower is steaming, whisk dressing ingredients in serving bowl. Toss cauliflower in dressing and serve immediately or at room temperature.

Skewer It!

For variety, color, texture, and the fun factor, kabobs are hard to beat. Your children can choose and arrange their favorite flavors, while you help them cut and skewer them. Try these options:

- VEGGIES peppers, mushrooms, cherry tomatoes, onions, eggplant, squash, zucchini, snow peas, sugar snap peas, asparagus, cauliflower, broccoli
- FRUIT apples, grapes, bananas, pineapple, mangos, melon balls, kiwis, strawberries, star fruit, pears, papayas, plums, tangerine slices

Make Your Own Five-Star Salad Bar

You and your children never have to have the same salad twice if you don't want to. You probably have more on hand in your refrigerator than you think to throw together a tasty salad. Try mixing and matching five main ingredients for something a little different every time.

BASE arugula, butternut, endive, escarole, iceberg lettuce, mesclun salad, mixed greens, red cabbage, romaine lettuce, spinach

FRUIT AND VEGGIES apple slices, artichoke hearts, avocados, bean sprouts, carrots, corn, grapes, tomatoes, green onions, jicama, mangoes, mushrooms, olives, pear slices, peppers, radishes, tangerine slices

PROTEIN GOODIES bacon, black beans, cheddar cubes, chicken, chickpeas, cottage cheese, feta, goat cheese, hard-boiled eggs, Swiss cheese, tuna

DRESSINGS blue cheese, buttermilk dressing, Caesar salad dressing, Dijon vinaigrette, Green Goddess, herbed oil and vinegar, lemon juice, ranch

ON THE TOP cashews, croutons, fresh herbs, pine nuts, raisins, sesame seeds, shaved Parmesan cheese, walnuts

What's For Dinner?

I work four days a week. We don't get home until 6:30 p.m. for baths, homework, dinner, and bedtime by 8:30. On Fridays, I am home with baby. Between taking care of her, errands, school drop-offs and pick-ups, and occasional play dates, I'm more exhausted at the end of a day "at home" than a day at work. I sympathize with both working and at-home moms. Getting a nutritious dinner on the table any day during the work week just isn't easy. Here are just a few of my tried-and-true recipes. On the weekdays, I simply can't make anything that takes longer than a half hour from start to finish. Pasta dishes or sauces made over the weekend and served with a salad do their duty at least once a week. The tofu dishes and the broiled salmon below are essential for quick dinners. I also rely on stir-fries a lot. They are a healthy way to cook up all sorts of meats and vegetable. It's useful to find a basic marinade and sauce for a one-dish stir fry you like, then do it so often you know the basic ingredients and steps by heart—so you can help with homework at the same time—and mix and match the meats and vegetable for variety. The fajita recipe is also great for the same reasons. The baked chicken recipe is really easy but has a relatively long cooking time in the oven—save it for a weekend treat.

Sizzling Fajitas

An easy way to turn dinnertime into fiesta time is by dishing up this sizzling serve-yourself meal. Keep tortillas warm by covering them with a linen napkin. If you have finicky eaters in your family, this dinner option lets them easily pick and choose how they'd like to fill their fajitas. You can serve also with guacamole (see page 93).

> 1 tablespoon oil
> 2 pounds skirt or flank steak OR 2 pounds shrimp, peeled, deveined OR 2 boneless, skinless chicken breasts OR 2 pounds zucchini, carrots, or squash, cut into diagonal 2-inch strips
> 3 yellow or white onions, peeled and sliced into strips
> 2 green onions, cut into 1-inch strips
> 1 red pepper, seeded and cut into 2-inch strips
> 1 green pepper, seeded and cut into 2-inch strips
> 1 yellow pepper, seeded and cut into 2-inch strips
> 8 to 10 flour tortillas

1. Heat oil in a large skillet on medium-high heat and cook meat on both sides. (about 10-12 minutes for steak, 6-8 minutes for chicken, 5 minutes for shrimp).
2. Remove meat from pan. Add onions and peppers and sauté until soft. (If you're making vegetarian fajitas, sauté all veggies at same time.)
3. Cut steak or chicken in diagonal strips and arrange on platter with sautéed vegetables.
4. Warm tortillas in skillet.
5. Serve immediately.

Yield: 4 to 6 servings

Thin Linguine with Turkey Meatballs

Every once in a while, my husband will make a large batch of these meatballs on a weekend afternoon. The extra is frozen for future low-hassle dinners. Individual meatballs with a bit of sauce are also stored in the refrigerator or freezer for our one-year-old's lunch and snacks.

> *3 tablespoons olive oil*
> *4 garlic cloves, minced*
> *5 cups canned, crushed tomatoes*
> *1/2 teaspoon dried oregano*
> *1/4 teaspoon dried thyme*
> *salt and pepper*
> *1 large egg*
> *1/3 cup milk*
> *1 white onion, finely chopped*
> *1/2 cup porcini mushrooms, finely chopped*
> *2/3 cup plain breadcrumbs*
> *1 cup freshly-grated Parmesan cheese*
> *1/2 cup chopped flat-leaf parsley*
> *1 pound ground turkey (light and dark meat mixture)*
> *1 pound thin linguine*

1. Make the sauce: In a large nonstick skillet, heat oil over medium-high heat. Add garlic, and cook about 1 minute. Stir in tomatoes, oregano, and thyme, and season with salt and pepper. Bring to a boil, lower heat, and simmer, covered, for 25 minutes.
2. Make the meatballs: In a large bowl, whisk together egg, milk, 1 1/4 teaspoon salt, and 1/4 teaspoon pepper. Stir in onion, mushrooms, breadcrumbs, 1/4 cup cheese, and parsley. Add turkey, and mix thoroughly. With slightly wet hands (to keep it from sticking), form mixture into 1 1/4-inch balls and place on a sheet of wax paper.
3. Using a wooden spoon, add meatballs to skillet and spoon sauce over to coat. Place over medium-low to medium heat. Cook until meatballs are just cooked through, about 8 to 10 minutes.
4. Prepare linguine according to package instructions, drain, and serve with meatballs, sauce, and Parmesan.

Yields: 4 servings

On Top of Spaghetti

Pasta is always a winner with kids. Add variety with some of these alternatives to your trusty marinara sauce:

- chopped clams sautéed in butter, garlic, and parsley
- stir-fried veggies in olive oil, garlic, and herbs
- black beans and salsa
- tuna, peas, light cream sauce, and Parmesan
- snap peas, soy sauce, ginger, chopped peanuts, and sesame oil

Baked Chicken with Garlic and Shallots

My mother-in-law is a fabulous cook, and this is one of my favorite recipes from her. We love smashing up the cooked garlic and shallots with a fork and smearing it over potatoes. Rather than doing potatoes separately, you can use a larger dish and add halved small potatoes, tossed with a bit of butter, to the edge of the pan. Serve this dish with sugar snaps or cilantro beans (*see page 94*).

> *1 chicken, quartered, or 2 Cornish hens, halved,*
> *(3 1/2 to 4 pounds)*
> *3 tablespoons unsalted butter*
> *6 medium shallots, cut in half and peeled*
> *12 large garlic cloves, peeled*
> *leaves stripped from 10 sprigs fresh thyme*
> *leaves stripped from 8 springs fresh rosemary*
> *salt and pepper to taste*

1. Rinse the chicken and pat dry.
2. Heat the oven to 425°F.
3. Put the butter into a 10 1/2" x 15 1/2" Pyrex pan or large shallow baking pan. Put the pan in the oven while the oven is heating.
4. When the butter is melted (about 10 minutes) remove the pan and set on top of stove. Add the shallots, garlic, and herbs, and coat with butter.
5. Dredge the chicken skin side down in the herb mixture. Arrange the chicken skin side up in the pan. Tuck garlic and shallots under the chicken pieces.
6. Add salt and pepper.
7. Bake until the chicken is browned and cooked through, 50 to 60 minutes (slightly less if using Cornish hens). Serve immediately.

Yields: 4 servings

Tofu Two Ways

The ingredients to two of my favorite tofu dishes are the same: tofu and ground meat. These dishes are easy to make and perfect for even young ones on solids. The stir fry tofu can be spiced up with chili paste for adult tastes after the kids' portion is removed from the pan. I serve these tofu dishes with rice and a vegetable. If you stir fry a vegetable, you can do it while the tofu is steaming, or after the stir fry tofu is done and in a warm oven. An easier accomplishment is steamed cauliflower (*page 95*). I use two packages of tofu in these recipes. One is never enough for my family with three little ones. With two packages, there are leftovers for baby's lunch the next day.

> *I teaspoon soy sauce*
> *I teaspoon dry sherry*
> *I teaspoon sweet bean sauce or hoisin*
> * sauce (optional)*
> *$^1/_2$ pound ground beef, pork, or chicken*
> *I tablespoon peanut oil*
> *two 14-oz packages of soft tofu*

Additional for stir fry tofu:
> *2 tablespoons peanut oil*
> *2 cloves garlic (minced if your children don't mind, or*
> * keep whole and remove after cooking)*
> *I cup frozen peas*
> *$^3/_4$ cup water or chicken broth*
> *2 tablespoons cornstarch*
> *$^1/_4$ cup water*
> *$^1/_2$ tablespoon hot bean sauce or chili paste (optional)*

Additional for steamed tofu:
> *2 tablespoons oyster sauce (optional)*

1. In a bowl, blend the soy, sherry, and hoisin; add meat and stir. Add 1 tablespoon oil and stir. Set aside.

FOR THE STIR FRY TOFU:

2. Cut the tofu in $^1/_2$-inch cubes; place in a colander to drain.
3. Heat a wok or large frying pan over high heat. When pan is hot, add 2 tablespoons oil. When oil begins to heat, add garlic and stir. And meat and stir fry until no longer pink (about 2 minutes, slightly less if using beef). Add tofu, peas, water or broth, and stir. Cover, turn heat down slightly, and cook for 3 minutes.
4. While tofu is cooking, blend cornstarch in $^1/_4$ cup water.

5. Uncover, add cornstarch mixture to side of pan, and stir until mixture bubbles and thickens.
6. If desired, remove a portion for children and add hot bean sauce to adults' portions in pan. Stir to mix well. Remove from pan and serve immediately or keep in warm oven.

FOR THE STEAMED TOFU:

2. Cut each tofu cake into eight pieces, roughly $^3/_4$-inch thick. Place in a shallow heatproof dish or pie plate in one layer. (I usually manage to fit most of the tofu, angling some at the rim of the plate. You can also do in two batches, steaming the second batch while you eat the first.)
3. Add a spoonful of meat mixture to the top of each piece of tofu. Press down slightly with back of spoon.
4. Place a rack in a wok or large frying pan with a domed lid. The lid needs to be 1 to 2 inches above the cooking food so steam can circulate. Add 1 inch of water to pan and bring to a boil over high heat. Place dish on rack, cover, and steam for 15 to 20 minutes.
5. Remove dish, pour off a bit of the juices, drizzle oyster sauce over top, and serve immediately.

Yield: 4 to 6 servings

One-Dish Stir Fry

Every once in a while I basically stir fry up lots of ingredients to make a one-dish meal to serve with rice. It's not the most elegant dish, but with kids, it works. It's basically the standard meat and veggie stir-fry, but I throw in some tofu cubes to satisfy my one-year-old, and two or three types of vegetables. I always include a vegetable I know my kids will eat and a vegetable I'm trying to get them to try or get used to.

> 2 teaspoons each soy sauce, cornstarch, dry sherry, water
> 1 pound skinless, boneless chicken breasts, cubed, or boneless lean beef, sliced
> 3 tablespoons peanut oil
> 1 clove garlic, smashed or minced
> 1 cup tofu cubes, drained (optional)
> $3/4$ pound vegetables: broccoli (blanched), asparagus (ends snapped off), red or green pepper (seeded), and/or onion (peeled), cut into bite size pieces; if you can get them: canned straw mushrooms, water chestnuts (sliced), and/or baby corn
> 2 tablespoons water

Cooking sauce:
> $1/2$ cup water or chicken broth
> 1 tablespoon dry sherry
> 2 tablespoons soy sauce or oyster sauce
> $1/4$ teaspoon sugar
> 1 teaspoon sesame oil
> 1 tablespoon cornstarch

1. In a bowl, blend the soy, cornstarch, sherry, and water; add meat and stir. Add $1/2$ tablespoon oil and stir. Set aside.
2. In a bowl, mix together the ingredients of the cooking sauce. Set aside.
3. Heat a wok or large frying pan over high heat. When pan is hot, add $1 1/2$ tablespoons oil. When oil begins to heat, add garlic and stir. And meat and stir fry until chicken is opaque (about 3 minutes) or beef is no longer pink (about $1 1/2$ minutes). Remove from pan.
4. Clean pan and add 1 tablespoon oil. When oil is hot, add vegetables and tofu and stir fry for 30 seconds. Add 2 tablespoons water and cover about 2 minutes for crisp vegetables, more for tender vegetables.
5. Return meat to pan. Stir cooking sauce, add to pan, and cook, stirring, until sauce bubbles and thickens. Remove from pan and serve immediately.

Yields: 4 servings

Broiled Salmon with Honey Dipping Sauce

This is the easiest meal I make at least once a week for my family. We also make it for our company holiday dinner for non-meat eaters. Everyone loves it! You can serve with just wedges of lemon or try the dip-

Salmon is a low-fat alternative to red meat and contains heart-healthy omega-3 fatty acids. Yet because of debate over levels of PCBs found in fish, it is recommended that children and pregnant or nursing women eat no more than 12 ounces of fish a week.

ping sauce below. Serve with steamed asparagus (*see page 95*) and rice.

> 4 salmon fillets (about 6 ounces each)
> Kosher salt

Honey Dipping Sauce:
> 3 cloves garlic, minced
> 2 tablespoons minced cilantro
> 1 tablespoon sesame oil
> 2 tablespoons soy sauce
> 1 tablespoon sherry
> 2 teaspoons rice or wine vinegar
> 1 tablespoon honey

1. Preheat the broiler.
2. In a bowl, mix ingredients of dipping sauce. Divide into 4 small bowls.
3. Arrange the fillets skin side up in pan. Lightly sprinkle with salt.
4. Place the fillets 4 inches from the heat and broil for 4 minutes. Turn, and cook another 3 minutes for slightly pink interior. Add a minute on each side to cook thoroughly.
5. Serve immediately with individual bowls of dipping sauce.

Yields: 4 servings

Fabulous Treats

I am not a baker. These recipes are all from my friend Sasha Perl-Raver, a talented young personal chef and caterer to actors, producers, and directors in Los Angeles, and they are all absolutely to melt for. I love carrot cakes—this one is THE best. I'm not much of a judge of chocolate desserts but my colleagues sigh at the mention of Sasha's fudge and brownies. So when all the veggies and nutritious meals of the day have been consumed, indulge a little with any of Sasha's fabulous and favorite treats. (Sasha would like to thank her parents, who denied her sugar as a child. It is now her addiction and inspiration.)

The Best Carrot Cake

This is the greatest carrot cake recipe ever. It makes three amazing, light, delicious layers of cake, or approximately 24 cupcakes. If you choose to make cupcakes, simply line a muffin tin with foil liners, and coat each with nonstick cooking spray. The cooking time will be 25 to 30 minutes.

3 cups flour
2¹/₂ cups sugar
1 tablespoon baking soda
1 tablespoon cinnamon
1 teaspoon salt
4 eggs
1¹/₂ cups vegetable oil
1 teaspoon vanilla
2 cups shredded carrots (approx. 6 carrots)
8 ounces chopped walnuts
1 (15 ounces) can chopped pineapple
1 cup raisins, plumped in hot water for 15 minutes
Zest and juice from 1 orange

1. Preheat oven to 350° F and grease three round 9-inch cake pans.
2. In a large bowl mix flour, sugar, baking soda, cinnamon, and salt.
3. In a medium bowl, mix the eggs with the oil and vanilla. Add the carrots, walnuts, pineapple, raisins, orange zest, and orange juice and stir.
4. Add egg mixture into flour mixture, and stir with a fork until flour is well moistened.
5. Pour batter into pans and bake for 40 to 45 minutes. Allow to cool, then remove from pans and frost with cream cheese frosting (see recipe following).

Yield: One three-layer cake or 24 cupcakes

The Best (and Easiest) Cream Cheese Frosting

This recipe is simple, easy, and so delicious. Don't even bother sifting the sugar.

24 ounces cream cheese, room temperature
8 ounces unsalted butter, room temperature
1 teaspoon vanilla
16 ounces powdered sugar
Zest and juice from 1 orange

Place all ingredients in a large bowl and beat until smooth.

Brownies Like No Other

These dense, fudgey brownies with all their variations are a guaranteed crowd pleaser. Remember not to overcook them!

1 pound of unsalted butter
1 pound semisweet chocolate
6 extra-large eggs, beaten
2 tablespoons vanilla extract
2¹/₂ cups sugar
1¹/₂ cups flour
1 tablespoon baking powder
1 teaspoon salt
1 cup chocolate chips (semi, bitter, or milk)

1. Preheat oven to 325° F and grease a 12" x 18" pan.
2. Melt the butter and semisweet chocolate together in a double boiler over simmering water. Allow to cool

slightly (do not let harden), then add eggs, vanilla, and sugar.

3. Sift dry ingredients together and add to the chocolate mixture. Then add the chocolate chips at the last minute, folding them into the batter.

4. Bake for approximately 35 to 40 minutes. Do not overcook—a toothpick WILL NOT come out clean when inserted! The center should no longer be jiggly, just slightly set, when removed from the oven. As the brownies cool, they harden and become like brownie fudge. Allow to cool completely before cutting and serving.

Yield: 16 to 20 brownies

VARIATIONS

- **Nuts** Add two cups of chopped nuts folded in with the chocolate chips.
- **Peanut Butter** Beat $1/2$ cup of creamy peanut butter into the batter, and add peanut butter chips.
- **Raspberry Nut** Add 1 cup of chopped walnuts, $1/2$ cup of raspberry jam, and 1 cup of fresh raspberries.
- **S'mores** Add 2 cups of miniature marshmallows and 1 cup of crumbled graham crackers.
- **Caramel** Swirl caramel (prepared caramel that is sold in grocery stores as an ice cream topping is perfect) over the batter just before cooking.
- **Chocolate Mint** Add 1 teaspoon of mint extract to the batter.
- **Candy** M&Ms are a fun, yummy addition that kids love, but just about any candy bar can be chopped up and added.

Fantastic Fudge

This fudge is really easy to make, but take care, as you will be working at very high temperatures. It will keep in an airtight container for several weeks.

> $2/3$ cup (1 small can) evaporated milk
> $1 2/3$ cups sugar
> $1/2$ teaspoon salt
> 1 jar marshmallow cream
> 8 ounces good quality semisweet chocolate, chopped (or chips)
> 1 teaspoon vanilla
> $3/4$ cup walnuts, chopped, optional

1. Butter an 8"x 8"square pan.
2. In a saucepan over medium heat, bring evaporated milk, sugar, and salt to a boil, stirring constantly. Boil 5 minutes, stirring occasionally, then remove from heat.
3. Place marshmallow cream and chocolate in a large bowl with high sides.
4. Carefully pour hot mixture over marshmallow cream and chocolate and allow to sit for 60 seconds. Stir vigorously until chocolate and cream have melted and are well blended. Add vanilla (and nuts, if using).
5. Pour into prepared pan and allow to cool before cutting.

Yield: 12 to 16 squares

Big Fat Oatmeal Raisin Cookies

These cookies are best when made huge. Serve them fresh from the oven with a large glass of milk or a steaming cup of apple cider.

> 2 cups all-purpose flour
> $1 1/2$ cups sugar
> 1 teaspoon baking powder
> $1/2$ teaspoon baking soda
> 1 teaspoon salt
> 1 teaspoon cinnamon
> 3 cups rolled oats, quick or old-fashioned
> 1 cup raisins
> 1 cup vegetable oil
> 2 eggs
> $1/2$ cup milk

1. Preheat oven to 400° F and grease a cookie sheet.
2. In a large bowl, sift together dry ingredients. Stir in rolled oats and raisins. Add oil, eggs, and milk to the

dry mixture and beat with a spoon until thoroughly blended.
3. Drop $^1/_2$-cup lumps of cookie dough on two greased cookie sheets.
4. Bake 12 to 14 minutes, rotating the tray halfway through cooking, until golden around the edges.

Yield: 12 large cookies

Cookie Brittle

Cookie Brittle makes a wonderful holiday present and is delicious sprinkled over ice cream.

> *1 cup butter, softened*
> *1 $^1/_2$ teaspoons vanilla*
> *$^1/_2$ teaspoon salt*
> *1 cup sugar*
> *2 cups flour*
> *2 cups semisweet chocolate chips*
> *1 cup chopped walnuts or pecans*

1. Preheat oven to 375°F.
2. In a large bowl, combine the butter, vanilla, salt, and sugar using a large wooden spoon. Gradually stir in the flour, then add chocolate chips and nuts.
3. Press cookie dough evenly into a 15" x 10" jellyroll pan and bake for 25 minutes, until light golden brown.
4. Let cool in pan. When completely cool, break into irregular pieces. Stored in an airtight container. The brittle will keep for several weeks.

VARIATION Try adding toffee, peanut butter, or white chocolate chips rather than semisweet, and toss in your favorite nuts. White chocolate with macadamia nuts are a great combination.

Yummy Banana Pudding

If you want to include more exotic flavors in this quick and simple pudding, try adding kiwi, mango, and pineapple to the layers of banana.

> *1 cup sugar*
> *3 eggs, beaten*
> *pinch salt*
> *2 tablespoons cornstarch*
> *2 cups milk*
> *5 to 6 ripe bananas, sliced*
> *1 teaspoon vanilla*
> *approx. 40 vanilla wafers*

1. In a medium saucepan, combine sugar, eggs, salt, cornstarch, milk, and ONE banana that has been chopped. Bring mixture to a boil over medium-high heat, stirring constantly, and cook until thickened.
2. Remove the pudding from heat. Add vanilla, mix well, and refrigerate until cool.
3. To serve, alternate layers of pudding, banana, and wafers trifle-style in a glass bowl.

Yield: 4 servings

Cereal Bars and Treats

This recipe is great with any cereal you choose. One to try is Cinnamon Toast Crunch with a little added nutmeg, cinnamon, and cloves. It tastes like eggnog.

> *1 10-ounce bag miniature marshmallows*
> *2 tablespoons butter or margarine*
> *6 cups Fruit Loops or similar cereal*

1. Grease a 12" x 18" pan or cookie sheet.
2. In a large pot, melt marshmallows and butter or margarine over medium-low heat. Remove from heat and stir in cereal until completely coated.
3. Spread mixture into prepared pan using greased hands and allow to cool.
4. Cut into squares and individually wrap in plastic. Store in an airtight container in a cool, dry place.

Yield: 12 bars

VARIATION Melt $^1/_3$ cup of creamy peanut butter with the marshmallow and butter in Step 2, and stir in 6 cups of crisp rice cereal and 1 chocolate covered peanut butter cups, chopped.

chapter three

Having Fun!

PLAYING WITH YOUR BABY

A baby's first and favorite playmate is Mom. From day one, babies are ready to start playing—at their own level, of course. For newborns, play can mean rocking in a rocking chair, listening to wind chimes, or feeling your heartbeat while lying on your chest. For older babies, play can mean throwing a ball, playing Pat-a-Cake, or knocking down a tower of blocks. At first, you'll use games to comfort and soothe your newborn. Eventually you'll use them to distract or entertain your child. Anything can be used for play—a glove, a wallet with photos, bangle bracelets, or keys. Sometimes props aren't necessary. A baby becomes familiar with the way Mom smells, smiles, and sounds through play. Through play, Mom learns about her baby's personality, preferences, and abilities. It's also through play that babies learn about the world around them.

Having a baby to play with is a true gift. It gives adults the opportunity to act goofy, sing songs, and make up stories. It lets them reconnect with the fun-loving, imaginative child within them. Be inventive. Make up a diaper-changing song. Take out pots, pans, and spoons for a drumming fest. Play heightens babies' interest in what's going on around them, helps them learn to concentrate, teaches them to communicate and cooperate, and aids the development of coordination. Babies who play well alone develop self-reliance, a valuable quality to have throughout life. There's no need to pack every moment with creative fun and learning. Babies have short attention spans and need down time. Give them time to cool down after intense play. Don't take them on outings if they're tired. There's nothing wrong with spending a quiet day at home. Your love, affection, and attention is all your baby really wants.

Ten Ways to Play with Newborns

- Make funny faces at your baby in the mirror.
- With your baby in your lap, cradle her head in your hands. Puff out your cheeks and use your baby's hands to press the air out in a whoosh!
- Move your face closer and closer to your baby's until you touch noses. Repeat a nonsense phrase as you do it.
- Wiggle your fingers in your baby's grasp.
- Clap your baby's hands or bicycle his feet.
- Dangle a rattle over your baby as she lies on her back.
- Put brightly-colored socks on your baby's hands.
- On a clean, well-padded floor, have your baby track a bright, squeaky, toy as you move it.
- While your baby is lying on his tummy, call his name and see if he turns his head.
- Roll a chime ball near your baby and see if she tries to reach for or scoot toward it.

Games to Play with Two- to Seven-Month Olds

- Peek-a-Boo is a classic, and there are several variations. Cover your baby's eyes with your hands, his hands, a diaper, or a scarf, and ask, "Where's baby?" You can cover a stuffed animal's eyes and ask the same question, or hide behind a scarf, pillow, or blanket and say, "Where's Mommy?"
- Sew a bell securely into your baby's sock so it rings when he kicks his feet.
- Roll your baby, tummy down, over a large, inflatable ball while holding him.
- Sing Pop Goes the Weasel; bend

knees and "pop" while holding your baby.

- Sit with your knees bent and your baby's tummy pressed against your shins, facing you. Then roll onto your back and raise your legs to give your baby a bouncy ride.

Games to Play with Babies Who Sit

- Let your baby fill up two plastic containers with objects too big to swallow. Show her how to move the objects from one container to the other. When she's ready, teach her how to pour them back and forth.
- Listen to your baby's sounds and gurgles, and repeat them back to him.
  - When your baby touches your nose, making a funny sound or stick out your tongue.
    - Splash your baby's hands and feet in the bathtub.
    - Blow bubbles and guide your baby's fingers to pop them.
  - Let your baby knock down stacked nesting cups. Timber!
- Play Pat-a-Cake. Babies love to clap. Use the traditional words

and then replace some of the words with your own. Lightly tickle your baby at the end.

- Read your baby a pop-up book.
- While standing, hold your baby around his upper chest and swing him back and forth between your legs.
- Give your baby a piggy back ride—beginner style. Hold both his hands, which are wrapped around your neck, with one hand. Bring your other arm around your back to support his bottom. Watch out for low clearances.
- Hold your baby securely around the chest and fly her around like an airplane. Vrrrooom!

> CAUTION! Never swing a child of any age by his arms alone. Dislocated shoulders can often happen.

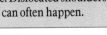

Finger Plays

Eensy, Weensy Spider ■ *This Little Piggy Went to Market* ■ *Ten Little Fingers* ■ *Where is Thumbkin?* ■ *Two Little Blackbirds* ■ *Five Little Monkeys*

- Have fun with blocks. Show your baby the domino effect. Arrange blocks by color and shape, announcing each color and shape. Count blocks as you stack them.
- Make a shoebox parking garage for toy cars, trucks, and buses.
- Draw pictures of objects your child is interested in.
- Say, "Look up!" When your baby looks toward the sky, tickle her under her chin.
- Point out your baby's shadow on a sunny day. Create shadows with some of his toys.

Games to Play with Crawlers

- Play hide-and-seek with toys. Bury a toy in the sand and let her find it. Hide a music-making toy and let your baby follow the sound to find it. Hide a toy under one of three cups, shuffle them around, and let him discover where the toy is.
- Play "advanced" Peek-a-Boo, in which your baby has to look for what's hidden.
- Have a crawling parade, or play a game of crawl tag.
- Explore smells: roses, shampoo, sliced oranges, scented candles, or pine trees.
- Explore textures: silk, satin, wet material, or a woven rug.
- Use a variety of objects—metal mixing bowls, rubber spatulas, wooden spoons, plastic flower pots—to make a drum set. Make music together.
- Teach your baby how to press your nose so your tongue comes out.

Games to Play with Cruisers

- Fill a box with different toys and objects. Name an object and ask your baby to take it out.
- Have a puppet show using a crib, playpen, or cardboard box as a theater.
- Teach your baby new words in a fun way. Smile when you say "happy." Look sad when you say "sad." Tell simple stories using the words your baby knows.
- Pretend to be absent-minded. Put a diaper on your baby's arm or a stuffed animal, instead of his bottom. Start to dress yourself in your baby's clothes, or try to climb into his high chair at mealtime.
- Crawl around the floor together, pretending to be animals. Moo! Grr! Meow! Woof!
- Supervise and teach your baby how to put coins into a piggy bank.

I love fingerplays like "Eensy, Weensy Spider" and "Five Little Monkeys". They are a great way to interact with your baby. There are so many new things for a baby to absorb that they take comfort and delight in the familiar. Just pick one fingerplay and do it for your baby again and again. He will soon watch very carefully; one day he will gurgle with delight when you start the motions; then he will do some of the motions. You can then try other fingerplays and see which ones he enjoys. I remember my eldest at five months cackling away when I first did "Five Little Monkeys"—she loved the "bump his head" motion. I like doing fingerplays after a reading session in bed, especially in the early months. It is a good way to have restful play with your baby.

Fun Songs and Games

Bingo ■ This Old Man ■ Pop! Goes the Weasel ■ Pat-a-Cake ■ Hickory, Dickory, Dock ■ I'm a Little Teapot ■ The Wheels on the Bus ■ Hokey Pokey ■ Head, Shoulders, Knees, and Toes ■ Ring Around the Rosie ■ Old MacDonald Had a Farm ■ There Was an Old Lady Who Swallowed a Fly

Rub-a-Dub-Dub

To keep little ones occupied and happy during bath time, think creatively. Lots of fun tub toys can be found in your cabinets, and others can be purchased inexpensively. Be sure plastic tub toys are airtight and dry fully after each use. To clean, wash in the top rack of the dishwasher, or rinse in a mild bleach solution to prevent bacteria growth. Replace or boil sponge toys every few months.

PLAYING BALL All babies love balls. Newborns enjoy touching soft, multi-colored balls made of fabric, watching weighted balls that don't roll away, and listening to balls with chimes inside. Babies who can sit enjoy having you roll the ball to them—don't expect them to roll it back, though. Roll a ball through a tube, down a ramp, or into another room. When your baby learns to roll the ball herself, set up some easy-to-knock-down bowling pins and guide her hand. Hold your baby and swing her legs so she can kick the ball soccer-style. Let her play with a large, colorful, inflatable ball. Help him hold a plastic ball underwater in the bath, and watch his surprise as it pops up. When your baby's hand-eye coordination is better developed, engage him in rolling several different-sized balls back and forth. Put a bucket on its side and encourage him to roll the ball in, and let him swat at the ball with a plastic bat or small broom. Guide him along until he can do it on his own. Older babies will enjoy throwing Ping-Pong balls and watching them bounce on the floor.

PLAYGROUND IDEAS
Bubbles, sand toys, balls, bread for ducks and birds, a doll stroller, and a water bottle will be useful at the playground. Put your baby in a bucket swing, placing her all the way in front. For fun, put another child behind your child, facing the other way.

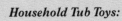

Household Tub Toys: Plastic Yogurt or Margarine Containers, Ladles, Strainers, Small Plastic Watering Cans, Plastic Cup to Pour Water. *Other Fun Ideas:* Animal-shaped Washcloths, Washable Tub Crayons, Floating Ball, Rubber Ducky, Sponge Blocks, Plastic Boats and Aquatic Animals. *Tub Songs: Splish-Splash; Baby Beluga; Rubber Duckie; This Is the Way We Wash Our (Ears, Hands, Toes); Row, Row, Row Your Boat; Sailing, Sailing.*

Nursery Rhymes

Nursery rhymes have entertained children for hundreds of years. Their easy rhythm, silly imagery, and gentle morals have made these poems irresistible to children all over the world. When you read nursery rhymes to your kids, they will develop favorites they want to hear again and again. The repetition of familiar stories actually builds your child's confidence. In a world where nearly everything is a new experience, they will feel comfortable knowing that they remember how the story goes and what comes next. Share these classic nursery rhymes with your children and watch them become favorites of a new generation.

Rub a dub dub, three men in a tub.
Who do you think they be?
The butcher, the baker,
    the candlestick maker.
Turn them out, knaves all three.

❖

Little Miss Muffet sat on her tuffet
Eating her curds and whey.
Along came a spider and
    sat down beside her
And frightened Miss Muffet away.

❖

Baa baa black sheep
Have you any wool?
Yes sir, yes sir
Three bags full;
One for my master,
One for my dame,
But none for the little boy
Who cries in the lane.

Georgie Porgie pudding and pie
Kissed the girls and made them cry
When the boys came out to play
Georgie Porgie ran away

❖

Little Bo-Peep, she lost her sheep,
And didn't know where to find them;
Let them alone, they'll all come home
And bring their tails behind them.

❖

Little Jack Horner sat in a corner,
Eating a Christmas pie;
He put in his thumb,
    and pulled out a plum,
And said, "What a good boy am I!"

❖

Peter, Peter, pumpkin-eater,
Had a wife and couldn't keep her;
He put her in a pumpkin shell,
And there he kept her very well.

Jack and Jill
Went up the hill
To fetch a pail of water
Jack fell down
And broke his crown
And Jill came tumbling after.

Who is Mother Goose?

While the real origins of Mother Goose are somewhat shrouded in mystery, most scholars agree that author Charles Perrault first coined the term "Mother Goose" in 1697. His book of well-known rhymes, entitled (translated from the French) *Histories and Tales of Long Ago, with Morals*, had a picture on the cover of an old woman spinning and telling tales with the caption "Tales of My Mother Goose". In 1765, John Newbery published more children's rhymes with the title *Mother Goose's Melody: or Sonnets from the Cradle*, which was widely pirated and reprinted in England and America. This further solidified the association between the name Mother Goose and the beloved nursery rhymes that we know today.

Little Boy Blue.
Come blow your horn
The sheep's in the meadow
The cow's in the corn!
Where is the little boy
minding his sheep?
Under the hay-rock
Fast asleep!

Paints, Scissors, & Paper

Art

Gooey paint, sticky glue, clumpy clay, colorful markers . . . most children can't resist the urge to explore their artistic side. No matter what the project is—and there are endless possibilities—children are natural artists. Unlike adults, whose inner artists are often buried beneath the more "serious" things in life, children are bursting with creativity. Show them an age-appropriate technique, and their wild imaginations will lead them to create a unique piece of art. Some children have a knack for realistic drawing. Others prefer being messy. Some work hard to master a technique. Others are more interested in pictorial storytelling. There is no "right" way to make art, and one child isn't a "better" artist than another child—they're just different. Inspire your child by doing weekend projects together, keeping art supplies well-stocked and handy, and taking day trips to galleries and art museums.

SCULPTURE Art doesn't have to always be two-dimensional. Sculptures can be made in any size, shape, or form, from a variety of materials. Keep pipe cleaners and toilet-paper and paper-towel rolls around for younger kids to experiment with. Older kids may enjoy working with Sculpy or other modeling clays.

TAKE YOUR CHILD TO AN ART SUPPLY STORE See which art supplies inspire her and suggest possible ways of working with them. You'll find the best prices at stores affiliated with art schools. You can also purchase children's art supplies through catalogs and websites, including *pearlpaint.com; shoptheartstore.com; utrechtart.com.*

FACE PAINTS Mix 1 teaspoon cornstarch, $\frac{1}{2}$ teaspoon water, $\frac{1}{3}$ teaspoon cold cream, and a few drops of food coloring to each cup in a muffin tin. Use a different color in each cup. Stir and paint.

COLLAGES Save magazines with lots of pictures—*National Geographic, Gourmet, Good Housekeeping,* and *Condé Nast Traveler.* Have your child leaf through the magazines, tearing out the images that catch her attention. Once she has her pile, it's time for cutting and arranging the images on a piece of fairly thick paper. Brush glue on the backs of the collage pieces. This is only one of the many collage possibilities. You can make a silly collage by cutting up animal pictures and interchanging body parts to create new, hybrid creatures. Or you can combine paint, cotton, and colored paper scraps to create a mixed media collage. Make a personalized photo-collage for a friend or relative by arranging photographs of the person (and yourself, if you'd like) on a piece of card stock, along with magazine images of bagels, beagles, balloons—whatever symbolizes relationship. Glue them down on heavy paper. Use large paper to make a poster. Use smaller paper to create a greeting card with a message.

DECOUPAGE Decoupage is the art of making collages on three-dimensional objects. Mix glue and a small amount of water for a soupy paste. Paste paper scraps or cutouts on an old cigar box or wood picture frame, overlapping to cover completely. Origami paper works great for decoupage, as do scraps of leftover wrapping paper. Apply a thin coat of glue mixture to the entire area to seal and create a glaze when dry.

Materials to Keep Around the House
construction paper ■ washable finger paints ■ sidewalk chalk ■ non-toxic glue ■ feathers ■ glitter ■ dried beans and macaroni ■ pads of thick paper in various sizes ■ tempera paint ■ watercolors ■ brushes of various thicknesses ■ jam jars to mix paints in (*encourage the invention of new colors!*) ■ crayons ■ oil pastels ■ felt markers ■ fabric markers and T-shirts or old sheets

If a local museum offers free art classes, consider signing your child up. If there is no such program offered, bring colored pencils and pads of paper to an art museum and sketch what you see or what certain pieces of art make you think of. If you do not live close to an art museum, find out if you can visit local artists in their studios. Many advertise in local papers or may work in local public schools. Visit your city's website as well as the websites of artists' organizations: often they will post dates for "open studio" tours. You can also take out some large-format art books from the library and create your own "museum" at home.

Straw Painting

straws, poster or tempera paint, paper

Place drops of paint onto the paper, aim your straw at the paint, and blow! Move your straw to send the paint in various directions. Encourage children to take breaks to avoid dizziness. Children of all ages will love this!

Papier-mâché

utility shears, chicken wire, tin cans, blown-up balloons, or other objects to use as forms, white flour, water, newspaper, tempera paints, paintbrush

1. Use tin snips or large utility shears to cut sections of "chicken wire" mesh (available at most hardware stores), being mindful of sharp edges. Help your child bend the wire mesh into the shape of an animal, mountain, house, or other object. For younger children or for a mask that a small child can wear, blow up an extra-large balloon to use as a form. Cans are good for modeling smaller objects.
2. In a large bowl, mix flour and water to form a thin paste.
3. Tear newspaper into strips, and one at a time, dip them in the paste. Do not allow to become soggy.
4. Hold each strip vertically and stroke off excess mixture by running two fingers down its length. Then drape it over your form. Keep layering the strips until they are about $1/4$ inch thick. If making a mask, leave a space at the bottom of the balloon large enough for your child's head to fit through, and holes for eyes. To add features to the face, dip a few strips of newspaper in the flour mixture and form them into the shape you want. Then paste on.
5. When the papier-mâché has dried, brush on finishing touches with tempura paint. Pop the balloon with a pin.

Box Town

boxes, milk and juice cartons, and other empty containers, glue or glue stick, scissors, construction or wrapping paper, crayons or markers

1. Cover boxes and cartons with paper—younger children will need your help.
2. Carefully cut windows, doors, tunnels, and other decorations from the construction paper, or simply draw them on.
3. Arrange the box buildings and houses into a town. As finishing touches, roll green paper into cone pine trees. Create road signs and store signs. You can also add building blocks wherever they seem to fit. Then it's time to play!

You can turn your Papier-mâché sculpture into a piñata for birthday parties. Simply cut out a small flap to insert wrapped candies and toys. Pierce two holes to loop through a cord to hang.

Rainy Day Fun

When storm clouds are gathering and the forecast is bleak, you'll need some new backup activities to keep the kiddies happily occupied indoors for the day. Though rain might be putting a damper on your outdoor plans, you can liven up the day with an indoor rainbow display and some colorful art. Spend some time in the cozy kitchen making treats or . . . play dough! Best of all, take a walk outside to enjoy the rain and show your kids that a rainy day doesn't have to be a dreary day.

Make Play Dough

Spend a chilly rainy day in a cozy kitchen. Of course you can bake cookies, but why not make play dough or (gasp) slime? It is easy enough to buy these things, but it is also very easy to make them. You and your child will have even more fun whipping up a batch of squishy stuff to play with than you would just opening a can.

> *1 cup water*
> *1 tablespoon cooking oil*
> *1 cup salt*
> *3 cups flour*
> *2 teaspoons cornstarch*
> *food coloring*

1. In a large bowl, mix flour and cornstarch. Add the water, oil, and salt.
2. Knead dough until smooth.
3. Divide dough into four small balls and color each one with different color food coloring. Colors will come off as you play, so cover stainable surfaces.

THINGS TO DO WITH PLAY DOUGH
- **Make a caterpillar.** Roll small balls of different-colored play dough and squish them together gently to form a caterpillar. Use toothpicks for antennae.
- **Build an igloo.** Make miniature play dough bricks and stack them in rings of decreasing diameter, pushing them together so they stick, until you are able to close up the dome. Remind your child to leave a hole for the entrance.

- **Make jewelry.** Roll out a ball of play dough into a snake shape and wrap it around your child's wrist or neck. Push little balls of other colors in for jewels.

Slime

> *¹⁄₃ cup Elmer's glue*
> *²⁄₃ cup warm water*
> *2 tablespoons Borax (supermarket laundry aisle)*
> *sealable plastic bag*
> *green food coloring*

1. Mix the glue and ¹⁄₃ cup water.
2. Mix Borax in remaining ¹⁄₃ cup of water.
3. In the plastic bag, add the glue mixture with the Borax mixture. Add a couple of drops of food coloring. Seal bag and knead the mixture.
4. Wash hands after playing with slime. Store slime in sealed bag in the refrigerator. When slime grows old or dry, add a bit of water or make new slime! (Do not leave in carpets or on furniture overnight.)

THINGS TO DO WITH SLIME
- Drape it over hands for creepy effect.
- Leave it lying around to surprise and disgust the unsuspecting.
- Hide a bit in your hand and pretend to sneeze.

Make a Rainbow at Home

Rainbows are a wondrous but rare occurrence. Instead of waiting for a rainbow to appear, create your own colorful display at home.

clear drinking glass, water, poster board, construction paper, flashlight, tape

1. Fill the glass with water and place it on the edge of a chair.
2. Cut a round piece of construction paper and make a small slit in the middle.
3. Use the circle of construction paper to cover the end of the flashlight. Secure it with tape. When the flashlight is on, you should only see one small beam of light coming through the slit in the paper
4. Have one of children hold the poster board about a foot back behind the glass of water.
5. Holding the flashlight about a foot from the glass, shine the light through the glass of water and onto the poster board. You may have to adjust the angle of the flashlight, but you should see a rainbow on the poster board.

Puddle Jumping

Just because it's raining doesn't mean you have to stay indoors. Don the raincoats and galoshes and let her splash in backyard puddles to her heart's content. Take a walk around the yard and check out worms crawling to the surface, or get a close-up view of how the raindrops cling to the flowers in the garden. On a warm rainy day, break out the bathing suits and the Slip 'n' Slide—you won't even need the hose!

What Makes A Rainbow?

While light may look colorless, it is actually made up of all colors: red, orange, yellow, green, blue, indigo, and violet. Shine a flashlight directly on the wall—when the light passes through air, it remains colorless. Shining light through a different medium, such as water, causes the beam of light to bend or refract, which splits out all the colors of the rainbow. When you see a rainbow outside, sunlight is passing through the little droplets of rain, producing the large rainbow that you see.

Take a Colorful Bath

Perfect after puddle jumping. Let your kids enjoy a hot soak and have colorful fun with bath paints.

shaving cream, food coloring, muffin tin or plastic containers

1. Squirt large dollops of shaving cream into each cup of a muffin tin.
2. Add a couple of drops of different-colored food coloring to each cup and stir. (Use food coloring sparingly to avoid staining skin. Test a bit of shaving cream on your child's arm before using.)
3. When the kids are in the bath let them paint themselves and the walls. Kids will love the squishy feeling of the shaving cream, and cleanup is as easy as hosing down the tub (and your little Picasso!).

The Dress-Up Box

- old dance-recital costumes
- old Halloween costumes ▪ old party
dresses ▪ toy "profession" hats
(fireman, policeman, cowboy, etc.)
▪ plastic tiaras ▪ colorful "silk"
scarves ▪ bandanas ▪ old hats
▪ wigs ▪ old neckties and shirts ▪
old costume jewelry ▪ fancy gloves
and handbags ▪ aprons ▪ old shoes
and high heels ▪ old baby clothes
(for dressing up stuffed animals)
▪ eyepatch ▪ fake mustache ▪

A Knight in Shining Aluminum

2 large rectangular sheets of posterboard, scissors, lots of aluminum foil, construction paper, markers, glue, hole puncher, 10 inch length of ribbon or string, long cardboard tube (from inside a wrapping paper roll)

1. Make a sandwich board for your little Sir Lancelot using two equal-size sheets of posterboard roughly the size of your child's chest.
2. To create "armor," cover the posterboard in foil and design a coat of arms in construction paper to glue on the front board.
3. Punch a hole near the top two corners of each board. Cut your ribbon in half. Connect the corners of the boards together by tying an end of ribbon through the holes. The completed sandwich board should fit over child's head and hang from the shoulders.
4. To make a lance, wrap tube in foil. Extend a bit of foil in one end to scrunch up and shape into a point.

Dragon Hat

green shirt or sweater, 1 piece of green felt (about 2 yards long and 1 foot wide), markers, fabric glue, long red scarf

1. Start by dressing in a green shirt or sweater.
2. Fold the felt in half (folded piece should be 1 yard by 1 foot). Mark a spiky, bumpy pattern from the top corner of the folded edge on the right to the bottom left corner.
3. Cut along the spikes. Glue the edges of the spikes together. Let dry.
4. Fit the felt on your child's head with the fold at the forehead. Glue together the tail part of the hat from the back of the head to the end of the tail. The dragon hat should fit securely on top of your child's head.
5. For fun, you can give your child a long red scarf to hold and flick. He can pretend it is the flame from a ferocious fire-breathing dragon and see who he can touch with his "flame".

Dress Up

Nothing is better than dress-up to spark your child's imagination. Keep some dress-up essentials in a big special box and periodically add to it with Halloween costumes or retired clothing items. On special days it is also easy to help your children make simple costumes. Try dressing them up as a brave knight, a beautiful princess, and a ferocious dragon!

Medieval Princess

plain white nightgown, colorful "silk" scarves, safety pins (optional), scissors, construction paper, aluminum foil, glue, pen, red glitter (optional)

1. For the princess's gown, decorate nightgown with scarves. You can simply tie corners of the scarves together to create a billowing skirt to tie around the waist or pin a bunch of scarves to the back to create a train or bustle. Scarves can also be pinned on each shoulder to create billowing sleeves.
2. Cut a strip of construction paper about 4 inches high and long enough to wrap around child's head. (Tape two strips together if necessary.)
3. Wrap and glue aluminum foil smoothly over the construction paper.
4. Draw a zigzag across the top of the strip and trim along the zigzag to form points of the crown.
5. Cut out gem shapes from construction paper, spread a thin layer of glue and add glitter, if desired, and glue to points of crown. Let dry.
6. Wrap strip around head and tape the two ends together to fit.

Insects

While you may have an aversion to all that is creepy and crawly, your child may love every little bug. Join your child in activities to learn about insects. Who knows? Your son or daughter may teach you how to see them through the wondering eyes of childhood. Discuss why spiders spin webs, why butterflies come in so many colors, and how crickets make such funny music. Soon, you will find yourself and your little entomologist fascinated by the insect world around you.

To order butterfly kits, ant farms, or ladybugs try *thenaturestore.com* or *brightworld.com.*

SEE BUGS WALK ON WATER Visit a pond or lake, and you will be able to show your child pond skaters (also known as water striders)—the small, long-legged bugs that skate along the surface of lakes. Your child may ask you how they do this without sinking. Here is a brief explanation: Water has surface tension—a kind of very thin layer on top. Pond skaters are so light that they are able to slide across the surface without falling through.

MAKE A BUTTERFLY FEEDER You can build a backyard or windowsill butterfly feeder to attract butterflies to your house. Keep a butterfly guide on hand to help you identify your glamorous guests. It's also fun to keep a record of which butterflies you have seen. Nail a board to a post or to your windowsill and paint it with a layer of butterfly food. To make the food, mix bananas, sugar, and a little self-rising yeast in a bucket; cover it and leave it for three days. It will get frothy (and quite smelly—so be careful where you put it). Or try skewering an orange half on the end of a sturdy branch or twig of a tree. Face the cut side outward so the butterflies can do some "fly-by sipping."

GROW YOUR OWN BUTTERFLIES Observe the magic of a caterpillar turning into a butterfly. You can buy butterfly kits online (*see page 118*) or go hunting for caterpillars yourself. Find a caterpillar on a plant. Remove the caterpillar carefully, using a leaf, rather than your hands. Take some branches and leaves from the plant on which you found it, and put them together with the caterpillar in large glass jar or fish tank. Punch some holes in the lid of the jar. Continue to feed the caterpillar pieces of the same plant on which you found it (check a caterpillar guide to make sure you are giving it the right food, as caterpillars are quite choosy). Mist the caterpillar's jar each day very lightly. In a short period, you will observe the caterpillar beginning to pupate. It will spin itself into a cocoon and appear to be lifeless. When it

MAKE AN INSECT INVESTIGATION Take a walk around your backyard or local park with your child and point out all of the insects that you see. Buy an insect guidebook to look up names and habits of more six-legged creatures. How many different insects can you find?

Ant Farm

large glass jar, soil, a piece of paper, ants, sponge, water, aluminum foil, food, plastic wrap, rubber band

1. Go outside to your backyard or park and hunt for anthills. Look for the telltale march of working ants carrying food, and follow them home.
2. Very carefully, without hurting any ants, collect the loose dirt around the anthill and put it into the jar. This makes for good ant-tunneling soil.
3. Before adding the ants, spray some water into the jar to lightly moisten the soil.
4. Use a small piece of paper to sweep the ants into the jar. Ask an adult to supervise, and be very careful, because some ants like to nip!
5. Once you have gathered a few dozen ants, wet a small bit of sponge and place it inside. Although ants get most of their water from food, this is always a good precaution.
6. Make a small food dish out of aluminum foil. For meals, ants love insects and sweet foods. A small piece of bread dipped in sugar water, tiny bits of watermelon, cookie crumbs, and dead caterpillars all make for good ant food.
7. Ants usually can't climb up the side of a jar, but you can seal it with a piece of plastic wrap punched with air holes and secured with a rubber band, just in case.
8. Every so often spray a little water into the jar to keep the soil moist for tunneling. Replace the foil dish and freshly wet the sponge each time you add food to the jar.

emerges—a butterfly—allow it to climb branches and dry its wings before releasing it. Release the butterfly near to where you found the caterpillar. For more information on gathering and rearing try *rearing-butterflies.com*.

BUY A HERD OF LADYBUGS Ladybugs are very good to have around your garden because they eat garden pests such as aphids. For this reason, many garden supply stores sell bags of ladybugs (*or see page 118*). Buy a bag and let your child help you free them.

GET WET A tub of water or a plastic inflatable pool, a sprinkler or a few water guns … it's simply a matter of space and how wet you want to get! When the weather is warm enough, set your kids out in swim suits and let them have a splash. A one year old is happy scooping and pouring little pails of water, older kids will enjoy tag games with water guns (or water balloons!), and all kids love running through sprinklers. (Remember to supervise carefully and empty buckets and pool after use. A baby or young child can drown in only 2 inches of water. Also, balloons are choking hazards, supervise accordingly and pick up all broken pieces.)

Discover the Mysteries of the Mundane

As familiar as your backyard or local park may be, there will always be something new to wonder about. Keep a few nature guides on birds, insects, and plants handy to satisfy curious minds. You might encourage your child to keep a nature journal about his own yard.

Backyard Adventures

If you have a backyard, you have an endless source of entertainment for your children. Fresh air, sunlight, contact with nature, and a chance to run around are wonderful things to give your child. Here are just a few activities that will provide hours of amusement and happy memories. Remember that backyards have something to offer in all seasons—and don't forget the sunblock!

GO DAYTIME CAMPING Set up a small pup tent outside. With your child, choose a destination—somewhere real or make-believe—and pretend that you are camping there. Pack a small backpack of camping items—a blanket, some bug spray, trail mix, a flashlight, and a map and compass. If you are comfortable with the idea, let the daytime camp-out turn into an overnight adventure.

Chart the Territory

Your child can have fun learning about maps by making her own map of your backyard. Provide some big pieces of paper and crayons or pens, establish which direction is north, and help your little explorer to chart the limits and features of her own kingdom. You can tell your child about some of the famous explorers. Let her name your backyard after herself if she likes!

MAKE A MUD PIE (This is the inedible recipe; see "Summer" for the edible kind.) All you need is dirt, water, and tolerance for a mess. Make a puddle somewhere in the yard and give your child some aluminum pie pans to play with. Add grass for a "coconut" effect. Twigs make good candles, and some small stones painted with red nail polish can be cherries.

MAKE A BEAN TEPEE Set up wooden dowels to form a child-size teepee frame. Plant beans at the base so that they will grow along the sticks. You and your child can do the planting and tending together, so then he'll have a nice, private leafy playhouse all summer long. Hungry kids? The bean tepee has healthy snacks built right in!

DIG FOR BURIED TREASURE This one takes a little planning. If you don't mind some holes in the lawn, you can bury "treasures" in the yard. Cigar boxes full of costume jewelry work well, as do plastic coins and secret messages in empty soda bottles. Use old teacups for an archeological experience, plastic dinosaurs for the future paleontologist. Give your child a plastic shovel and a treasure map indicating where to dig.

Variation: Hide one prize and a number of clues (it's fun to write rhyming hints) that connect to each other. For example—the clue in the hollow log leads to the clue hidden in the wheel barrow, which leads to the clue under the doormat...and eventually to the hidden treasure.

Giant Soap Bubbles

Fill a bucket with a mixture of one part dishwashing liquid to between four and six parts water. Add a little glycerin for extra-durable bubbles. Make a loop out of a wire coat hanger, or use an old tennis racket with some of the strings removed. Dip the loop in the soap mixture and wave it gently back and forth. Huge, wobbly bubbles will be released to shimmer across the yard.

HAVE A SACK RACE Have little contestants step into pillowcases and hop their way toward a predetermined finish line. They may fall down along the "racecourse," but if they're outside on the grass they won't hurt themselves too much, and everyone will be laughing all the way.

A Child's Garden

*L*et your children enjoy the miracle of life in plant form. Whether it is grass seed on the lawn or a flowering bulb in a pot, teach your child the art of gardening and show him how to care for his own plants. Grow vegetables outside and use them in a favorite dish, or create a beautiful arrangement of cut flowers from the blooms you've planted together. Indoors, potted herbs will add spice to your family dinner as flowering bulbs add fragrance to the air.

OUTDOOR GARDEN If you have extra backyard space for gardening, cordon off a small area for a garden for your child. Pass on your knowledge and enthusiasm for cultivating flowers and vegetables by working side by side with your child. Ask her what she would like to grow and decide together what plants to put in the garden. Your child will probably enjoy growing foods and flowers that she's familiar with. Plants with large seeds like beans and sunflowers will be easier for your child to sow.

PLANT A PIZZA GARDEN! What better way to get your kids interested in gardening than by planting the ingredients of their favorite food? Help your child plant peppers, onions, tomatoes, basil, oregano, and any other type of veggies he likes on a pizza. When your vegetables and herbs are in full bloom, plan a pizza party for the family.

A FLOWERING SALAD Your child will probably be fasci-nated to learn that there are actually many types of edible flowers. Plant a few different types of lettuce, some cucumbers, and tomatoes, and then nasturtiums, violets, and pansies. Once the harvest is in, mix up a beautiful fresh salad and top it off with a few flowers. Show your children how gourmet chefs garnish their favorite dishes, and arrange a couple of edible flowers on your child's dinner plate.

Sponge Grass

*T*his is a good first activity for little ones who just can't wait.

sponge, grass seed, water, saucer

1. Moisten the sponge.
2. Dip and rub the sponge in grass seed.
3. Put the sponge in a saucer of water.
4. Place the saucer in the sunlight.
5. After a few days grass should sprout on the sponge.

Stately Sunflowers

*S*unflowers are dramatic in their height and spectacular in their beauty. Create a secret room for your child in the garden by planting a circle of tall sunflowers. Cut a few of the giant blooms and hang them upside-down to dry. Once they have dried out, pick the flower apart for the seeds and roast them (*same method as for pumpkin seeds, page 198*) for a tasty and nutritious treat for the kids.

Forced Bulbs

Paperwhite narcissus bulbs are fragrant, easy-to-grow plants that will add beauty to any windowsill. Unlike other bulbs, paperwhites do not require any chilling or rest period before growing, which makes them an ideal choice any time of the year.

clear vase or other container without drainage holes, clean 1/2-inch pebbles, large, firm paperwhite bulbs, water

1. Fill the chosen container with pebbles until about one inch from the rim.
2. Add water to the container until it is just below the top of the pebbles.
3. Place the bulbs close together in the container on top of the pebbles. Be sure that the bulbs themselves are not actually touching the water, or they may get moldy.
4. Add more pebbles to the container, covering the bottom third of the bulbs.
5. Leave the bulbs in a cool, dark place, maintaining the water level. This will encourage root growth.
6. After about a week or two, gently tug on the bulbs to see if they feel rooted. Once they have rooted, move the container to a bright spot without direct sunlight.
7. The paperwhites should flower in three to five weeks.

WINDOW BOX

Another beautiful way to teach your children about flowers is to plant a lush window box. When choosing plants to put in the window box, choose ones that will grow to different heights, and ones with bright, complementary colors. Make sure the window box has good drainage, with holes in the bottom. Cover the holes with a small piece of window screen, or place pebbles at the bottom. Use potting mix to loosely fill the rest of the box. Unpot the plants you will be using, and gently loosen the roots. Nestle the tallest plants (like geraniums) in the potting mix at the back of the box, spacing them apart for growth, and the trailing plants (like petunias) in the front. Water well and place on a sunny windowsill or mount outside.

HERB BOX Culinary herbs are easy-to-grow plants for indoor spaces. You can plant various herbs together in a long, rectangular box, or choose small decorative individual pots for each herb. Choose herbs that your child is familiar with and branch out a bit to enhance her palette. Basil, thyme, dill, chives, and rosemary should work well indoors, and together you can plan a meal featuring your child's fresh herbs. When planting, be sure each pot has drainage, and fill each one with potting mix. Drop the seeds in according to the packet directions, and water well. The herbs should sprout in about two weeks.

They worked in their garden, As good children do, And truly enjoyed it Until they were through.

Just Say The Magic Word

Here are some classic magic words that your little magician can use: Abracadabra, Open sesame, Hocus pocus, Shazam, Alakazam.

You can easily make up your own magic words by combining ordinary words to make a silly phrase. Say them with a magician's flair and you are sure to get both giggles and awe. Here are some examples: Cauliflower kerfuffle, Anemone spumoni, Cantilever lobsterpot. You can make magic words by rearranging the letters of your child's name or simply by saying it backwards.

Magic!

You may not be Harry Houdini, but your child looks to you to provide much of the magic in his or her life. Here are a few simple tricks that every parent can learn to entertain a child. These are the sorts of tricks that do not require complicated props, so you can do them practically anytime or anywhere. Tricks may require some practice to perfect, but when you find yourself performing to a rapt audience of wonder-filled children, you will see that it has all been worth it.

COIN FLIP This one takes some practice, but once you show your child this trick, he will spend hours trying to learn it, too. Place your right hand on your right shoulder (or left hand on left shoulder if left-handed). Set a quarter or silver dollar on your elbow and, in one movement, flip the coin off your elbow and catch it with your right hand.

MAGIC MONEY CLIP Fold a dollar in thirds to form a flattened Z. Clip the first and middle section together near the left edge of the dollar. Clip the middle and bottom sections together near the right edge of the dollar. Tell the audience you can magically link the paper clips together without touching them. Tug both ends of the bill to straighten it out. The paper clips will pop off and link together!

KNOT TRICK Take a three-foot-long piece of string and challenge your child to tie a knot in the string without letting go of either end of it. They will be unable to do it. Then place the string on a table. Fold your arms in such a way that one palm ends up under your elbow and the other on your upper arm. Now, without uncrossing your arms, stoop and pick up an end of the string in each hand. Uncross your arms, and—Voila!

FUN WITH STATIC This is a good one to do at a birthday party, a parade— or anywhere you are likely to find balloons. Take a balloon and rub it against clothing or hair to create friction and static. Hold the balloon against your child's head, then let it go. It will stay stuck there. Or you can stick the balloon to a wall or other surface.

Why does this happen? Static electricity created by rubbing the balloon against a "rough" surface like hair or fabric removes some electrons, giving the balloon a positive charge. The molecules that lost electrons bond with molecules on your head or wall.

FLOATING NEEDLE Tell your friends you can make a needle float in a glass of water. Let your friends try first. The needle will sink. Cut out a piece of paper napkin longer than the needle. Place the napkin flat on the water. Lay the needle on top of the napkin. The napkin should sink when wet. If not, push it down carefully with your finger. The needle will stay afloat. Amazing.

Funny Business

Kids are natural comedians. They enjoy laughing and making others laugh. Around age six, most children begin to enjoy wordplay. Knock-knock jokes and variations of chicken crossing the road jokes are sure favorites.

    Knock-knock!
    Who's there?
    Boo.
    Boo Who?
    Don't cry.

Other things knocking and responses:
Al: Al be seeing you.
Tank: You're welcome!
Aitch: Gesundheit!
    Thea: Thea later alligator.
    May: Maybe I'll tell you, maybe I won't.
Tania: Tania self around and you'll see.
    Thistle: Thistle be the last time I knock on your door.
    Wooden: Woodn't you like to know?
    Albert: Albert you don't know who this is.

There is no one who will not remember the endless fascinations of a certain chicken poised on the edge of a busy road.

Why did the chicken cross the road? To get to the other side.

Other things crossing the road and responses:
chewing gum: Because it was stuck to the chicken.
cow: To get to the udder side.
dinosaur: Because the chicken hadn't evolved yet.
egg: To get there before the chicken.

Card Games

Card games have entertained adults and children all over the world for centuries. From the simple fun of Go Fish and Old Maid to the more sophisticated Crazy Eights and Gin Rummy, card games are a fun and easy way to pass time, teach kids about strategy, and promote fair play. Create a family game night that features a different game each week. Cards also work especially well on rainy days or long road trips!

Memory

- *Number of players:* two or more
- *Age:* 3 and up
- *Setup:* Take a deck of cards and place them all facedown in rows.
- *Goal:* To collect as many pairs as you can
- *How to play:* Flip one card over. Then choose a second card to flip and try to make a matching pair. If they match, remove those two cards from the table and continue. If not, turn both cards back over and let the next person try to find a pair.

Old Maid

- *Number of players:* three to five
- *Age:* 4 and up
- *Setup:* Remove the Queen of clubs, the Queen of diamonds, and the Queen of spades. Deal out all the cards to the players (it doesn't matter if some players have more than others).
- *Goal:* To avoid becoming the "Old Maid"
- *How to play:* If any player has a pair of matching cards (such as two 7s or two Kings), he discards them on the table. The player to the dealer's left fans out his cards so nobody can see them. He offers them to the player on his left, who pulls one out of the fan without seeing what it is and adds it to his hand. If it makes a pair with anything he has, he discards the pair. That player then lets the next player pick a card from his hand in the same way. The game continues until the only card left is the Queen of hearts, the Old Maid. The player left holding the Old Maid is the loser!

Go Fish

- *Number of players:* three to five
- *Age:* 4 and up
- *Setup:* Deal out seven cards to each player, and put the rest facedown in the "pool." Players remove any four-card sets from their hands. Players then organize their hands so that all cards with the same value (such as Jacks or 3s) are together.
- *Goal:* To get the most four-card sets
- *How to play:* First player asks one of the other players for a card that matches one she already has in her hand. If the player she asks has the denomination—let's say Jacks—the player must give her all the Jacks she has. If the first player gets the card she wants, she asks for another card from the player again. If the other player doesn't have the card the asker wants, the player tells the asker, "Go fish," from the pool. The asker takes one card from the pool. The player who said, "Go fish," becomes the next asker. Whenever a player collects all four of a kind, she puts the set faceup on the table. The game ends when one player is able to get rid of all her cards.

Memory, Uno, and Go Fish have been favorites in our family and I look forward to introducing the kids to Spit soon. But our big craze right now is Set: A Family Game of Visual Perception. The object of the game is to identify a "set" of three cards from 12 cards laid out on the table. Each card has a variation of four features: color, symbol, number, and shading. Age is no advantage in this award-winning game, in fact, my seven year old has beaten me too many times. For ages 6 and up; for 1 or more players. Try it!

Crazy Eights

- *Number of players:* two to five
- *Age:* 4 and up
- *Setup:* Deal out seven cards to each player and leave the rest facedown in a stack. Take one card from the top of the stack and place it faceup on the table. This will be the discard pile.
- *Goal:* To be the first to get rid of all your cards
- *How to play:* The player to the dealer's left goes first. He looks through his hand for a card that matches the one on the discard pile, either in value (for example, both are Jacks) or suit (both are spades). If he finds one, he places it on top of the discard pile. If the player doesn't have a card that matches, he draws from the deck until he gets one that does match. The exception: Eights are "wild cards"—meaning that you may play them on any card. Whoever plays an 8 of any suit gets to choose the next suit to be played. The winner is the player who gets rid of all his cards first, but the game may continue until there's only one player left standing.

War

- *Number of players:* two
- *Age:* 5 and up
- *Setup:* Deal out the cards, half to yourself and half to the other player. Hold your cards facedown in a stack.
- *Goal:* To get all the cards in the deck
- *How to play:* You are the dealer. Your opponent places the top card from her stack faceup on the table, and you do the same. Whoever played the higher card (the Ace is the highest, the 2 the lowest) takes both and adds them to the bottom of her stack. If both cards have the same value, it means "war." If the cards starting the war are both 2s, place two cards facedown and a third card faceup. Likewise, if the cards are 7s, place seven cards facedown, and so on (Jacks are worth 11 points, Queens 12, Kings 13, and Aces 1). If the deciding cards again match, the war continues in the same way. Whoever wins the war takes all the cards on the table. Continue in the same way as before, turning cards over, one pair at a time. When one player wipes the other out, the game is over!

Spit

- *Number of players:* two
- *Age:* 8 and up
- *Setup:* Deal out all the cards to both players. Players arrange their cards into five stacks, facedown and solitaire-style (from right to left, the first pile has one card, the second has two, the third has three, and so forth). Turn the top card of each stack faceup. If any top cards match (say two Jacks or three 4s), the player can put them together in a separate stack and turn the next cards up. Each player places his leftover cards in a pile in the middle.
- *Goal:* To be the first to get rid of all your cards
- *How to play:* Players flip over the top cards from their leftover piles into the middle space between them. These are the "spit" piles. The players then try to get rid of all of their cards from their five stacks into these spit piles as fast as they can, in sequence. Numbers can go up or down (2-3-2-A-K). As each player places faceup cards onto the center piles, the next facedown cards on their stacks are turned faceup. Matching cards can be placed together, and if any stack is finished, a faceup card from another stack can be moved into the empty space, and the card beneath it turned up. (Players are allowed five cards facing up.) If at any time neither player can put any more cards onto the spit piles, both players take the next cards from their leftover piles and place them on their spit piles. When one player has finished all of his stacks, he quickly slaps the spit pile he thinks has fewer cards and takes possession of it—if the other player notices, he can try to slap it first. The players then set up all of their cards again in solitaire-style stacks, and the next round begins. The game ends when one player has discarded all his cards.

Ball Games

*D*o you have fond memories of lazy summer days where all you did was play ball with your friends? Why not introduce your kids to some timeless favorites? Teach your children and their friends some games and they will amuse themselves for hours outside. When they are looking for something a little out of the ordinary, grab some bottles from the recycle bin and set up "Soda Bottle Bowling" in the street. Or if the temperature is climbing, cool off the kids with an impromptu game of water balloon "Hot Potato".

SODA BOTTLE BOWLING For one or more: Fill ten empty plastic two-liter soda bottles with about two inches of water and seal them. Set the bottles up like bowling pins, with one pin in the front, two in the next row, three in the third row, four in the fourth row, and five in the fifth row. Mark a starting line about fifteen feet away. Using a playground ball, try to bowl down the pins from the starting line. Each person gets two turns per round, and a point is given for every pin knocked down. The winner is the one with the most points after five rounds. Playing alone? Set up the pins and see how many strikes you can get!

STICKBALL For two or more: Who doesn't love to play this old-fashioned favorite? All you need are a few friends, a ball, a stick, and you are ready to go. Stickball is played like baseball. Mark off four bases and have someone be the pitcher. Each hitter gets three strikes for a strikeout; each team gets three outs for

their inning. The strike zone is very wide, and there is no such thing as a walk, so start swinging. The players can determine the dimensions of the field to decide which hits are home runs. Play as many innings as you like, and the team that scores the most runs wins! If there are only two of you, turn it into a home run derby! Choose a distance that would qualify as a "home run" and see which player can rack up the most.

BALL BETWEEN THE KNEES RELAY RACES For two or more: Create teams for this game, and give each team a ball. (The smaller the ball, the harder the race will be!) The first person on each team places a ball between their knees. When "Start!" is called, each person must run to an appointed target and back, keeping the ball between their knees. When the team members get back to the starting line, they pass the ball to their next teammate who must do the same. The first team to have all of their members run the course

and keep the ball between their knees is the winner. You could also play this game against just one other player; race to the finish line and the first one there with the ball between her knees wins.

MONKEY IN THE MIDDLE For three or more: One person is the "monkey" and stands in the middle, while the other players throw a ball over the monkey's head. The object of the game is for the monkey to catch the ball. The person who threw the ball then becomes the new monkey.

WATER BALLOON HOT POTATO For three or more: Fill up some small balloons with water and gather your friends in a circle. Have one person be the leader, and stand in the center with a water balloon. The leader tosses the balloon to a player in the circle and then closes his eyes. The players then toss the balloon around the circle to each player. When the leader yells "Hot Potato!" the person left holding the balloon is out. To make this game a little harder, have the players in the circle stand farther apart. Be prepared to get wet.

Sidewalk & Playground Games

If you live in a city or suburban neighborhood, the sidewalks and playgrounds can offer your children a great space to play. If you're lucky enough to live in a safe and low-traffic area, there will often be neighborhood children out and about. Set your children up with an activity or two and watch other children come and join in the fun.

JACKS Bounce the ball and scoop up a jack and the ball before the ball bounces twice. To increase the difficulty, play twosies, threesies, and foursies; toss the ball and scoop up two, three, or four jacks and the ball before the ball bounces twice. Continue until you have picked up all the jacks.

MARBLES Young children (but not so young that marbles would be a choking hazard) can play a simplified game of Ring Taw, the most popular marble game during settler times. Draw a ring on the ground and place several marbles inside. Children practice shooting a marble from outside the ring, trying to knock other marbles out of the ring. Older children can play against each other "for keeps," keeping marbles they knock out. The one with the most marbles wins.

BEANBAG TOSS Grab a beanbag, some chalk, and a friend for a beanbag toss competition. Draw a target with chalk on the ground and be creative: make a circle or square and draw different segments with various point values. Take turns tossing the beanbag, and see who can score one hundred points first.

SIDEWALK ART The sidewalk is a perfect canvas for a creative outlet. Get a box of large sidewalk chalk and let your kids draw pictures to their hearts' content. Gather more neighborhood children to create a large sidewalk mural.

KICK THE CAN The player who is "it" kicks an empty aluminum can as far as possible. Once the can starts rolling, all the other players run for hiding places. "it" retrieves the can, puts it back in the original place, and counts to fifty. After "it" has finished counting, he or she must find other players. Once someone is found, "it" calls out their name and must rush back to beat the player to the can. If "it" gets there first, the hider is captured. Captured players can be set free if a hider gets to the can before being spied by "it," kicks the can, and yells "Home free!" Everyone can then hide again.

HOPSCOTCH Use your imagination and draw a creative hopscotch pattern. Make blocks in a traditional straight line, a circle, or a zigzag pattern. Grab a stone or coin, toss it on the first numbered block, and hop your way to the end. Keep your balance, don't step on the lines, and don't forget to pick the stone up on the way back!

Remember these favorites from the schoolyard? Remind your kids how much fun they can be! *Follow the Leader, Hide and Seek, Leapfrog, Touch Football, Tug-of-War, Blind Man's Bluff*

Playground Games

Looking for a fun way to amuse a group of kids? If you have plenty of running room and lots of children to entertain, here are some suggestions:

BARNYARD PEANUT HUNT Requires about twelve kids divided into four teams. Each team is assigned an animal (cow, pig, horse, etc.) and a captain. Peanuts are hidden in the playground, and all the teams search for them. Only a captain can pick up the peanuts, so if another member of the team finds a peanut, he or she must make the sound of their team animal to alert the captain of the location of the peanut. The sounds of all the "animals" will resemble a barnyard ruckus! The team with the most peanuts wins.

RED ROVER Divide into two teams of at least five members each (the more the merrier with this game). Teams should be evenly divided, and line up holding hands opposite from each other. One team calls out, "Red rover, red rover, send (the name of one player) right over!" The team member who was called will run across and try to break through between two people on the opposing team. If he cannot break through, he now joins the opposing team. Each team takes turns until there is only one team left.

FRISBEE GOLF For two or more players. You will need a Frisbee, a large open area, and paper and pencil for keeping score. Before play begins, everyone decides on what the "hole" will be—it can be a particular tree in the field, a pole, or whatever else serves as a large target. To make things interesting, the players also might

Jump Rope Rhymin'

Kids love to jump rope whether it be alone or in groups. Teach your children these jumping rhymes and they will entertain themselves and their friends for hours.

> Cookies, candy in a dish
> How many pieces do you wish?
> 1, 2, 3, 4…
>
> Ice cream, soda, lemonade, punch
> Spell the initials of your honey bunch
> A, B, C, D…
>
> Policeman, policeman, do your duty
> Here comes [*Name of next jumper*]
> And she's a cutie;
> She can jump and she can twist,
>   [*Jumper does activities*]
> But I bet she can do this! [*Jumper does a trick*]
>
> A, my name is *Alfred*,
> My wife's name is *Allison*,
> We grow *Apples*
> In *Alabama*.
> [*Repeat with words starting with B, C, D…*]

decide on what "hazards" and obstacles to put on the way to the hole, like having to throw through an empty jungle gym, or a tunnel perhaps. Each player then takes a turn throwing the Frisbee as many times as it takes to reach the target. The fewer number of throws, the better. You can design numerous "holes" like these for an entire course.

TAG Here are some variations on the classic game of tag:
- **Regular** One of the players is "it," and he chases the others around, trying to tag them. Whoever gets tagged becomes the new "it."
- **Ball** Same as regular tag, but instead of touching other players, "it" tosses a soft rubber ball to tag others.
- **Blob** Only one player starts off as "it," but as he tags other players, they join hands with "it," eventually making one massive "it" blob.
- **Freeze** Whoever gets tagged becomes "frozen," and has to stand perfectly still until he is touched by an unfrozen player.

Paper & Pencil Games

No matter how many plush toys, picture books, and building blocks you accumulate, there are going to be times when your child says, "Mom, I'm bored." When this happens, it helps to have some simple games in your mental bag of tricks. Games that are played with a piece of paper and a pencil can be especially useful when you are away from home: waiting in a doctor's office, for instance, or riding on a train. Here are a few old standbys to keep young minds and fingers busy.

TIC-TAC-TOE This simple game has the power to fascinate young children. While older children can easily figure out how to block their opponent at each turn, making it impossible for either side to win, children under the age of 5 usually do not understand the basic nature of tic-tac-toe. Therefore, you can win or let your child win quite easily. A combination of the two is probably best.

HANGMAN This old favorite is great for building the vocabulary and spelling skills of children six and older. Hangman is best played with more than one child.

EXQUISITE CORPSE
The Surrealist artists in France invented this game in the 1920s. It is a good game for practicing art techniques, stretching the imagination, and making children (and yourself) laugh. Take a blank piece of paper and draw—or ask your child to draw—the head and neck (if there is one) of a person or creature. Whoever is not drawing should not look at the page. Once the drawing is completed, fold—or ask your child to fold—the top of the page so that the head is concealed. The next artist will draw the middle section of a person or animal. The third artist completes the picture with the bottom section. You then unfold the drawing to find a unique creature, perhaps with the head of a lion, the belly of your child's grandma, and the tail fin of a fish. You might then want to encourage your child to make up a story about the creature you have created. Where does it live? What does it eat? What does it like to do for fun? Who are its friends?

Exquisite corpse can also be played using words. In this case, the first person writes the first sentence or paragraph of a story or first line of a poem. Each person adds to the work without seeing what went before. The result may surprise you with depth beneath the absurdity.

ANAGRAMS Older children may enjoy this vocabulary builder. Think of a word and write it down with the letters scrambled. Give your child a set amount of time—five minutes, say—to figure out the word. A variation on this game: Challenge your child to make new words out of the letters of his name. This may result in a new nickname!

I always bring a pad and pencils when I go out to eat with my kids. The wait for food can be quite long, especially when you have hungry and fidgety kids. Children can draw or practice writing. My husband is a great maze maker and would create quick mazes for them to solve. When they were younger, I would create connect the dot patterns for shapes or letters. Now that they are slightly older, tic-tac-toe and hangman are favorites.

Car Games

"**A**re we there yet?" "How much longer?" "Danny is hitting me!" "I'm soooooo bored!" Yikes. The next time you decide to brave a road trip with children, arm yourself with a handful of car games. These will sharpen eyes and minds, and hopefully make the trip seem faster.

ALPHABET GAME Players look for words that begin with each letter of the alphabet on road signs, billboards, buildings, train cars, or semi trucks. (License plate letters don't count.) When you find your A word, you must call it out so that no one else can claim it. Then you can go on to B, and so forth. (You can't call words out of order!) The tough letters are usually Q, X, and Z. So be sure to look for a Quick Mart after the RR Xing where there's a Speed Zone Ahead. Younger children can simply look for each letter of the alphabet in order.

ALPHABET SPY Each player must find three things that start with each letter of the alphabet. The first player to finish the Z's wins. For example, a Southwestern trip might include armadillos, adobes, and Appaloosas. A trip to the city might include buildings, billboards, and bridges.

GOING ON A PICNIC The first player recites the phrase, "I'm going on a picnic and I'm bringing _____." He or she fills in the blank with a word beginning with the letter A, such as APPLES. The second person recites the phrase and adds a B word: "I'm going on a picnic and I'm bringing APPLES and BANANAS. Each additional turn requires reciting the whole phrase and adding a new word that begins with the next letter of the alphabet. Whoever can't recite the growing list of items in proper order loses.

GEOGRAPHY Players choose a category, such as cities, countries, rivers, or landmarks. The first player names something from that category. The next player must think of another name that starts with the last letter of the first name. For example, a city list could start: San Francisco, Omaha, Akron, New York, Kansas City. If a player can't think of another city, that person is out. The last player in the game wins.

GHOST The first player says a letter. The next player must think of a word that starts with that letter and give a second letter. The object is for each player to add a letter without ending the word. (Two- and three-letter words don't count). For example, the letter called out is B. The next player adds U, thinking of BUSY. The third player adds M, thinking of BUMP. If the next player adds a P, he would lose the round. A smart choice would be the letter B (for bumble), to continue the round. The first player to end the word gets a letter

G. A person who gets all the letters to spell GHOST loses.

SMOKE One player thinks of a famous person or character. The other players must guess by asking metaphorical questions. Sample questions and answers for Sherlock Holmes would be: "If this person were a story, what kind would he or she be?" (*A mystery*) "If this person were glass, what kind would he or she be?" (*A magnifier*)

BOTTICELLI One player thinks of a famous person or character. Everyone else takes turns asking yes or no questions. The player who guesses correctly wins the round and gets to lead the next one.

Water Games

On a hot summer day, slather the kids with sunscreen and get them into the water to sharpen their swimming skills while having a blast with their friends. When they start saying, "Mom, we're bored!" suggest the next game to keep them entertained for the day.

MARCO POLO When the person who is "it" closes his eyes and shouts "Marco!" everyone else in the water must respond "Polo!" Marco will now try to swim towards the person who sounded the closest and tag them. The person who gets tagged becomes the new Marco.

SAND BANK A form of freeze tag you can play in the water! "It" swims around tagging people. Once tagged, the person must swim to the shallow waters and remain there until a "free" teammate comes and swims between their legs.

FOLLOW THE LEADER Everyone lines up in back of a leader, who will swim around performing different tricks. The leader can turn, swim, flip, blow bubbles, hold her breath under water, stand on her hands and everyone must mimic her. After a set amount of time, the leader swims to the back of the line and the next person is the leader.

SHARKS AND MINNOWS The person who is "it" is the Shark, and the goal is to tag as many Minnows as possible. When a minnow gets tagged, they also become a shark and try to tag other swimming minnows. Make the game trickier by only letting the Sharks tag the Minnows when they come up for air. The last Minnow remaining becomes the new Shark for the next game.

UNDERWATER TUNNEL RACE Children are divided into equal teams of no more than four. The team lines up single file, with the last person touching the edge of the pool. Everyone else stands with legs spread apart to make a tunnel. On the count of three, the last person in line swims forward through his teammate's legs. When they reach the front of the tunnel, he surfaces and stands at the head of the line with legs spread. The race goes on like this until one team reaches the other side of the pool and wins.

DIVE FOR PENNIES With goggles and a fistful of change, you can test your children's underwater skills and their math knowledge at the same time. Throw the change in the water and ask them to bring back, say, seventeen cents. For older kids, challenge them with a figure like $2.38.

UNDERWATER TEA PARTY For two to four kids: Sit underwater and pretend you are sipping tea, eating cakes, and having a tea party.

WHIRLPOOL Any amount of kids: Start walking around the perimeter of the pool, creating a current that gets stronger and stronger. Once the current is very strong, let it carry you. If someone yells "whirlpool," everyone turns around and tries to fight against it.

CHICKEN FIGHT Two kids (a smaller child and a larger child) team up. The smaller child gets on the larger child's shoulders. On the count of three, the pair "fights" other pairs by trying to knock the smaller child off of the larger one's shoulders. The winners are the last team left standing.

Birthday Parties

For your one-year-old, there's no need to throw an extravaganza—
a few family members and a cake will be more than enough for
some good pictures. As your child grows older though, the annual birthday party can become a highlight of his year. Because birthdays are so
precious to children—a whole day during which the child is THE most
important person—they can be a little too stimulating. You can make
sure your child's party is an enjoyable experience for everyone by planning ahead and keeping it simple.

THEME Take your child's favorite interest at the moment, from ballet to barnyard animals to backyard campout, and plan the entire party around it. Choose decorations, invitations, games, and activities that enhance the theme.

BUDGET To save money, be creative. Print out party details on plain paper, glue onto construction paper, and let you child decorate borders on each invitation. Bake cupcakes for favors and prizes. Instead of hiring an entertainer, enlist relatives or friends to perform (a puppet or magic show) or handle activities. Make your own cake.

GUESTS Invite as many child guests as your child is old, plus one or two more. It's fun to have friends, but too many kids can be overwhelming for you and your child.

INVITATIONS Send invitations at least two weeks in advance to give guests ample time to respond. Remember to include information about whether parents can drop off kids and what time party ends.

DECORATIONS Once you decide on the theme and activities, shop for decorations and supplies. *(See resources on page 141.)*

SCHEDULE Two hours is plenty. You don't want the children overexcited or over-stimulated.

LOCATION PARTIES If you prefer not to have a party with a dozen energetic little ones at home, here are some ideas for different party locations: bowling alley; ice or roller skating rink; pizza parlor; pottery studio; children's museum; zoo or aquarium; gymnastic or sports center; movie theater; miniature golf center; playground; sports field; park; pool; or small amusement park. The best source of information is a mother with a slightly older child. She's probably been to a dozen parties and knows which ones were the hits.

Have a sing-along or a video of cartoon shorts handy in case you run out of steam at the end of the party. The children can watch while waiting for pick-up.

HELPERS Whatever you do, don't do it alone. Ask another adult or two to help you at the party. You'll at least want someone by the door to greet the guests while another adult makes sure the other guests are entertained (and safe).

A good reference is the book series: Your One-Year-Old *up to* Your Ten- to Fourteen-Year-Old *by Louise Bates Ames. A small section of the book provides a birthday party schedule and list of activities geared specifically to the abilities and interests of the age group discussed in each book. At Sylvia's fifth birthday party I was surprised to discover the game "telephone" did not work with this age group. They were too shy. At Chi Chi's seventh birthday, I was amazed at how fast and efficiently the kids followed instructions and flew through the activities. The books actually pointed these characteristics out. So now I'm more prepared to tackle oh, thirty or so more birthday parties?!*

ENTERTAINERS If you choose to hire an entertainer, keep in mind children under four can get easily frightened by a six-foot version of their favorite character or a heavily made-up clown. A guitar player or just someone to blow balloon animals is less overwhelming for the younger set. Otherwise, clowns, puppeteers, magicians, costumed characters, and naturalists with animals are all excellent options. Ask mothers with slightly older children for recommendations of entertainers they have used or seen at other parties.

FOOD Keep the food simple. Most children don't have very sophisticated tastes, so small sandwiches or pizza will do for the main course; pretzels, tortilla chips, carrot and celery sticks are fine for snacks. Serve the cake at the end.

GAMES Plan more activities than you think you can do in the party time frame. This will give you the flexibility to skip a game the kids don't like, or have more activities if they breeze through them. Some favorite games: Duck Duck Goose; Hot potato/hot dinosaur egg/hot water balloon; Catch (plastic ball for little ones); Water-balloon fights (bathing-suit party); London Bridge; Ring around the rosy; Gossip; Candy Bingo; Name that tune; Treasure/scavenger hunt; Bowling (tennis ball and plastic bottles); Pin the tail on anything; Musical chairs; Red light, green light; Charades.

FAVORS Favors should not be extravagant. Some good party favors: yo-yos, slinkies, jacks, glowsticks, stickers, kazoos, costume jewelry, crayons or colored chalk, temporary tattoos, small balls, bubbles, magnets, and small candies.

PRESENTS It is best not to open presents during the party. It's hard for those not getting presents to just sit and watch. If you do, try handing out a wrapped special favor to the guest whose present your child is opening. Remember to keep track of gifts and their givers for thank-you notes.

Resources

- *Parents.com/other/birthday_planner.jsp* has a great party planner section where you can enter your child's age and select a theme to get a list of invitation and game ideas, and even cake recipes for a theme party.
- *Birthdaypartyideas.com* Hundreds of birthday and holiday party ideas are listed here with instructions and suggestions.
- *Iparty.com* This retailer provides one easy place to purchase all the party goods you need.
- *Birthdayexpress.com* or *1-800-4-BIRTHDAY* This mail order and online catalog has complete party packages for popular themes and favorite characters.
- *Oriental.com* or *1-800-327-9678* A great source for a large selection of favors, prizes, and gifts for children's and holiday parties.

Once upon a time....

Fairy Tales

When you share a fairy tale with your child, you visit magic worlds together. Whether you read your son one of the classics or make up your own tale of wonder and adventure for your daughter, you and your child will soar on the wings of the imagination, to lands where anything is possible, and where the strangest things are ordinary. Fairy tales are stories that involve magical events and creatures in fantastical settings. They stimulate your child's creative powers, curiosity, and awareness of the extraordinary. A character is often transformed in one of these stories, from a frog to a prince, for instance, or from a scullery maid to a queen. Your child will carry the gift of fairy tales throughout his life, as he keeps his mind always open to the idea that magic is everywhere.

FAVORITE FAIRY TALE COLLECTIONS
Aesop's Fables, Grimm's Fairy Tales, Hans Christian Andersen: Fairy Tales and Stories, 1001 Arabian Nights

WEBSITES
- *www-2.cs.cmu.edu/~spok/grimmtmp/*—Grimm's fairy tales.
- *childrenstory.com*—Other fairy tales.

FAIRY TALES FROM AROUND THE WORLD
- *Jeweled Sea: A Book of Chinese Fairy Tales*, edited by Hartwell James with illustrations by John R. Neill.
- *The Magic Drum: Tales from Central Africa*, by W. F. P. Burton.
- *North American Legends*, edited by Virginia Haviland, illustrated by Ann Strugnell.
- *Yule-Tide Stories: A Collection of Scandinavian and North German Popular Tales and Traditions*, edited by Benjamin Thorpe.

FAVORITE FAIRY TALES
For centuries, children have listened in awe and puzzled over the strange happenings of countless fairy tales. You may remember the following favorites, find them in collections, or even look them up on the Internet: Rumpelstiltskin, Cinderella, Snow White, The Little Mermaid, Hansel and Gretel, Puss in Boots, The Princess and the Pea, The Frog Prince, and Jack and the Beanstalk. You can also find four favorite tales on pages 144 and 145.

USE SPECIAL EFFECTS
You can easily make great sound effects to go along with your storytelling. All you will need are a few items that everyone has around the house:
- Hit a cooking pot lid gently with a spoon for the sound of the clock striking midnight in "Cinderella."
- Take a pair of shoes with hard heels and gently knock heels and then toes together for the sound of walking. You can use this for "Little Red Riding Hood" or "Hansel and Gretel."
- Cup your hands and knock them against your chest for the sound of a horse galloping.
- Rustle a newspaper or paper bag for the sound of the wind in the trees. This is good for any story that involves a walk in the woods.

PERSONALIZE A FAIRY TALE
Fairy tales are the common property of all who have heard them, and can be altered in any way you like. There is no reason at all why you cannot tell the story of "Ella and the Beanstalk" instead of "Jack and the Beanstalk," or why Jack can't trade a bike rather than a cow for the handful of beans. Giving your child ways to connect to fairy tales can help capture her attention and stimulate her imagination. If she sees herself as a fairytale heroine, there is no telling what other great ambitions she may come up with.

GOLDILOCKS

Once upon a time, a little girl named Goldilocks got lost in a big forest. As she went deeper into the forest, she came across a quaint, little cottage and knocked. No one answered. Through a window she saw three bowls of porridge. Feeling hungry, she let herself inside.

Goldilocks tasted the porridge in the largest bowl. "This is too hot!" she cried. Next she tried the medium-sized bowl. "This is too cold!" she said. Finally, she tried the smallest bowl. "Yum! This is just right!" she said, and ate it up.

With a full tummy, Goldilocks went to sit by the fire. She sat in the biggest chair, but it was too high. Then she sat in the medium-sized chair, but it was too low. Finally she sat in the smallest chair, and it was just right! She sat and sat until—crack! The chair broke into pieces. "Oops!"

Feeling sleepy, Goldilocks went upstairs. She tried the largest bed, but it was too hard. Next she tried the medium-sized bed, but it was too soft. Finally she tried the smallest bed, and it was just right. She fell asleep.

Meanwhile, the bear family who lived in the cottage returned home. "I'm starving!" said Papa Bear. When he saw his large bowl, he grumbled, "Someone's been eating my porridge!" "Someone's been eating my porridge, too!" gasped Mama Bear. Then Baby Bear cried, "Someone's been eating my porridge, and there's none left!"

They went to sit by the fire. "Someone's been sitting in my chair," Papa Bear growled. "Someone's been sitting in my chair, too!" Mama Bear cried. "Someone's been sitting in my chair, and they broke it into pieces!" Baby Bear shouted.

The three bears went upstairs. "Someone's been sleeping in my bed!" Papa Bear roared. "Someone's been sleeping in my bed, too!" Mama Bear cried. "Someone's been sleeping in my bed and THERE SHE IS!!!" Baby Bear cried, waking Goldilocks.

"Aaahhhhh!" screamed Goldilocks, diving under the covers. When she peeked out, she realized that the bears were just a nice, normal family. She explained that she had gotten lost and apologized for all she had done. The three bears were very understanding and Baby Bear said he'd be happy to help her find her way home. •

THREE LITTLE PIGS

Once upon a time a mama pig sent her three little pigs off to start lives of their own. "Don't forget to take the money you've earned from delivering newspapers," she said. "But I spent most of my money on candy!" squealed the youngest pig. "I spent mine on new clothes!" chimed in the middle pig. "I'm afraid I have no more money to give to you," mama pig said sadly. The oldest pig was the only one who had saved all his money in a piggy bank.

The youngest pig quickly built a house of straw. The middle pig quickly built a house of twigs. And the oldest pig worked hard and built a beautiful mansion of bricks.

One day, while the youngest pig was napping, a big bad wolf banged on the door. "Little pig, little pig, let me in!" he growled. "Not by the hair on my chinny chin chin!" cried the little pig. "Then I'll huff, and I'll puff, and I'll blow your house in!" barked the wolf, and that's just what he did.

"Oh no!" squealed the little pig. He hurried over to his middle brother's house.

Minutes later, the wolf banged on that door. "Little pigs, little pigs, let me in!" he growled. "Not by the hair on our chinny chin chins!" cried the two little pigs. "Then I'll huff, and I'll puff, and I'll blow your house in!" barked the wolf, and that's just what he did.

"Oh no!" the pigs squealed, and ran over to their older brother's mansion.

Soon, the wolf came knocking. "Little pigs, little pigs, let me in!" he growled. "Not by the hair on our chinny chin chins!" cried the three little pigs. "Then I'll huff, and I'll puff, and I'll blow your house in!" barked the wolf. He huffed, and he puffed, but the sturdy brick walls wouldn't budge. The wolf leapt up to the chimney and called down, "Oh little pigs! I'm coming down!"

"Be our guest!" called the three pigs. The big, bad wolf slid down the chimney and landed smack-in-the-middle of the roaring fire the pigs had quickly made. "OUCH! OUCH! OOOUU-UCH!" he yelled as he bolted from the fire and out the door.

The oldest pig invited his brothers to live with him and they all got jobs. They all worked hard and made sure to save money for far more important things. •

LITTLE RED RIDING HOOD

Once upon a time there was a little girl called Little Red Riding Hood. One day she set off into the forest with some chicken soup to take to her sick grandmother. Suddenly, a wolf jumped into her path. "Hello there," he said in a sweet voice. "Where are you headed?"

"To my grandmother's house," said Little Red Riding Hood.

"Where does she live?" asked the wolf. "Maybe I can give you a shortcut."

Not wanting to be late, Little Red Riding Hood gave the wolf her grandmother's address, and he pointed out a shortcut. (The wolf had tricked her. It was really the long way.) Then, the wolf raced over to her grandmother's house and found her in bed. Just as he was about to eat her, Little Red Riding Hood arrived. (She had walked very fast!) "Hi, Granny!" she said as she headed up the stairs. Thinking fast, the wolf locked the grandmother in a closet, put on her glasses and nightcap, and crawled into bed.

"Granny?" Little Red Riding Hood said, entering the room. "I've brought you chicken soup."

"Come closer so I can see you, dear," the wicked wolf called kindly. Little Red Riding Hood moved forward. "Granny, what big eyes you have," she remarked.

"The better to see you with, my dear. Come closer," replied the sneaky wolf. Little Red Riding Hood came closer, and said, "Granny, what big ears you have."

"The better to hear you with, my dear," said the wolf.

"And what a big nose you have, Granny," Little Red Riding Hood observed.

"The better to smell you with. Come a little bit closer, dear," the wolf beckoned, and Little Red Riding Hood did. "Granny, what a BIG mouth you have!" she exclaimed.

"The better to eat you with!" growled the wolf. But just as he was about to eat Little Red Riding Hood, her grandmother burst out of the closet. (She had picked the lock.) She and Little Red Riding Hood chased the wicked wolf out of the house and into the woods.

"I feel better already," said the grandmother before she even tasted the soup.

"Good!" said Little Red Riding Hood. And she never talked to a stranger again. •

THE BOY WHO CRIED WOLF

Once upon a time, a shepherd boy lived in a tiny village, high in the tallest mountains. Every morning, he led the villagers' sheep up a steep, grassy hill to graze.

From the shady spot where he sat, he'd often look down at the ant-size villagers and wondered what it would be like to bake bread or cobble shoes for a living, surrounded by other people instead of sheep. "It wouldn't be as boring as watching sheep," he muttered. "All sheep do is eat and sleep and say Baa all day. I'm sooooo bored!"

Suddenly, he had idea.

"Wolf! Wolf!" he cried loudly. "A wolf is chasing the sheep!"

The villagers immediately hurried up the hill.

"I don't see a wolf," said the butcher, huffing and puffing from the steep climb.

"Our sheep are fine. What is going on here?" said the doctor.

"Oh! I just wanted some company!" said the shepherd boy.

"Don't cry 'wolf' when there's no wolf, or you'll be sorry," the villagers scolded the shepherd boy. But the boy was laughing so hard that tears ran down his cheeks.

The next day, the boy looked down at the ant-size villagers again. And again he said, "All sheep do is eat and sleep and say Baa all day. I'm sooooo bored!" So again the boy yelled, "Wolf! Wolf! A wolf is chasing the sheep!"

Again, the villagers climbed the steep hill.

"I don't see a wolf," said the butcher.

"He did it again!" yelled the doctor.

"DON'T CRY 'WOLF' WHEN THERE IS NO WOLF, OR YOU'LL BE SORRY," they warned. But the shepherd boy just laughed, entirely thrilled.

The next day it happened. From the top of the hill the boy saw a REAL wolf—furry, fierce, and drooling—sneaking from tree to tree, closer and closer.

"Wolf! Wolf!" the shepherd boy shouted in a panic. But the butcher said, "He's doing it again!" And the doctor said, "I'm not running up that hill again." This time the villagers didn't come. And, with no one to help him, the shepherd boy lost all his sheep to the wolf. •

chapter four
Stepping Out

Top 10 Largest U.S. Cities by Population[*]

1. New York, NY 8,084,316
2. Los Angeles, CA 3,798,981
3. Chicago, IL 2,886,251
4. Houston, TX 2,009,834
5. Philadelphia, PA 1,492,231
6. Phoenix, AZ 1,371,960
7. San Diego, CA 1,259,532
8. Dallas, TX 1,211,467
9. San Antonio, TX 1,194,222
10. Detroit, MI 925,051

[*]according to the 2002 population estimate from the U.S. Census Bureau

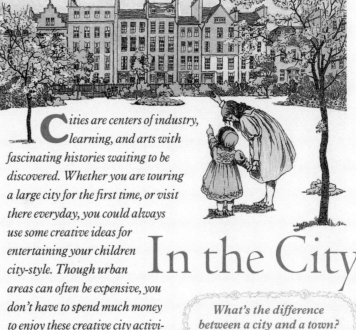

Cities are centers of industry, learning, and arts with fascinating histories waiting to be discovered. Whether you are touring a large city for the first time, or visit there everyday, you could always use some creative ideas for entertaining your children city-style. Though urban areas can often be expensive, you don't have to spend much money to enjoy these creative city activities with your family.

In the City

DITCH THE CAR Public transportation may seem like just another convenience of city life, but to your child it is uncharted territory. Take an outing and travel by train, bus, or subway. Let your child buy the fares (if he's old enough) and pay his own way through the turnstiles. Your child will get a great understanding of how busy people move around in a big city.

SEE THE SKYSCRAPERS The tallest building in any large city usually has some sort of observation deck. Take your child to the top and let them get a good look at the city below. Bring binoculars so they can see the detail of different neighborhoods from such a height. A view of the city can be even more magical at night—be dazzled by all the twinkling city lights.

Oldest U.S. City
The oldest U.S. city is St. Augustine, Florida. Established in 1565 by Spanish settlers, St. Augustine is the oldest continuously occupied city of European origin in the United States.

EASY LUNCH Most large cities have a variety of lunch carts and food vendors near tourist or shopping areas. Pick an area with a few different choices and let your child decide on lunch for the day. This might be a great time to try a new food or enjoy a favorite treat. Find a bench under a shady tree; watch the hustle and bustle, and enjoy an easy lunch with your child.

ENJOY THE SHOW Most big cities have street performers in crowded areas. If you see one, stop for a minute and let your kids check out the show. Of course, be sure to watch your belongings in a busy area, but let your kids enjoy the music and magic. If they like the entertainment, give your child a little money to toss in the hat, and have them thank the performers.

What's the difference between a city and a town? Simply put, incorporated cities in the U.S. have their own form of government, delegated by the state and approved by the voters of the city. The city can provide local government and services to the residents. A town, village, or other unincorporated community does not have these governmental powers. Some towns do have limited governmental powers, but they vary from state to state.

TOURISM BUREAUS Most cities have websites that provide travel deals, ideas, and schedules of events:
New York: *nycvisit.com*
Los Angeles: *ci.la.ca.us*
Chicago: *ci.chi.il.us*
Houston: *houston-spacecityusa.com*
Philadelphia: *pcvb.org*
Phoenix: *phoenixcvb.com*
San Diego: *sandiego.org*
Dallas: *dallascityhall.com*
San Antonio: *sanantoniocvb.com*
Detroit: *visitdetroit.com*

It is never too early to interest your child in the natural world. Hold baby up in the sunshine or let your toddler crawl around in the grass and you will see their faces light up with joy. As children grow they will ask many questions about the natural world. You can share a variety of sights and sounds with them, from the roar of a mighty waterfall to the quiet pleasures of a woodland walk. Sharing your love of nature with your children will feed their natural curiosity and give them a lifelong source of peace and contemplation. There are many activities you can do to develop your child's interest in the natural world.

In the Woods

PRESS LEAVES AND FLOWERS Keep a roll of wax or parchment paper handy, and take it on nature exploration trips. Press leaves and flowers between two sheets of wax or parchment paper. Place them between the pages of a clothbound blank book. (If you use a regular reading book, you might stain the pages.) Write the date of your trip and location where you found the leaves and flowers on each page, along with what species you think it is.

LOOK AND LISTEN FOR FROGS Locate a body of fresh water, like a pond or marsh. Visit early in the morning or at sunset, when frogs are most talkative and stationary. You can hear frogs calling out to one another. They create their croaking sounds using large pouches under their chins that vibrate and amplify the sound of their calls. The louder a male frog can croak, the more likely he can attract a mate.

Encourage your child to start her own nature journal from an early age. Keep track of animals seen and observations about changes in the environment. (For example, a tree turns red in the fall and, violets come up in the shade in the spring.)

GO FOR A NATURE WALK Most state parks provide free nature walks led by knowledgeable park rangers. Rangers provide a wealth of fun facts about your local ecosystems and can answer many of the questions that your little naturalist will ask.

AMATEUR GEOLOGY Not everything in nature is lively. You can help your child foster a lifelong interest in geology by starting a rock collection. Rocks are found in every backyard and park and tell us about our environment and the earth itself. You will find dif-

ferent kinds of rocks depending on where you live. Buy a rock guidebook and a fishing tackle box to hold small rocks. The U.S. Geological Service has a helpful website at *pubs.usgs.gov/gip/collect1/collectgip.html*.

BIRD WATCHING Bird watching is a wonderful way to learn about nature and develop powers of concentration. Start with your local birds. Buy a guide to birds in your area and identify the birds you see in your backyard. You can bring the birds to you by setting up a bird feeder. Hang a feeder from a tree near a window in your house and fill it with birdseed. Keep a pad of paper near the window and help your child record the types of birds that come to your feeder. As you become accustomed to the birds in your yard, begin exploring other areas. If you live near the seashore, you may notice different birds on the beach compared to those inland. Take a bird guide (a general one, or one specific to the area) with you on your family vacation.

For the advanced amateur birdwatcher, an organized annual bird count can be a great learning experience. Contact your local or state wildlife department and ask about bird counts in your area. You will be given a particular area to count and identify all the birds you see during a set time period. At the end of the day, you gather with other birders to share your information.

Keep a number of guidebooks on hand, especially ones for your specific area. Books on birds, plants, insects, and local mammals are useful.

Camping

Nervous about taking your children camping? Why not have a trial campout in the backyard? Set up the tent and spend the night outdoors, complete with snacks, sleeping bags, and a flashlight. This will give the reluctant camper the chance to see how fun a campout is without being too far from home or mom.

Be a Junior Ranger

A great program offered by the National Park Service is the Junior Ranger program. Your child can take part in activities that will help him learn about the park, its history and significance, and ways to preserve it for future generations. Visit the National Park Service website for participating parks, or call the Visitors' Center at the park you will be visiting to find out more information on how to participate.

National Parks

One of the greatest treasures America has to offer is our collection of National Parks. They are found in every state in the nation, and provide an inexpensive and invaluable place to teach your children about the world around them. Visit one locally for a day trip, or plan the next family vacation around a tour of several parks. Each park is loaded with activities from hiking, fishing, and canoeing, to cave tours, and volcano explorations. Our National Parks will inspire your children to explore the natural world on their own.

Whether planning a day trip or a week's vacation to a national park, your first stop should be the National Park Service website at *nps.gov*. You can search by state, activities, park type, cultural heritage, and topics of historical or scientific interest. Should you already have a park in mind, use the website to learn additional information about your destination or locate a few nearby parks.

For information that travels well, pick up a copy of *National Geographic's Guide to the National Parks*. This extensive paperback contains information on all of the national parks, and breaks down each site into manageable trips focusing on the highlights of the particular park. The book offers suggestions for activities and accommodations at each park, and provides information on the park fees, facilities for the disabled, and special advisories.

Best National Parks for Families

- *Grand Teton National Park*—Moose, Wyoming. Take a rafting trip down the Snake River and get an up-close view of moose, blue herons, and pelicans.
- *Lassen Volcanic National Park*—Mineral, California. Kids can check out the Volcano Discovery Lab, where rangers simulate different types of volcanic eruptions using shaving cream or popcorn.
- *Voyageurs National Park*—International Falls, Minnesota. Home to more than 1,000 glacial islands, all accessible by boat.
- *Rocky Mountain National Park*—Estes Park, Colorado. Try Rocky After Dark—ranger-led flashlight tours where kids identify trees by touch and learn about animals that see well at night.
- *Big Bend National Park*—Near Marathon, Texas. This park boasts more types of birds, bats, and cacti than any other national park.
- *Mount Rainier National Park*—Ashford, Washington. Take a walk on the gentle Nisqually Vista Trail for a great view of a glacier.
- *Great Basin National Park*—Baker, Nevada. Take a tour of the Lehman Caves, a five-million-year-old single limestone cavern!
- *Mesa Verde National Park*—Mesa Verde, Colorado. Home to ancient Pueblo cliff dwellings.
- *Denali National Park and Preserve*—Denali Park, Alaska. Check out the dogsled demonstrations in the summer.
- *Yosemite National Park*—Yosemite, California. Don't miss Yosemite Falls, the tallest waterfall in the U.S.

Museums are wonderful resources to share with your children as they grow. Natural history, art, science, and children's museums will fascinate your kids and spark their natural curiosity. Even very young children will benefit from a museum visit: most have specific programs geared for kids that introduce subjects in a fun and creative way. Here we've gathered great museum options for you and your children, and offer a few tips to make this the first of many enjoyable returns.

Museums

Natural History Museums

Though they house amazing and varied exhibits, natural history museums are some of the best places to check out dinosaurs—and what kid doesn't love those? Bring your children to one of these museums and let them try to find their favorite dinosaur, learn about where and when it lived, and impress you with all their new dino-knowledge.

- *American Museum of Natural History, New York, NY*
  The museum just completed a $48 million renovation to their dinosaur exhibit and they have the world's only intact velociraptor skull.
- *National Museum of Natural History, Washington, D.C.*
  One of the leaders in dinosaur research, this museum is situated on the Mall near other national landmarks and Smithsonian museums.
- *The Field Museum of Natural History, Chicago, IL*
  Home to Sue, the most famous Tyrannosaurus Rex skeleton in the world.
- *Natural History Museum of L. A. County, Los Angeles, CA*
  Visit the amazing recreation of a Tyrannosaurus Rex doing battle with a Triceratops, built with cast and real bones.

Art Museums

While strolling through an art museum may seem like an adult activity, most major art museums offer programs and exhibits for children filled with activities to spark their interest and creativity. Local museums and galleries are great for a first day trip too; they will be smaller and less crowded, allowing your child to get a better look at the art.

Tips for Visiting an Art Museum with Children:

- *Decide on specific exhibits* Choose one or two exhibits and focus your time there. Talk to your child about what they will see so they have time to think of questions to ask.
- *Limit your time* Children tire easily, so make your first trip to an art museum with your child focused. Don't forget to bring a few snacks and sit down to a take a break if your kids get tired.
- *Let them be inspired!* Have your child bring a small sketchpad and pencil (check first to see if your museum allows it) and let them draw what they see. If they love an abstract painting, lay out some fingerpaints and paper when you get home, and let them go to town. By making their visit to the museum a positive experience, your children will be excited to return.

Art Through Books

The innovative children's books series, *You Can't Take A Balloon...* by Jacqueline Preiss Weitzman and Robin Preiss Glasser, can serve as an introduction for your child to the world of museums. The three books follow a young girl as she explores the Metropolitan Museum of Art, the National Gallery, and the Museum of Fine Arts, while her wayward balloon causes havoc in the world outside. Illustrated reproductions of famous artworks and the hilarious antics of the balloon are sure to keep your child interested.

Science Museums

Few places do a better job of making learning fun than science museums. Most museums throughout the country offer specific camps and workshops geared for young children. Many organize sleepovers for groups of kids, so stop at the information booth and see what your local museum offers.

- *Museum of Science and Industry, Chicago, IL* Visit the Great Train Story, 1,400 feet of track that models the trip from Seattle to Chicago and the logistical transfer of goods.
- *Exploratorium: Museum of Science, Art, and Human Perception, San Francisco, CA* Kids age seven and older can check out the Tactile Dome, an exhibit that forces you to use your hands as eyes to identify your surroundings as you explore in the dark.
- *Carnegie Science Center, Pittsburgh, PA* Here, kids will encounter the UPMC Sports-Works Building, which is loaded with sports-related activities emphasizing the connections between science, health, and fitness.

Children's Museums

Great children's museums take the ordinary world and make it extraordinary. From learning how electricity is generated, to discovering how a television and recording studio work, these museums empower kids to explore new horizons.

- *Children's Discovery Museum of San Jose, San Jose, CA* Take a tour with Power Girl and learn how electricity is generated, distributed, consumed, and converted into other forms of energy.
- *Please Touch Museum, Philadelphia, PA* Here children can play the role of *Alice in Wonderland* using puzzles, riddles, and oversized props to recreate her adventures.
- *Children's Museum of Boston, Boston, MA* In the Construction Zone exhibit, kids get to try out a life-sized Bobcat construction vehicle and build miniature skyscrapers.
- *The Magic House, St. Louis, MO* Be a star on KIDS TV where children can be news anchors.
- *Minnesota Children's Museum, St. Paul, MN* Your child can don a costume and pretend to be a busy beaver in the Earth World gallery.

Off the Beaten Path

There is a museum for almost any child's interest or favorite hobby...

- *World's Largest Toy Museum, Branson, MO* This museum has thousands of toys on display from the 1800s up through today. *worldslargesttoymuseum.com*
- *San Diego Model Railroad Museum, San Diego, CA* Located in Balboa Park, this museum houses the largest indoor model railway display in the world. *sdmodelrailroadm.com*
- *Ripley's Believe it or Not Museum, Orlando, FL* Devoted to the "World's Strangest Oddities!" collected by Robert Ripley, this "odditorium" is full of wacky spectacles sure to entertain the whole family. *ripleysorlando.com*
- *Matchbox Road Museum, Newfield, NJ* With over 29,000 Matchbox vehicles on display, this museum offers little collectors an overwhelming selection of cars, trucks, and planes to enjoy. *mbxroad.com*

Looking for a great place to teach your children about wildlife? Zoos and aquariums are wonderful venues for learning about animals, sea life, and the habitats where they live. Many zoos and aquariums are involved in research and conservation efforts. Not only are they giving top-notch care to the animals in their parks, they are also ensuring the survival of these animals in the wild. Check out these top zoos and aquariums from across the country.

Zoos & Aquariums

Aquarium Art

Your child can create her own aquarium to remember her day exploring underwater life.

crayons, white or natural-colored construction paper, watercolor paints

1. Have your child draw the sea floor at the bottom of the page. Color the sand, shells, and draw long green seaweed reaching for the surface. Be sure to color all the items heavily with the crayons.
2. Add some tropical fish to the mix. Let your child draw some of the fish that she saw at the aquarium. Color heavily on the whole paper with bright colored crayons.
3. When the sea floor and fish are complete, you are ready to add the ocean. Using shades of blue and green, paint over the entire piece of paper. The blue and green paint will fill in all the blank space, while everything drawn with crayons with resist the paint and pop out from the background.
4. Let the art dry, and hang it in a prominent place.

Top Zoos

- *Audubon Zoo*—New Orleans, LA
- *Baltimore Zoo*—Baltimore, MD
- *Bronx Zoo*—Bronx, NY
- *Cleveland MetroPark Zoo*—Cleveland, OH
- *Columbus Zoo*—Columbus, OH
- *Denver Zoo*—Denver, CO
- *Fort Wayne Children's Zoo*—Fort Wayne, IN
- *National Zoo*—Washington, D.C.
- *San Diego Zoo*—San Diego, CA
- *Toledo Zoo*—Toledo, OH

Zoo Books for Little Ones

Goodnight Gorilla by Peggy Rathmann ■ *If I Ran the Zoo* by Dr. Seuss ■ *Curious George Feeds the Animals* by H. A. Rey and Margaret Rey ■ *Zoo Do's and Don'ts* by Todd Parr ■ *Polar Bear, Polar Bear, What do you Hear?* by Eric Carle

Other Places of Interest

- *Wildlife Waystation, Angeles National Forest, CA* This refuge was founded to rescue and rehabilitate wild, native wildlife and exotic animals from around the world. One of the Waystation's main focuses is to educate the public about the global plight of wildlife, especially near cities.
- *Audubon Aquarium of the Americas, New Orleans, LA* This amazing aquarium lets you explore four distinct aquatic environments: the underwater world of the Caribbean Sea, the Mississippi River, the Amazon Rainforest , and the Gulf of Mexico—all without leaving New Orleans. The Aquarium features 10,000 animals representing 530 species. It also houses a Touch Pool where visitors can pet a baby shark.

Top Aquariums

- *John G. Shedd Aquarium*—Chicago, IL
- *Monterey Bay Aquarium*—Monterey, CA
- *National Aquarium*—Baltimore, MD
- *New England Aquarium*—Boston, MA
- *Sea World*—Orlando, FL; San Diego, CA; San Antonio, TX

The Zoo

When William Henry went to the Zoo
    He kept very close to Nurse.
He didn't know what the lions might do,
    And tigers, he thought, were worse:
The bars of the cages looked so thin
    And animals walked about.
Although he had asked to be taken in
    He longed to be taken out.

And safe at home he sorted with care
    The toys in his nursery box,
The wooly lamb from the grizzly bear,
    The yellow cat from the fox.
"I'm sorry," he said to the yellow cat,
    That you have been frightened so;
I did not think they were fierce as that,
    But now, little cat, I know."
          —Florence Hoare

Events & Shows

When the kids are looking for something new and exciting to do, look for events and shows in your area. No matter what your child's interest is, you can find a show that celebrates it.

Air Shows
- U.S. Air Force Thunderbirds ▪ U.S. Navy Blue Angels ▪ Canadian Airforce Snowbirds ▪ The Biggest Little Air Show in the World

CAR SHOWS There are all kinds of automobile shows around the country, usually grouped by type of car: Antique, European, Muscle Cars, etc. Local enthusiasts abound, so if your child can't get enough of his toy cars and trucks, take him to see the real thing! A great resource is *car-shows.com* where you can find special interest car shows in your area.

CAT SHOWS The Cat Fanciers' Association sponsors the largest international pedigreed cat show in the western hemisphere. Held every year in a different location, this three-day event draws competitors from around the world. Check out *cfainc.org* for show details and a listing of regional cat shows closer to home where you can bring the kids.

DOG SHOWS Have you ever watched TV and found dogs weaving through poles and diving for distance off docks? These amazing dogs train diligently for agility events, and you can see them live! The American Kennel Club website provides a listing of dog shows and agility events in your area—go to *akc.org* for more information.

WILD WEST SHOWS *The Great American Wild West Show* in Denver, Colorado, is patterned after the

Offbeat Festivals
Check your community paper for details of festivals in your state or try festivals.com. *Here are some favorites:*

- *Laura Ingalls Wilder Festival*, Mansfield, MO ▪
- *National Storytelling Festival*, Jonesborough, TN ▪ **Chicago International Children's Film Festival**, Chicago, IL ▪ *Chuck Wagon Gathering and Children's Cowboy Festival*, Oklahoma City, OK ▪ *Tom Sawyer Days and National Fence Painting Contest*, Hannibal, MO ▪ *National Baby Food Festival*, Fremont, MI ▪ *Mighty Mud Mania, the Original Mud Obstacle Course*, Scottsdale, AZ ▪ *Rattlesnake Festival*, San Antonio, FL

Westminster Kennel Club Dog Show

- Oldest continuous sporting event in America besides the Kentucky Derby
- Held annually at Madison Square Garden, New York, in February
- Terriers have won the most Best in Show awards—42!

- The Herding group has only ever won one Best in Show award.

wild west shows of old, including a six horse stagecoach holdup, world champion trick roping, dance hall girls and tributes to the Native Americans. National Western, the venue, also sponsors rodeos, livestock events and a miniature horse show.

HORSE SHOWS For the little one who loves everything horses, visit a horse show or jumping competition. The USA Equestrian website has a list of shows, competitions, and contacts for every state in the nation. For information go to *equestrian.org*.

Why Three Rings?
In the late 1800s, P. T. Barnum's circus was so popular that he decided to add additional rings with sideshows to accommodate more people under the big top. The circus became as large as seven rings at one time, but was scaled back to the traditional three-ring version we see today.

Circus Day at Home
✳ Round up all of her stuffed animals and let her be the master of ceremonies in her own big-top show. ✳ Dig out the face paints you saved from last Halloween and turn your child into a clown. Complete the transformation with a silly, mismatched outfit from your closet and watch him get into the act. ✳ Let her amaze you with the fantastic tricks she's trained her favorite stuffed bear to do. ✳ Stretch a length of rope across the floor and practice your "high wire" act together. ✳ Try juggling with marshmallows. ✳ Turn a hula hoop into an amazing act as his stuffed animals go flying through! ✳

Circus Time!

What child doesn't love the magic and wonder of the circus? Death-defying aerials, astonishing animal stunts, and comical clowns all under the big top. Extend the excitement and amazement of the circus with fun activities and treats at home the next day.

Great American Circuses

RINGLING BROTHERS AND BARNUM AND BAILEY'S CIRCUS Billed as the Greatest Show on Earth, this iconic circus has been travelling the nation for 133 years, visiting more than 90 cities each season. In addition to the show, families can come an hour early to talk with the performers, meet the clowns and even learn how to juggle!

BIG APPLE CIRCUS This one ring, non-profit East Coast circus creates an amazing show while donating part of their proceeds to worthy causes. Their charities bring underprivileged kids to the circus, support clowns in hospitals entertaining critically ill children, and help broaden the circus experience to include the blind and the deaf.

CIRQUE DU SOLEIL For a more sophisticated theatrical experience, try Cirque de Soleil. Though no animals are used, each show embraces a theme and articulates it through acrobatics, clowns, aerials and dance. Three shows are currently in residence in Las Vegas, and five are touring the U.S. and abroad; the shows are generally recommended for children over 5.

CARSON AND BARNES CIRCUS With the world's largest big top and travelling zoo, this five-ring show travels coast to coast to exhibit more than 40 acts from around the world.

Circus Camps
Check out Circus Smircus of Greensboro, Vermont. With beginner, intermediate, and family camps, Circus Smircus promises that anyone can improve her circus skills, boost her self-esteem, and have loads of fun!

Big Top Sipper

Serve this colorful drink with other circus-inspired snacks, like popcorn and shell-on peanuts; be sure to share with the (stuffed) animals!

8 ounces orange juice
8 ounces cranberry juice
16 ounces white grape juice or seltzer

1. Freeze orange and cranberry juices in ice cube trays.
2. When frozen, divide ice cubes into six tall glasses.
3. Add grape juice or seltzer. Stir and serve with colorful straws.

Serves 6.

Parents are probably more excited than the kids before that first circus experience: they are envisioning enraptured and joyous faces. Take steps though to prepare young children. If a child is under five, the crowd, the strange environment, and the darkening of lights and loud noises before the show can be terrifying. Tell your child what to expect beforehand and perhaps let him sit on an adult's lap in the beginning.

My eldest daughter spent the first 15 minutes of her first circus with her face on my chest. When the horses showed up she peeked; when the trapeze artist started swinging, she was sitting straight up, eyes huge and completely entranced.

Caramel Apples

These gooey delights are a crowd pleaser—just get the facecloths ready!

14 ounces individually wrapped caramels, unwrapped
2 tablespoons milk
6 Granny Smith apples
Popsicle sticks

1. Place the caramels and milk in a bowl and microwave for about 2 minutes, stirring once.
2. Stick one Popsicle stick into the end of each apple.
3. Dip the apples into the caramel mixture and place on a greased cookie sheet.
4. Refrigerate for 15 minutes or until caramel sets.

Serves 6.

Easy Outings

*L*ooking for some *interesting and easy outings for the family? There are many places to take your child exploring, and most are close to home. Children will be fascinated to learn how everyday tasks are accomplished. How does the mail get from here to there? How is a restaurant run? How does a sports arena operate? Kids would love to get a behind-the-scenes glimpse of their favorite baseball park or an insider's view of what happens at a fire station. These suggestions will get you thinking about other locales that you and your child would both enjoy discovering.*

GO TO A MINOR LEAGUE BASEBALL GAME
Lots of small towns and cities have minor league baseball teams that are looking for fans. Tickets are generally inexpensive, and games often include family-friendly activities like base-running contests at the seventh inning stretch, wacky mascots, and team memorabilia give aways. Visit *minorleaguebaseball.com* for the team nearest to you.

TOUR A PROFESSIONAL SPORTS ARENA
If you live in or near a large city, take a tour of the major league ballpark, professional football stadium, or basketball arena. Nearly all professional sports teams offer guided tours of their home turf, and your child will get the inside scoop on his favorite team. Check your local team's website for more details.

CHECK OUT THE LIBRARY Local libraries sponsor lots of free activities for children, like weekly story hours or small art projects. Check with your local library, and get your kids hooked on reading at an early age.

EXPLORE YOUR LOCAL PARK If you have a Parks and Recreation department in your town, call to get a

schedule of activities for the year. You may be able to sign your child up for free or low-cost tennis lessons, or meet some new kids and learn how to swing a golf club.

VISIT LOCAL HEROES What kid isn't fascinated by that bright and shining fire truck? Call your local fire department and ask if they will give your child a tour of the firehouse and engine.

VISIT THE POST OFFICE The mail arrives on time every day. Ever wonder how that happens? Drop in on your local post office and ask if they will give you a behind-the-scenes tour showing how the mail gets from here to there.

GO TO LOCAL EATERIES Do you know a friend who works at a restaurant? Why not ask for a kitchen tour? Your child can see all the hard work that goes into each order and learn a little bit about cooking restaurant style. Also, some chain restaurants like Papa Gino's will let kids get behind the counter and make their own pizza from scratch. Call ahead for best times and details.

TAKE OFF TO THE AIRPORT Despite tightened security, smaller airports provide a great vantage point for watching planes take off and land—a thrill for any small child. Spend some time watching all the activity, and then make some paper airplanes at home for fun.

GO TO A FARM OR ORCHARD If you live near farmland, a tour of a neighbor's farm or orchard can be a great activity. Kids can see how the animals are cared for and fed, or pick some apples for a pie to make at home. You can talk to your kids about what is grown on the farm and how it eventually ends up at the grocery store.

Have A Picnic

When the weather is beautiful, pack some tasty nibbles and a few distractions to enjoy a leisurely day in the sunshine. Here we've gathered a few kid-friendly foods (and a recipe for a fun treat) that are great for picnics, although with a good cooler and lots of ice you can make almost any meal travel well.

Peanut Butter and Jelly ■ Peanut Butter and Banana ■ Ants on a Log—*Celery sticks spread with peanut butter and dotted with raisins* ■ Apples ■ Crackers ■ Pretzels ■ Trail Mix ■ Rice Krispie Treats ■ Granola Bars ■ Brownies and Cookies

Also great for a picnic, but be sure to keep cool: Fried Chicken ■ Potato Salad ■ Pasta Salad ■ Watermelon ■ Nectarines ■ Grapes ■ Berries

Picnics are not just about food! Bring along these fun, easy-to-pack items: Frisbee ■ Kite ■ Deck of Cards ■ Jump Rope ■ Wiffle Ball and Bat ■ Baseball and Glove ■ Soccer Ball ■ Bubbles

Berry-licious Cream Cones

This handy treat is an easy and fun way to get kids to eat their fruit. Throw the ingredients into your basket and assemble at the picnic.

    6 plain ice cream cones
    1 can of whipped cream
    $1/_2$ pint blueberries, washed
    $1/_2$ pint raspberries, washed
    $1/_2$ pint blackberries, washed

1. Squirt a little whipped cream into the bottom of the cones.
2. Fill cones with alternate layers of whipped cream and berries.
3. Top it off with a little squirt of whipped cream and enjoy!

For a healthier alternative to whipped cream, try mixing all the berries with a small container of flavored low-fat yogurt and filling the cones with the mixture.

My family loves picnics. We live a block from Prospect Park in Brooklyn, and picnics there are an easy Sunday afternoon for us. We vacation in the summer at our old family cottage on Lake Huron, Canada, and picnic practically every day at favorite swimming spots. A favorite is definitely hot dogs. You can cook turkey dogs at home and pack them into Thermos bottles with the hot cooking liquid. Bring buns and pack ketchup, mustard, and relish in baby food jars. You can have hot and fresh hot dogs with the works anywhere! (Our Canadian friends call it Alice's New York treat.)

At the Beach

If you live near the coast, you know that nothing can top a glorious, sunny day at the beach. There is built-in entertainment for the kids everywhere you look. Bring along a bucket and shovel and give your budding architect some help with her newest sand creation, or grab your boogie board and head for the waves. Need some fun activities or new vistas to explore? Here you'll find some excellent beaches to visit with your family—some local and some exotic—as well as some easy ideas to keep the kids busy while you are there.

Best Beaches

- CAPE COD NATIONAL SEASHORE, MA In addition to abundant hiking and biking trails in the area, these beaches on Cape Cod are known as some of the cleanest beaches in America.
- CORONADO, CA This quiet "island" community is actually situated at the end of a peninsula that connects it with mainland San Diego. The main beach stretches 1.5 miles along Ocean Boulevard, framed by luxurious homes, and provides ample opportunity for swimming, surfing, and exploring the tidal pools.

- HILTON HEAD, SC With a variety of beach locales, plentiful golf and tennis, and even a Disney resort, Hilton Head Island has all the activities and amenities for a fabulous family beach vacation.
- KA'ANAPALI, HI Stretching three miles from Hanaka'o'o (Canoe Beach) to Honokowai Beach Park, Ka'anapali Beach is surrounded by lush resorts, fine dining, and some of the best shopping on Maui. The beach is accessible to the public, and activities from snorkeling trips to windsurfing expeditions can

all be arranged by the nearby hotels and resorts.
- SIESTA KEY, FL Renowned for its beautiful white quartz sand beaches, Siesta Key has been cited as one of America's best beaches. Accommodations are family friendly, and facilities include volleyball, tennis, and a playground at the Siesta Key public beach, as well as picnic areas and fitness trails.

Catch the Waves

For a far out family vacation, why not try a surf camp? San Diego Surfing Academy offers overnight surf camps for all ages. Here beginners can learn about ocean safety, the basics of board paddling and riding, and are guaranteed to catch a wave into shore by the end of the camp. Go to *surfsdsa.com* for more information. Or be a spectator at these amazing surf competitions:

- *East Coast Surfing Championships* Every year in August at Virginia Beach, VA.
- *Vans Triple Crown of Surfing* Every year in November and December in Oahu, HI.

Building Sandcastles

Sandcastles are all about creativity. Use hard-packed sand in different sized plastic pails to form the base of your castle. Decorate with shells, rocks, sticks—whatever interesting things you can find on the beach. For older children, impress them with these sand structure techniques:

DRIBBLY SAND

1. Select a spot not so close to the shoreline that the waves will reach you, but not too far away, either. Dig a hole until the sand has a very watery consistency.
2. Build a small mound of sand that you can dribble onto.
3. Scoop up a bit of wet sand from the hole. Shape your hand into a fist, hold it a few inches above the mound, and allow sand to "leak" from the bottom of your fist. The wet sand should stick and form dribbly shapes along the sides of the mound.

TOWER BUILDING

1. Squeeze handfuls of wet sand into a pancake shapes by patting your hands around and using slight pressure. Don't press too hard or the water will be squished out the sides.
2. Stack the cakes on top of one another. As you near the top, begin to use smaller cakes so that the tower will taper off. This will allow for more stability as you and your child carve a fanciful tower with your own decorations.

Feeling like a pro? Enter the Sandcastle Contest at Cannon Beach, Oregon, held yearly in June. There are divisions for all ages and skill levels, so the whole family can participate. Spend the afternoon admiring the sculptures before the next tide sweeps them away!

Beachcombing

The ocean's waters turn countless treasures out onto the beach. Spend some time by the water's edge checking out the smooth rocks and shells. Gather some favorites to bring home for future arts and crafts projects—a shell necklace or a jewelry box mosaic made from tiny rocks. Beach glass makes another great take-home memento. Start a collection of rare colors like blue, pink, and aqua, and add to it with each successive trip.

DON'T FORGET THE TIDAL POOLS! Each little rocky puddle is a giant ecosystem that kids will enjoy exploring. Check out the tiny crabs, shrimp, worms, and snails living under the rocks. Try organizing a scavenger hunt to see how many different types of sea creatures they can find. But tread lightly! Most marine creatures cannot survive outside their habitat, so be sure to leave them where you found them.

Don't Forget: Beach Umbrella ▪ Sunblock—*The sun can burn sensitive skin in minutes. Layer on SPF 15 or higher throughout the day to prevent a nasty sunburn* ▪ Cooler of Cold Drinks—*Stay hydrated in the hot sun* ▪ Wide-brim Hat ▪ Sunglasses ▪ Snacks ▪ Plastic Bags—*Use them to collect trash or keep wet bathing suits off dry clothes* ▪ Towels ▪ Sand Chairs ▪ Plastic Pail and Shovel ▪ Beach Reading—*For that spare moment when the kids are happily occupied*

Fun Extras: Squirt Guns—*Just watch out for your neighbors on the next towel over!* ▪ Paddleball—*Great way to play a little "tennis" at low tide* ▪ Boogie Boards, Body Boards—*Check with the lifeguard to see if they are allowed at your beach* ▪ Mask and Snorkel—*See undersea life up close in the shallow tidal pools* ▪ Wiffle Ball and Bat—*If you have space to spare, organize a pick up game with friends.*

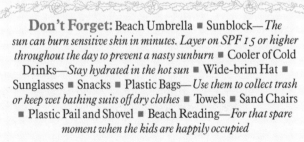

Amusement Parks

Remember the thrill you felt racing down the steep track of a roller coaster for the first time? Share the excitement with your children by taking them to an amusement park. When deciding which park to visit, consider your child's age. Make sure there are plenty of age-appropriate rides available, and choose a time to visit when the park won't be as packed with people, since little ones are easily overwhelmed.

Great Theme Parks

BONFANTE GARDENS, Gilroy, CA. This family-oriented theme park is home to more than forty rides, beautiful gardens, and the world-famous Circus Trees. Created by Axel Erlandson and rescued by Michael Bonfante, these trees have been intricately grafted and woven into amazing shapes and are displayed in the park.

LEGOLAND, Carlsbad, CA. An entire theme park dedicated to Legos! Walk through Miniland USA where America's achievements are celebrated in Lego form—the cityscapes of New York, the New Orleans French quarter, and the California coastline are all on display in Legos at $1/20^{th}$ of their actual size.

SESAME PLACE, Langhome, PA. Perfect for the younger set, Sesame Place is the only Sesame Street-themed amusement park in the world. In addition to character-themed rides, there is also an educational component found in Sesame Studio Science and a live show with Elmo and his friends.

Favorite Amusement Parks

- *Astroland, Coney Island*—Brooklyn, New York
- *Busch Gardens*—Tampa, Florida and Williamsburg, Virginia
- *Cedar Point*—Sandusky, Ohio
- *Hershey Park*—Hershey, Pennsylvania
- *Kennywood*—West Mifflin, Pennsylvania
- *Knott's Berry Farm*—Buena Park, California
- *Knott's Camp Snoopy*—Bloomington, Minnesota
- *Six Flags Astroworld*—Houston, Texas
- *Universal Studios*—Orlando, Florida and Hollywood, California
- *Walt Disney World and Disneyland*—Orlando, Florida and Anaheim, California

Amusement Parks are places where you have to be especially vigilant. In the excitement of having fun, it is easy to let your guard down. Children can get lost in the crowd easily. Notice height and weight requirements, but also be aware of your child's maturity, experience, and tolerance. Kids can become overwhelmed or frightened during a ride, unbuckle their safety belt, and try to scramble out of moving rides. Or in the all the enthusiasm, you may find yourself on a roller coaster with a suddenly terrified five-year-old, and it's only the beginning of the ride. Do not take a child on adult rides unless they've been on kiddie versions first.

DISCOVERY COVE, Orlando, FL. A new idea in amusement parks. Admission is limited to about 1,000 guests per day, so there is never a line. Advanced reservations are required. The highlight of the experience is a swim with dolphins.

Fun Facts

TALLEST ROLLER COASTER The Top Thrill Dragster at Cedar Point, Sandusky, OH, towers 420 feet at its highest point and has top speed of 120 mph!

OLDEST AMUSEMENT PARK Lake Compounce, Bristol, CT. Opened in 1846, it's been recently refurbished to balance modern rides with nostalgia.

OLDEST CAROUSEL The Flying Horse Carousel at Watch Hill in Westerly, RI. Built around 1876, this hand-carved carousel is the oldest in America. Each horse has real horsehair for the mane and tail, and genuine agate eyes. The solid wooden horses are suspended by chains and swing out farther the faster the ride goes, hence the name Flying Horse Carousel.

chapter five
Seasons &
Holidays

FORREST W. ORR

Mud Pie

Spring is the time of thaw and also the time of mud. Explain to your child how melting snow makes big mud puddles and brings worms up to the surface of the earth. Create this edible masterpiece together and serve it honor of Earth Day on the first day of Spring.

chocolate pudding (prepared)
chocolate cookies, crumbled
gummy worms
flowerpots lined with aluminum foil or plastic wrap
artificial flowers

Fill the lined pots with a mixture of pudding, crumbled cookies, and worms. "Plant" the flowers and serve. Eat with a big spoon or plastic shovel.

Signs of Spring

Spring flowers emerge one after the other in a seemingly choreographed parade. Tell your child what to watch out for:

Crocus	Snowdrop
Daffodil	Tulip
Hyacinth	Bluebell

Harbinger of Spring

Spring begins around March 21, on the vernal equinox, when the day and night are of equal length. Once spring arrives, you and your child will be eager to get out and explore the world again without being weighed down by layers of winter clothing. Flowers poke out of the frozen ground to brighten the world and there are wonderful sights to see everywhere, from magnolia trees bursting into bloom to ducklings taking their first swim with their mama.

Spring!

TAKE A NATURE WALK

Take a flower guide outside to a park, botanical garden, or wilderness area. Bring along a blank book and some colored crayons or pencils. Help your child identify the flowers you find. Depending on the species, you might be able to take a few domestic blooms (unless you are in a botanical garden) and press them between pages of the blank book, but remember to teach your child: Never pick delicate wildflowers, as these are endangered. Instead of picking a flower, your child can use the blank book to draw pictures of it and describe where it is, what it smells like, and what other plants are around it.

Mistress Mary,
Quite contrary,
How does your garden grow?
With silver bells,
And cockle-shells,
And pretty maids
all in a row.

Visit Your Local Zoo

Spring is the time of year when most animals give birth. Zoos will almost always have a bunch of new baby animals for your own "little creature" to visit. As much as children love the adult animals in zoos, there is something particularly appealing about miniature versions of critters from chimpanzees to giraffes and lion cubs, and even boa constrictors to penguins. Feeding times may offer an especially good opportunity to observe the newborns. Petting zoos within larger zoos also feature young animals— lambs and kids and young rabbits—at this time of year. Prepare for your visit by finding out which animals have had babies and looking them up in an encyclopedia or on the Internet.

Most zoos have websites that announce the births of new animals. Ask your child questions about each animal's distinctive features, behavior, and native habitat. Then help him or her find the answers. Look out for books about the animals you have seen, too, or ask your child to write a story about the zoo babies. What will they grow up to be? What sorts of adventures might they have in the wild?

LEARN ABOUT MAPLE SUGARING Early spring is the time when maple trees produce the sap that is used to make maple syrup. In some areas (particularly New England), sugarhouses offer tours where you and your children can see sap buckets hanging from the trees and tour the facilities where sap is processed into syrup. A visit to a sugarhouse provides lessons in math (it takes forty gallons of sap to produce one gallon of syrup!), cooking (maple syrup can be used as a sweetener in many recipes), and history (people have been making maple syrup the same way for centuries).

Maple Sugar Candy

Whether or not you live in the Northeast, you can celebrate maple-syrup season by making this candy at home. Follow this simple recipe.

$^1/_3$ cup butter or margarine, softened
$^1/_3$ cup maple syrup
1 pound powdered sugar

Mix the first two ingredients and then add the sugar, mixing first with a spoon and then with your hands until it is smooth. Press into plastic candy molds (maple-leaf shapes are nice for this) or roll into small balls and set on a cookie sheet. Allow to harden. The candy will become firm, but still be somewhat soft.

PLANT YOUR GARDEN Spring is the time to plant your garden. If you do not have a yard, or access to one, you can give your child a planter box to fill with seeds or

More Signs of Spring

SMALL BUDS ON TREES *Look for pussy willows.* TADPOLES *Visit a local pond and see if you can catch any tadpoles. Take one home and watch it grow into a frog.* WORMS *Worms come up when the soil gets warmer.* FULLER RIVERS AND STREAMS *Make a paper boat and drop it from a low bridge. Watch how quickly it moves away.*

young plants, and teach him how to tend it throughout the summer. Visit your local nursery and help your child decide on the types of plants that are appropriate for your climate and setup. Choose plants that will blossom or bear fruits at different points throughout the summer to keep your child's interest. Plants like beans, which grow quickly and are hardy, are a good choice to start a small garden. If you do use bean plants, you will need to tie them to a makeshift wooden framework or sticks on which to grow.

It may help to buy your child his or her own watering can to give the daily chore a more personal feel. Plant your garden together and mark days on the calendar when you can begin to expect growth or maturity in the plants. If you are planting vegetables or herbs, while you are planting them discuss with your child how you may use them later in the summer in meals. If you grow some flowers, make a bouquet of them and put them in a place of prominence in the house so that your child feels proud of what she has accomplished.

Summer

For most children, summer is their favorite season. Out of school and out of doors, life seems an endless parade of fun and adventures. For school-age children it is a welcome rest from the discipline and expectations of the classroom. There is no reason, however, why kids can't continue to learn during the summer, just as long as they can do it in a stress-free way. In fact, a summer spent in activities that are both fun and educational can help prepare a preschooler for kindergarten and ease the transition back to school in September for older kids. Because you can spend time outside, summer is a great time to teach children about nature, the planet, and even the universe. Here are some summer things to do that allow you and your children to relax and learn new things at the same time.

GO BERRYING Summer is berry time. In some parts of the country you may encounter wild blackberry patches, while in others you will need to look out for the "Pick Your Own Strawberries" signs along the roadside. You might ask sellers at your local farmers' market if they let people pick on their farms or if they know anyone who does. Blueberries are particularly fun for children to pick, as they grow on low bushes. Because the temptation to simply eat every berry you pick can be overwhelming for a child, establish an amount you would like to bring home before you start. Two cups' worth of most berries will make a pie, cobbler, or crumble, so let this be the minimum. While you pick, you can sing songs together or talk about what you are going to do with the berries when you get home.

ATTEND AN OUTDOOR CONCERT As much as kids seem to love music, it can be hard to get them to sit still for it. Outdoor concerts mean that they don't have to. Most towns and cities offer free outdoor concerts during the summer. It is probably best to attend free concerts, as even the best-behaved child may tire before the last movement of a

Signs of Summer

Tell your child to look out for these indications that summer is on the way: *Longer days.* ❀ *Rising temperatures.* Give your child an outdoor thermometer to keep track of changes. ❀ *Flowering trees and green leaves.* Help your child draw pictures of a local tree in all four seasons. ❀ *Blooming flowers.* Look for roses in June and tiger lilies in July.

Beethoven symphony and you may want to leave early. Pack a picnic, a blanket, some books, and (quiet) toys, and you are ready to introduce your child to live music. Festivals in city parks include symphony orchestras, performers from around the world, jazz ensembles, and contemporary pop artists. Give your child a range of listening experiences throughout the summer. One way to both entertain a child during a concert and help her develop skills of expression is to ask your child to "draw what you hear," or, for older children, "write how what you hear makes you feel." This kind of activity keeps a child focused on the music without putting too much pressure on her to respond to it analytically. The resulting masterpieces of art or poetry can be kept for posterity.

VISIT A FARMERS' MARKET

A weekly visit to a farmers' market with your child can be wonderfully educational as well as appetizing. Your child will learn the many varieties of vegetables and fruits, and will get a sense of the growing seasons of each as new things appear and disappear in market stalls throughout the summer. Obliging

> ## What Makes Fireflies Glow?
>
> The glow is caused by an enzyme on the insect's body that is activated by other chemicals in the body to create light energy. Fireflies are flying beetles (not flies). The male of the species glows to attract females, who may flash in response. Fireflies are quite slow moving, and it is easy to capture them in a jar. Make sure to poke holes in the lid of the jar that are big enough to let air in but not let the fireflies out. Let your child enjoy this natural lantern for a few hours, but be sure to release the beetles, as there is nothing sadder than a jar full of dead bugs.

he will learn about menu planning and cooking, lessons that will be invaluable later in life.

GAZE AT THE STARS Summer is a great time for stargazing. It is pleasant to be outside at night and there is much to watch for in the heavens. If there is an observatory in your area, it will probably offer programs for visitors. Experts who work at the observatory will be able to help you and your child see planets and galaxies and explain something of the nature of the universe.

You can become amateur astronomers together. A telescope and star map are all you need. Set the scope up in your yard if you have one, or take it to a state park or beach for better visibility. Astronomy Watch posts bulletins on star activity on their website *Astronomy-watch.com*. The annual Perseid meteor shower usually happens in August and can be quite spectacular, depending on conditions.

farmers will explain what they expect to produce at different times, and perhaps describe for your child how various fruits and vegetables grow and how they are harvested. It may interest a child, for instance, to see that Brussels sprouts grow on a big stalk and that potatoes come out of the ground. As you choose your produce together and talk about how you will use it,

Astronomy may prompt your child to ask big questions about the universe, and our existence in it. This can provide a wonderful opportunity to have a deep conversation with your child and share with him some of your ideas about the meaning of life.

Summer Mysteries

Here two questions and answers your curious youngster may ask this summer:

When does summer begin? Explain that summer begins around June 21, on the summer solstice, which is the longest day of the year. Celebrate the solstice by waking up at dawn and making sure to watch the sunset.

Why is it warmer in the summer? Summer is the period when our part of the earth is tilted on its axis towards the sun. This makes the days warmer.

Autumn is a great time to go on adventures with your child. The air is cool but not cold, and golden light gives every building and tree a soft, warm glow. There are many seasonal activities for you and your child to

Autumn

share. They will get you out of doors and in touch with nature, before winter chases you inside. Here are a few ideas for activities that you can enjoy together.

Autumn Mysteries

Why are the leaves changing color? Since most of us are not professional foresters, this brief explanation may help. During the spring and summer, chlorophyll, a green-colored chemical in plant cells, processes light and nutrients to make food for a tree. The leaves only look green because there is so much chlorophyll present at this time. In the fall, as the days get shorter and the air gets colder, the chlorophyll breaks down, revealing the many other pigments (colors) that are in each leaf, such as yellow, orange, and red. So the leaves don't become more colorful, they just become a lot less green!

When does Autumn begin and end? Dates of autumn: Autumn begins on the autumnal equinox, a day when light and darkness are of equal length. In the northern hemisphere, this happens around September 21 and lasts until the first day of winter, around December 21.

What's special about autumn? Autumn is harvest time, when all the hard work that farmers do during the summer finally ends and they collect all the fruits and vegetables from their fields.

Harvest Time

Roll the golden pumpkins
  Through the harvest corn,
Pile them high from earth to sky,
  Let them hide the morn.

See the Indian tents a-field,
  Shocks of corn are they.
Set them high from field to sky,
  They will close the day.

Go Apple Picking

In the fall, many orchards invite paying visitors to pick apples, taste cider, and sometimes go for hayrides. Look in your local Yellow Pages or call your chamber of commerce for information. Children of seven or eight and older will enjoy climbing ladders to pick apples, while younger children will like to play in the grass under the trees. Older children can race with one another to fill a bag or basket. Most orchards grow more than one variety of apple. Help your child learn the names of these; taste them and try out new words to distinguish among flavors. If you have apples left after you make your apple pie and apple-sauce, try these treats.

Apple Fritters

For something decadent, try these deep fried apple fritters as a special dessert for the family.

1 cup sifted all-purpose flour
1 1/2 teaspoons baking powder
1/4 cup sugar
1 teaspoon salt
1 egg, beaten
1/3 cup milk
1 tablespoon melted shortening
2 large apples
5 cups vegetable oil for deep frying
Confectioners' sugar for dusting

1. In a large bowl, sift together flour, baking powder, sugar, and salt.
2. Combine egg and milk and add to the flour mixture. Beat until smooth.
3. Add melted shortening to the batter and mix well.
4. Peel, core, and quarter the apples.
5. Heat the oil to 375°F in a deep, heavy-bottomed pot.
6. Dip the apple wedges in the batter, and drop into the oil about 4 at a time.
7. Fry the wedges for about 1 1/2 to 2 minutes per side or until golden brown.
8. Place cooked fritters on a paper towel to drain.
9. Serve warm, dusted with confectioners sugar.

Makes about 8 fritters.

Dried Apple Rings

Use your microwave to make dried apple ring snacks for your kids in a fraction of the time it would take to dry them in the oven.

2 apples, peeled and cored
1 tablespoon lemon juice
1 quart cold water
Wax paper

1. Slice the apples in rings about 1/4 inch thick.
2. Mix the lemon juice and the water in a bowl.
3. Dip the apple rings in the lemon water to prevent the apples from turning brown.
4. Arrange the rings on a sheet of wax paper so that they are not touching.
5. Put the rings in the microwave on Defrost for 35-45 minutes. The apples will be rubbery and dry when done.
6. Store apples in an airtight container. Apple rings should keep for three to six weeks if completely dried.

Makes about 2 to 3 cups.

PLANT BULBS If you have a garden, or know someone who can lend you a small part of theirs, plant bulbs with your child. It's easy to do: Simply dig a small indentation in the ground with your hands or a trowel and drop the bulb in, covering it up loosely. Plant a mixture of bulbs chosen by your child—hyacinth, daffodil, tulips, narcissi—and explain that they will sleep all through the winter and come up in the spring. You can even mark dates on the calendar together when you will come back to check on them.

CHOOSE A PUMPKIN OR THREE Although most people only buy pumpkins to turn them into jack-o'-lanterns, they make cheerful decorations without being carved, and last much longer this way. Visit a pumpkin patch in mid-October and let your child make a selection of sizes, shapes, and shades. Draw faces on some, or just leave them plain. You can also spend time together spooning out the seeds of a pumpkin and toasting them for lunchbox snacks (*see page 198*). Or your child may want to watch you cut up a pumpkin, bake the pieces, and puree them to use in pie or soup.

Go Frolicking in the Leaves

MAKE CLAY LEAF IMPRINTS Take a piece of clay and flatten it with a rolling pin. Press a leaf into the clay and roll over it with the rolling pin. Remove the leaf and let the clay dry. You can also add acorns and cattails, or use more than one leaf to create an interesting design. The clay impression can be painted when dry.

MAKE A LEAF PILE If you have a big yard and a rake, make leaf piles and jump in them. This is an excellent way to get young children to help you with a chore. Explain that you are making a leaf pile and at the same time clearing the lawn so that it will not be suffocated under wet leaves during the winter, and your child will get a lesson in ecology and gardening, too.

LEAF PRINTS Brush paint onto leaves and press them against construction paper to make a print. Metallic colors are especially fun for this.

PRESERVE AUTUMN LEAVES Take your child on a walk to choose some branches of bright autumn leaves and/or rushes. Pound the stems and place them in a jar filled with a mixture of one part glycerin (available at most drugstores) to two parts water. Explain how the glycerin travels up the veins of the branches, showing your child the parts of the leaf or drawing the process on a piece of paper. In two weeks the branches will be preserved, giving your child a little bit of autumn to remember for the whole year.

TAKE A "LEAF-SHUFFLE" WALK This is a great activity for the end of the season, when most of the leaves have fallen. You will find them dried and piled up along the walkways in most parks. Simply walk along, shuffling your feet in the leaves, kicking them up in the air a little. This is especially fun for smaller children, who are closer to the ground, but it also can be an enjoyable way for older kids to kick out frustrations or just enjoy the rustling sounds and rich colors of the season.

Dancing Leaves

Swaying gently to and fro,
　　Weaving patterns as they go,
Now in stately step and slow,
　　Now like driving, wintry snow.

How they scamper on their way,
　　From pinky dawn 'till close of day!
How they laugh and how they play!
　　Dancing leaves in colors gay!

MAKE SNOW ANGELS
Dress your child warmly, ideally in a snowsuit, and go out to a snow-covered area. Drop backward into the snow. Wave arms up and down alongside your body and open and close legs. Get a hand up from the snow so as not to ruin the picture. With a stick you can draw a halo over the angel's head. Your child can also make a snow bunnies! Keep legs together and only move the arms in small waves along the top of the head for bunny ears.

CUT OUT SNOWFLAKES
Take a sheet of square white paper and fold it in half on the diagonal and again on the diagonal. Snip the corners off.

Despite the chilly air, winter is full of fun and wonder. From the quiet magic of snowflakes to the high-speed thrills of sledding, there is much in the season for children to enjoy. It is a time of gathering together around fireplaces or in warm, fragrant kitchens, a perfect time of year to spend together doing things that will bring you closer. Here are some winter activities to share with your child. The happy memories will last a lifetime. Winter begins around December 21, the winter solstice. This is the shortest day of the year, when we are tilted farthest away from the sun. Help your child take note of sunrise and sunset on this day by finding out the times from your local newspaper.

Winter

Make triangular cuts of varying sizes along the edges. You can also poke your scissors into the middle and cut diamond shapes there. Unfold page for snowflake. Try making snowflakes out of tissue paper, silver foil, wrapping paper, doilies, or waxed paper.

BUILD A SNOWMAN
Start with a snowball and continue adding snow, patting it onto the ball and rolling it around until it is the desired size. Start with a large ball for the base and then add a somewhat smaller ball for middle and a smaller one for the head. Prunes make good eyes and carrots are perfect for noses. A scrap from your sewing basket makes a jaunty scarf. An easy fun shape to build is a snow caterpillar. Assemble six to ten large snowballs in a slightly squiggly line. Stick two long twigs in the first ball for antennae. You can also make more fantastic creations. Use sticks or PVC pipe and some duct tape to form the basic shape of your animal or fantasy creature. Push it deep into the snow so that it stands by itself. Then, starting at the bottom, pack on the snow, layer by layer, until it looks the way you imagined. If it is really cold, and there's no possibility of the snow melting, you can drape your snow creatures in twinkling lights!

GO SKIING
The younger children start skiing, the better they tend to ski as adults. It's something to learn when you are low to the ground and not so fearful of breaking bones. All ski slopes offer beginners' lessons where your child will learn on a "bunny" slope and no doubt soon amaze you with her alpine talents. Remember the sun block, as glare reflected off snow can burn little faces.

Winter Wonders

What makes snow? Snow crystals
are a kind of ice formed when water
vapor becomes solid. Crystals can
form around tiny particles of dust in
the atmosphere when the temperature falls below 32°F (0°C). The
resulting snowflakes are six sided and
symmetrical. Snowflakes appear
white because they have so many
facets reflecting light.

Where do fish go in the winter?
Fish do not hibernate like bears.
They remain in rivers, ponds, lakes,
and oceans, but are much less active,
thereby using less energy. They live
off the fat reserves that they build up
during the summer, when it is easier
to find food.

How do penguins stay warm?
Penguins have many tricks for keeping warm in very cold water. They
have a layer of blubber, a layer of
downy feathers, a layer of thicker
feathers and a coat of oil on top.

    Be a penguin! Coat one hand in
petroleum jelly, immerse it in water,
and show your kids how the water
rolls off in droplets. Cover your
child's hand in a woolly winter glove
and then a rubber glove. Have him
put his hand in a pot of cold water
and ice cubes. Ask, "Do you feel
the cold?"

Marshmallow Snowmen

Marshmallows are delicious homemade. For even more winter fun, try
making marshmallow snowmen! Sweet, fluffy, and plump, these marshmallow snowmen bring winter fun into the kitchen. You can add a few
drops of red food coloring to make pretty pink marshmallows. To make
flavored marshmallows, use 2 teaspoon of peppermint, coffee, almond,
or other essence in place of the vanilla.

3 packets unflavored gelatin; 2 cups white sugar; pinch of salt;
2 cups water; 2 teaspoons vanilla; 2 teaspoons baking powder; 2 cups icing
sugar; sweetened; shredded coconut; toothpicks, melted chocolate (optional)

1. Mix gelatin, sugar, salt, and water in sauce-pan and simmer for 10
   minutes. Let cool.
2. Add the vanilla, baking powder, and icing sugar. Beat until thick.
3. Spread mixture into a buttered 9" x 11" pan and refrigerate for
   3 hours.
4. Cut out four 1½" and four 2" circles. Roll circles in coconut.
5. Attach each small circle to a larger circle with a toothpick. Add dots of
   melted chocolate for eyes, noses, and buttons.   *Makes 8 snowmen.*

Snow Globe

Create a little magical snow world of your own! Snow globes are so easy—
make several with different scenes to enjoy or give away.

small glass jar with lid, 1 eggshell, small plastic reclosable bag, rolling pin,
strong waterproof glue, small plastic toys or ornaments (snowman, angel,
Santa, trees, star, cabin, etc.), baby oil, glitter, pie tin

1. Wash and dry the jar inside and out.
2. Wash and dry the eggshell. Place in the plastic bag, pushing as much
   air as possible out of the bag before sealing it. Crush the eggshell with
   the rolling pin until it is as fine as sugar.
3. Glue toys to the inside of the jar lid, making sure finished scene will fit
   inside closed jar. Sprinkle a little bit of the eggshell over any exposed
   glue. Let dry.
4. Fill the jar three-fourths full with baby oil. Add the crushed eggshell
   and some glitter to create sparkle in your snow. Allow the snow to settle
   at the bottom of the jar.
5. Place the jar on a pie tin to catch any overflow of baby oil.
6. Put beads of glue on the threads of the lid and carefully lower the
   ornaments into the oil. Screw the lid on tight.
7. Allow 5 minutes for the glue to set, and then give it a shake!

Suggestions: Use different sized baby food, jam,
or pickle jars. Use plastic jars if you have
small children (i.e., plastic peanut-butter
jars). Try cutting up aluminum foil or
shaving different colored crayons for snow.

A HAPPY NEW YEAR

MAKE RESOLUTIONS Ask your child what he would like to do or be in the coming year. Without suggesting that there is room for improvement, you can ask your child if there is anything he would like to do differently in the future. Make it plain that you won't punish him for not living up to his resolution. Explain that resolutions are just an opportunity to think about things we would like to accomplish or change.

After your child makes her own resolutions, think about some things you'd like to do together. Make some joint resolutions, like the ones here:

Watching the sunrise together
at least once per season

Telling each other secrets

Writing a letter to someone far away

Seeing an elephant

Going for a walk together

Jumping in a puddle

Going to the highest point in
the area to enjoy the view

Going to the lowest point (a beach or a valley, for example) to enjoy the view

Eating a food you've never tried before

New Year's Eve

The transition from one year to the next, the excitement of a whole new year about to begin, is just as fascinating to youngsters as it is to older people. Although most children will not be able to stay up until midnight on New Year's Eve, they will want to be part of the festivities. Include them in family discussions about how time passes and what the future holds; afterward, make some noise to mark the momentous occasion!

Celebrate with kids before they go to bed, or wait till New Year's morning, if you prefer. Here are some must-haves for a child's celebration: *noisemakers, party hats, sparkling apple cider in a bottle with a popping cork, confetti.*

Sing Auld Lang Syne Together

This traditional Scottish song, with lyrics by Robert Burns, is always sung on New Year's Eve, although few know what it means. Explain to your child that it is a song celebrating old friendships.

Original lyrics appear on the left and translation on the right for the first verse and chorus below.

Should auld acquaintance be forgot,	Should old friends be forgotten,
And never brought to min'?	And never remembered?
Should auld acquaintance be forgot,	Should old friends be forgotten,
And days o' lang syne?	And the days they shared together?
CHORUS	CHORUS
For auld lang syne, my dear,	For days now in the past, my dear,
For auld lang syne,	For days now in the past,
We'll tak a cup o' kindness yet	We'll drink a toast of kind
	remembrance,
For auld lang syne!	For days now in the past.

THROW A NEW YEAR'S EVE PARTY FOR KIDS Invite your child's friends over for a celebration. Help your child decorate the room ahead of time with streamers and homemade pictures of the "old year" and the "Baby New Year." Set a clock ahead as many hours as you'd like, and when guests arrive, hand out party hats and kazoos or other noisemakers. Serve sparkling cider in plastic champagne glasses. Gather the kids together and count down to "midnight," and then toss confetti in the air.

MAKE A LIST OF IMPORTANT EVENTS OF THE PAST YEAR Sit down with your children on New Year's Eve and ask them to think of all the important things that happened during the year. This might include starting school, losing teeth, getting a pet, or making a friend. Keep these lists to refer to each year as you make a new one. You will be creating little autobiographies for your kids.

A Dozen Red Roses

*red tissue paper, scissors, 12 green pipe cleaners
(or wires wrapped tightly with green tape), tape, perfume*

1. Cut ten slightly different-sized circles of red tissue paper, from 2" to 4" in diameter. Place circles on top of each other, from smallest to largest.
2. Poke the stem wire through the middle of the circles. Make a small loop at the top of the wire; wrap a bit of tape at the bottom of the tissue flower to secure.
3. Separate the tissue paper by lifting each piece and pulling it toward the center to "fluff out" the petals of the flower.
4. Repeat to make a dozen roses.
5. Spray a bit of perfume into the air several inches above the roses to scent them.

ALL OUR LOVES One of the nicest things you and your child can do together on Valentine's Day is make a list of all the people that you love and who mean something to you. Use a big piece of paper and some red magic markers or crayons. Rather than writing the names in a column, you can draw a heart around each one. Around each heart you can write something about that special person. Tape this list up in your child's room to remind him of how many people he is close to.

SING A SILLY LOVE SONG TO-GETHER Choose a love song with simple words, such as "I Want to Hold Your Hand," by the Beatles, or "You are My Sunshine." Play a recording on the stereo and invite your child to sing along as loud as she can. Shout it through the house.

WRITE AN ODE Explain to your son or daughter that an ode is a poem of praise to a person or object. Sit down with your child and think of something you both love—like chocolate ice cream or the family dog. Come up with a few reasons why you love this food or your pet so much. Make a list of your "love object's" best qualities. Add some "even though's" for humor and sincerity. Read your ode aloud together to the object of your affections.

MAKE PASSION-FRUIT SMOOTHIES For a Valentine's Day refreshment, mix passion-fruit nectar (available in the Spanish food sections of most supermarkets) with plain yogurt or vanilla ice cream in a blender. Mix and serve with half a strawberry (heart-shaped) on the edge of the glass.

MAKE VALENTINES Make memorable valentines together. Put out markers, scissors, tape, glue, gold and silver glitter, ribbons, stickers, doilies, red and pink tissue, construction, and aluminum paper and see what your children can create for friends and family.

Valentine's Day

Valentine's Day can be about more than romantic love. You and your child can set the day aside to celebrate all kinds of love and affection. It's a great time to spend together talking about how much you love each other and the many special people you know. Making valentines and distributing them to all the people who are part of your child's life can be a wonderful experience in which you share the delights of giving and receiving friendship. The history of Valentine's Day is obscure, but you might explain to your child that our culture likes to take one day out of the year—February 14—to celebrate the feeling of love, an emotion that binds us tighter and compels us to take care of one another.

Easter

Easter comes at that delightful time of year when the air finally starts to become warm again and the world seems full of babies and delicate flowers. You can have a wonderful experience with your child celebrating the spring season by sharing Easter activities that range from the artistic to the madcap. What is Easter? You can help your child enjoy the holiday even more by sharing a little of its history with him or her. Easter has a long history, rooted in the joy that people have always felt when winter ends and warm weather returns. Ancient Saxons celebrated the rebirth of nature at the end of winter with a festival honoring the goddess of spring, Eastre. Christians combined this holiday with their celebration of the resurrection of Jesus.

DYE EASTER EGGS You will need a half dozen hard-boiled eggs. Fill some paper cups with food coloring or special Easter-egg dye. Make a loop out of picture wire to hold an egg as you lower it into dye. Dye one end of an egg one color and the other end another color, or dye an egg one solid color and then dip it into another for a mixed effect. Allow to dry.

VARIATIONS

- *Magic marker eggs:* Use magic markers to decorate eggs, either previously dyed or undyed.
- *Batik eggs:* Use a candle to drip wax in a pattern onto an egg. Dip the egg in dye and then, when it is dry, scrape off the wax and either dip the egg again or leave these parts white.
- *Blown eggs:* Do not boil eggs. Make a small pinhole in each end of an egg and, holding the egg over a sink, gently blow the yolk and white out. Dye eggshells. You can use blown eggs as containers for small wrapped candies. Simply use a needle to make a hole about the size of a quarter in one end of the egg, rinse, dry, and fill with candies.
- *Shiny eggs:* To give eggs an extra shine, wait till they are dry and polish them with a drop of cooking oil.

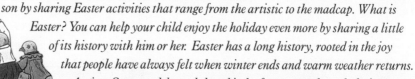

FAVORITE BOOK A beautiful book guaranteed to charm young ones and bring tears to any mother's eyes is *The Country Bunny and the Little Gold Shoes*, by DuBose Heyward. Find out how a mother bunny attains the exalted position of Easter Bunny in spite of her responsibilities as the mother of twenty-one little bunnies!

BE A BUNNY Start the day right by making sure everyone in the house is wearing their bunny ears and tails. Bunny ears are easy to make. Cut out a pair of long, pointed ovals from construction paper or stiff felt. Attach them to a plastic hair band. You can fluff your bunny ears up by gluing cotton balls all over them. For a tail, glue three or four cotton balls together and attach to your clothes with double-stick tape. Add a pink nose and black whiskers with face paints and hop away!

Decorate an Easter Bonnet

Help your child make a unique Easter bonnet by taking a hat and covering it in cloth flowers, plastic fruit, feathers, bright ribbons and bows, and whatever else seems pretty. You can use scraps of wrapping paper and tissue paper by bunching them into flower shapes and gluing them onto your holiday hat. The more flamboyant the better!

HOLD AN EASTER-EGG RELAY RACE You will need at least two teams of three people each. Set up a start and finish line about ten feet apart. Give each team member a spoon. Each team member carries an Easter egg on a spoon from start to finish line and back, where he or she passes it to the next team member. If an egg falls, it can only be picked up using the spoon. The first team to complete the relay wins.

Magic Rainbow Eggs

When March winds blow so blithely,
And whistle through the air,
The March hares are preparing
Their usual Easter fare.

Their rabbit feet go dancing
About a magic brew,
While Easter eggs so dainty
Are tinted many a hue.

Sing A Rousing Rendition of "Yankee Doodle Dandy"

This song, written by an Englishman to mock the ragtag American troops, was quickly adopted by the proud revolutionaries as their own jingle. It has many verses, but most people just sing...

Yankee Doodle went to town, riding on a pony,
Stuck a feather in his hat
*   and called it macaroni!*
Yankee Doodle, keep it up, Yankee Doodle Dandy,
Yankee Doodle, keep it up,
*   and with the girls be handy.*

The last line simply means "flirt with the girls," a concept that is sure to make youngsters giggle and run for cootie shots.

4ᵗʰ of July

The Fourth of July is an exciting holiday for children—noisy and festive and full of bright lights. It literally ushers the summer in with a bang. Many towns and cities have parades and there are always fireworks shows to see or, in some states, set off. The traditional barbecue is lots of fun for kids, who love the freedom of eating outdoors, where table manners aren't so strictly enforced. Independence Day offers many opportunities for fun and creative activities.

HAVE A RED-WHITE-AND-BLUE BREAKFAST Have cereal with milk, strawberries, and blueberries. Or slather your toast with a little cream cheese and blueberry and raspberry jam.

GO TO A PARADE Take your homemade flag and/or wear your flag T-shirts to a parade. Colorful floats, marching bands, firetrucks, and the inevitable cotton candy are sure to entertain your little patriot. Encourage loud cheering and applause—it's nice to have one day when it's okay to make a racket.

MAKE NONFLAMMABLE SPARKLERS This is perfect (and safe) for young children. Dip an ordinary bottlebrush in glue, then glitter. Let it dry and give it to your child to wave around. Glow sticks, which can be bought at many toy stores, also safely satisfy the urge for pyrotechnics.

HAVE A BARBECUE Invite over some friends of all ages. Let your child help you with messy tasks such as loading charcoal in the grill or making hamburger patties. Let him or her help plan the menu and prepare the food. Decorate the yard with streamers and balloons in patriotic colors.

MAKE FLAGS You can use many materials to make flags. Stitch old clothes together and glue them to a wooden dowel. Or cut up construction paper and paste together the pieces. Trace stars using a cookie cutter or use star stickers, available in most stationery stores. Explain that each star is a state. See if you can name all fifty states together while you work on your flags.

WEAR A FLAG Use fabric markers to draw flags on plain white T-shirts.

MAKE A FLAG CAKE All you need is a rectangular cake, some vanilla frosting, and red and blue food coloring to color the frosting. Make your stars out of jellybeans, Sno-Caps, or sugared almonds.

START A REVOLUTION Set up a tent in the yard and call it Revolutionary Headquarters. Hang red, white, and blue streamers. Invite some of your child's friends over and give them all new names—General Washington, Molly Pitcher, Ethan Allen. Ask them to come up with a "constitution," or list of rules that ought to be followed in their tent. Dip feathers in ink and let them sign their document. Celebrate with an outdoor feast.

CELEBRATE AMERICAN HEROES Read a book or tell a story about an American hero. Some suggestions: Harriet Tubman, Neil Armstrong, Lewis and Clarke, Susan B. Anthony. Ask your child who he or she thinks is a hero.

What is Independence Day?
The Fourth of July is a day when we celebrate our special form of government and our history. On July 4, 1776, America broke away from Britain, the country that had been ruling it. Today we celebrate some of the best things about our country, such as freedom of speech and diversity.

Halloween

Halloween is a holiday made for children. It is a time of spooky decorations, fantastical costumes, strange traditions, and, of course, bags of treats. It is a time to enjoy the fall and to celebrate the imagination as you and your child devise mysterious disguises or carve a pumpkin. Here are some ideas for activities to share with your child and his or her friends. Your little monster is sure to have a great time going door to door or telling ghost stories. And if the eerie atmosphere gives your children the creeps, remember that a nice warm hug is all it takes to reassure them.

WHERE DOES HALLOWEEN COME FROM?

Your child may ask you why exactly we dress up and demand candy from our neighbors on Halloween. Here is a brief answer to satisfy the curious mind. Halloween is a combination of holidays celebrated in ancient Europe. Samhain (pronounced SOW-in) was a Celtic festival to mark the day when the spirits of the dead were supposed to return to earth. Celts wore costumes so the dead would not recognize them. This tradition was joined to the Roman festival Feralia, which honors the dead, and the Christian holiday of All Hallows' Eve, the night before All Saints' Day, November 1, when saints and souls are celebrated. The practice of giving cakes to the poor on this day in return for their prayers for the dead became our custom of trick-or-treating.

Roasted Pumpkin Seeds

Instead of throwing away those slippery pumpkin seeds when you carve your jack-o-lantern, put them aside and roast them for a tasty Halloween treat.

1 1/2 cups pumpkin seeds
2 tablespoons of butter
Salt to taste

1. Preheat oven to 300° F.
2. Scoop out seeds from a fresh pumpkin. Wash seeds under cold water, removing any stringy fibers. Blot dry with paper towels and set aside in a bowl.
3. Melt butter in a saucepan and pour over the bowl of seeds. Sprinkle with salt to taste and mix until the seeds are well coated.
4. Spread the pumpkin seeds evenly in a single layer on a baking sheet. Bake for approximately 45 minutes, stirring occasionally, until seeds are golden brown.

CARVE A PUMPKIN Jack-o'-lanterns were made to frighten spirits away on Halloween. If you can, buy a pumpkin carving kit—it will make the carving easier and safer. Choose a pumpkin with a fairly even surface. Cut a lid out of the stem end, set it aside, and remove the pulp and seeds with a large kitchen spoon. Scrape out some of the meat of the pumpkin to make the inside clean and smooth. Draw a face on the outside with a magic marker. Use a sharp knife to carefully cut out the design. Choose a short, fat candle to illuminate the pumpkin. Light the candle and anchor it in some soft wax dripped in the bottom of the pumpkin. Put the lid back on the pumpkin (tilt it slightly to leave a space; the flame gets more oxygen and burns brighter this way). If you are wary about using lit candles to illuminate your pumpkins, you can use special electric lamps, which are also available at many stores in October. Place your jack-o'-lantern in a window or on a porch to light up the night. (Your pumpkin will last longer if you spray a 5 percent chlorine solution on the cut areas and the interior of the pumpkin.)

MAKE A HAUNTED HOUSE

Decorate one or two connecting rooms in your house with glow-in-the-dark skeletons, cobwebs (you can make these by hanging up strands of thread), plastic spiders on strings (hang from the ceiling) and black streamers. Place creepy things around the room: a bowl of peeled litchi nuts or grapes (eyeballs), a bowl of cold spaghetti (brains), a bowl of warm tomato juice (blood). Invite some of your child's friends over for a party. Play some eerie music and dim the lights. Blindfold each guest or trick-or-treater in turn and lead them through the haunted house. Let them put their hands in each bowl, walk them through cobwebs, and let them bump into plastic skeletons.

TELL GHOST STORIES

Scary stories help put us in the Halloween mood, but you don't have to give your child nightmares. Tell scary stories that end with a laugh. The headless horseman, for instance, might search frantically for his head and then suddenly find it somewhere silly, like the refrigerator. Or a witch might try to cast a spell on someone only to hiccup in the middle and accidentally turn herself into a frog.

MUMMY RACE

Invite some of your child's friends over for a mummy race. Pair kids off, and give each pair a roll of toilet paper. One member of the pair "mummifies" the other by wrapping him or her in toilet paper. Then the mummies race across the yard or down the hall.

EAT SLIME

Make a bowl of green Jell-O with gummy worms in it. Eat with hands.

DO SOME SPELLS

On Halloween night, catch an autumn leaf as it falls from its branch and before it touches the ground. Your family will have a year of good fortune. At bedtime, here is a handy spell to get rid of any monsters who may still be hanging around. Flick the bedroom light switch on and off thirteen times and say:

> Monsters lurking far and near,
> Your jaws of death I do not fear.
> There are no children sleeping here,
> So scamper off and disappear!

Five Little Witches: Fingerplay

Five little witches (*five fingers*)
Standing by the door.
One flew out (*flying motion with hands*)
And then there were four.
Four little witches (*four fingers*)
Standing by a tree.
One went to pick a pumpkin (*picking motion*)
And then there were three.
Three little witches (*three fingers*)
Stirring their brew. (*stir*)
One fell in
And then there were two. (*two fingers*)
Two little witches went for a run. (*run with fingers*)
One got lost
And then there was one. (*one finger*)
One little witch, yes, only one. (*one finger*)
She cast a spell (*clap hands quickly*)
And now there are none.

> A turkey is a funny bird,
> Its head goes wobble, wobble,
> All it knows is just one word,
> "Gobble, gobble, gobble."

MAKE A FLOCK OF TURKEYS

Take some pieces of construction paper (brown and orange work well) and some magic markers. Help your child trace his open hand on a piece of paper. Draw a beak, eye, and wattle on the thumb, and a pair of turkey legs extending from the heel of the hand. Cut out a bunch of turkeys, decorate with glued-on feathers, and tape them up around the house. You can also write the names of your guests on turkeys and use them as place cards.

GIVE THANKS Help your child make a list of things that he or she is grateful for. Using construction paper and magic markers, you can make thank-you notes together to send or give to people who have made a difference in your lives (teachers, doctors, sports coaches, grandparents) during the year. Some families like to take a moment during Thanksgiving dinner for each person to say aloud what they are thankful for. Once they start talking, even the youngest child will have something to say—even if it is "I am thankful for apple pie"—and will enjoy being part of the tradition.

DRESS LIKE PILGRIMS If you have any old belts that you are not using anymore, snip off the buckles and attach them (use twist-ties or string) to black shoes. It is easy to make a pilgrim hat from pieces of black construction paper or felt. Simply make a witch hat, cut off the point and add a piece of paper for the flat top. Attach a buckle (real or paper) to the front. For girls, make a bonnet by folding a white napkin over head and tying it with attached strings under chin.

HANG COLORED CORN Visit your local farmer's market and buy some ears of colored corn. You may find red, blue, white, or even multicolored corn. Help your child tie a ribbon around the husks of the corn and loop this over a nail or hook on your front door. You can also pop this corn simply by scraping it off and tossing it into a heated and buttered stewpot. While not the most delicious popcorn, it can be used to make popcorn wreaths for decoration.

Thanksgiving

Americans celebrate Thanksgiving on the last Thursday in November. The holiday began as a celebration of the first harvest after the Pilgrims came to Massachusetts. Arriving late in 1620, they had suffered through a hard winter, but in the spring of 1621, with the help of Squanto, a local Native American, they were able to plant crops. That fall they reaped a rich harvest, and they shared their feast with the Native Americans who had helped them survive. Thanksgiving is a day when we express our gratitude for the bounty of the earth and the help of others.

While you are busy in the kitchen, you may want to point out to your child that many of the foods are native to America, which means that the Pilgrims had never had them before they arrived on this continent. Some foods that are native to America: turkey, corn, squash (including pumpkin), beans, and cranberries.

Corn Soup

To commemorate Native American contributions to American history, you might want to make a dish based on a native recipe. This corn soup is an Abenaki recipe. The first native person whom the Pilgrims met was an Abenaki.

1 gallon water
4 ounces salt pork or bacon
2 cups hominy corn
1 can kidney beans
1 onion, chopped
1 potato, peeled and diced

Combine all ingredients in a large pot. Stew over low heat, covered, for about an hour.

Christmas

For many children, the whole year is a buildup to Christmas. They carefully write and revise their wish lists throughout the year and long for those magical days when the tree is trimmed and the whole family comes together to exchange presents and holiday cheer. Christmas is a wonderful holiday to spend with children, who bring so much wonder and joy to traditional events. From the hanging of stockings to the placing of a star high atop a fragrant tree to the crumbs of a cookie left by Santa himself, every moment and every detail of the season is captivating to a child. There are many wonderful ways to celebrate Christmas with children. Here are just a few.

READ A SPECIAL BEDTIME STORY When you put your kids to bed on Christmas Eve, read them *The Night Before Christmas* or *A Child's Christmas in Wales*. These magical poems will send children off to sleep in a Christmas spirit.

LEAVE A SNACK AND A NOTE FOR SANTA This tradition is a wonderful way to help children develop a sense of gratitude, and to preserve the delightful belief in Santa's magic. Tell your child that because Santa has so many deliveries to make on Christmas Eve, he will very much appreciate a snack. You can let your child decide what this snack should be. A small mince pie or cookie is traditional, but there is no reason that a bowl of macaroni and cheese would not do just as well. Help your child write a note to go with the snack thanking Santa in advance for his visit and the gifts he brings.

Remember: It is very important that someone eat Santa's snack, so eat it! You may also want to write a thank-you note from Santa to your child.

Because he travels through chimneys, it might be fun to write this note in charcoal.

MAKE WRAPPING PAPER Help your child wrap your family's Christmas gifts in truly personalized paper. Buy a pad of large newsprint paper (available at art supply stores). Use Christmas cookie cutters dipped in finger paint to stamp designs on paper or allow your child to draw Christmas scenes with magic markers or crayons. Even the youngest children can get in on the action using red and green finger paint to create festive works of art.

Decorate Christmas Stockings

These easy-to-make holiday stockings will become a part of your family tradition as they are brought out (and stuffed) each year. Buy men's large socks or soccer socks, which are extra long for extra stuffing. Encourage your child to adorn his own stocking with sequins, feathers, beads, and any other eye-catching materials. Cut out your child's initials from a piece of felt and sew or glue them onto the sock. Or write them in glitter glue.

Classic Sugar Cookies

These can be enhanced with lemon or orange zest if you choose. But even plain, they are the perfect holiday treat.

1 cup butter (2 sticks), at room temperature
1 cup sugar
2 eggs
1 teaspoon vanilla extract
3 cups flour

1. Cream the butter and sugar. Beat in the eggs and add the vanilla. Add the flour and mix well. Refrigerate for at least 2 hours.
2. Preheat the oven to 375°F and line baking sheets with parchment paper.
3. Roll the dough out on a lightly floured surface (marble or wood) and cut with a cookie cutter. Transfer the cookies with a spatula to cookie sheets. If you are going to decorate without icing, decorate with sprinkles and move the sheets into the oven. Bake for approximately 10 minutes. When the cookies are beginning to brown, remove them from the oven and slide the parchment off the baking sheet. When the cookies have cooled a bit, slide them off the parchment. Cool the cookie sheets before using them again. If you have baked the cookies without decorations, wait until they are completely cool before icing with Snow Icing.

Snow Icing

1 package (16 oz) confectioners sugar
3 egg whites
1 tablespoon white vinegar
Assorted food coloring

1. Place the confectioners sugar in a mixing bowl.
2. In a separate bowl, beat the egg whites lightly with a fork. Add them to the sugar and beat with an electric mixer on the lowest speed for 1 minute. Add vinegar and beat for 2 more minutes at high speed, or until the mixture is stiff and glossy, as for stiff meringue.
3. Separate the mixture into small bowls and tint with different color.
4. When not working with the icing, keep it covered with plastic wrap so it doesn't dry out. If you don't use it all, you can keep it covered in the refrigerator for up to 2 weeks.

Mistletoe Mysteries

In their excitement over the Christmas season, children will have many questions for you. Here are some brief answers to help explain (and preserve) the magic of the holiday.

Why do we have a tree in our house? Ancient Romans, Egyptians, and Druids all decorated their homes in wintertime with branches of evergreen trees to symbolize the continuation of life through the winter. Christians in Germany adapted the tradition by bringing pine trees into their homes and decorating them with lights to symbolize the stars in the sky over the manger in which Jesus was born.

How does Santa visit all the houses in the world in one night? The answer to this pesky question is easy: magic reindeer. The reindeer of the North Pole are famed for their incredible speed, faster than the speed of light, many say.

How does Santa get in if we don't have a chimney? Santa is not an ordinary person. He is a kind of Christmas sprite who is able, portly though he is, to squeeze through the tiniest spaces—under doors or through mail slots. If you don't have a chimney, you may want to designate a "Santa entrance" and help your child hang a sign over it, just to make sure he finds his way in.

chapter six

Preserving Memories

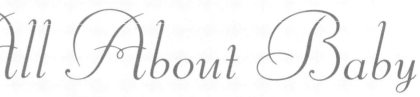

All About Baby

Have you ever caught yourself thinking, "Oh! My child is growing up too fast!"? The desire for our children to leisurely linger in childhood is a natural one. The fun, innocence, wonder, and joy that mark this special time create magical experiences and beautiful memories. Here are some ways to preserve those memories.

FIRST PHOTOS Keep your print camera loaded with film, your digital camera charged, and your video camera ready to record your baby's milestone moments. Some of baby's firsts will be spontaneous, such as the first smile or word or those brave first steps, so keep your cameras in an easy-to-grab location for quick snapshots. Other milestones will be easy to plan for—the first bath or haircut or cutting that first tooth.

Mama's Baby

Big, bright eyes and fuzzy head,
Lips like cherries, rosy red,
Cunning feet, with wee, pink toes,
Rose-leaf hands, and tiny nose,
Dimpled elbows, shoulders, knees,
Round her wrists a little crease,
One white tooth just peeping through
When she tries to say "Goo-goo!"
What if ev'ry one must walk
All a tip-toe, scarcely talk,
When she takes her morning nap?
That is nothing. Though a lap
Is the only place at night
That will suit her fancy quite.
Though she screams and shrieks with rage,
Did you do less at her age?
What if she must clutch and tear
From its roots her mama's hair?

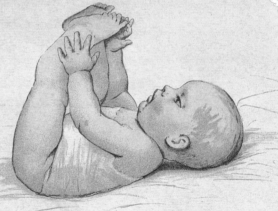

If your watch will keep her quiet,
Why, my dear, of course you'll try it.
Bang the tongs, she's fond of music.
Does she cry? You would, were you sick.
Spoiled, you say? You think so, maybe.
But, you see, she's Mama's baby.

A Beautiful Day in the Neighborhood

Whether you grew up in a small town, big city, or somewhere in between, you can never quite revisit the neighborhood of your childhood, but you can capture it in photographs. Document your home, town, and the surrounding area. Capture your baby's room décor and the playground with the favorite sandbox. Include letters and hand-written notes in a scrapbook that express special moments or favorite daily routines. When your child is old enough to enjoy photos, you'll both be able to see how much the world has changed.

GET THOSE PRINTS Baby hand and foot casting kits are readily available online and in craft stores. These print kits allow you to create 3-D impressions of your baby's hands and feet at home. You and baby can have fun preserving those tender fingers and toes with exquisite detail—including fingerprints!

THE NEXT GENERATION FAMILY ALBUM

🌿 Remember the look on Grandma and Grandpa's faces when they first laid eyes on your little angel? Invite them to share those early memories in letters or record them on videotape to include in a family album or family video documentary.

🌿 When extended family comes to visit or you take baby on trips to see them, capture shots of great-grandparents, uncles, aunts, cousins, godparents, friends, and pets.

🌿 Gather and include stories from family members in the album.

🌿 Compile a family tree at the beginning of the album. Where possible, include pictures and birth dates of family members.

🌿 Capture the memories of elderly relatives and record the special bond they have with baby. You may be surprised to learn new stories about your own youth when Grandma remembers how you behaved or responded the same way as your little one is at this age.

Date and label photos, including your baby's age, when you get them developed. Time has a way of passing quickly during these early years, and dates of events may be hard to remember later.

Picture of the Month

Your baby goes through more changes in the first year of life than any other year. Capture those subtle—and not so subtle—changes by documenting the first year with at least one great picture at the beginning of each month. At the end of the year, create a large matted frame picture of the first twelve months. Here are some suggested shots:

1 month: I'm here! *2 months*: Smiling *3 months*: Holding and shaking rattle *4 months*: Holding head and shoulders up while on stomach *5 months*: Starting solids *6 months*: Sitting supported or unsupported *7 months*: Teeth *8 months*: Crawling *9 months*: Standing or Cruising *10 months*: Waving goodbye *11 months*: "Reading" favorite book *12 months*: Walking or First birthday

GERTA RIES

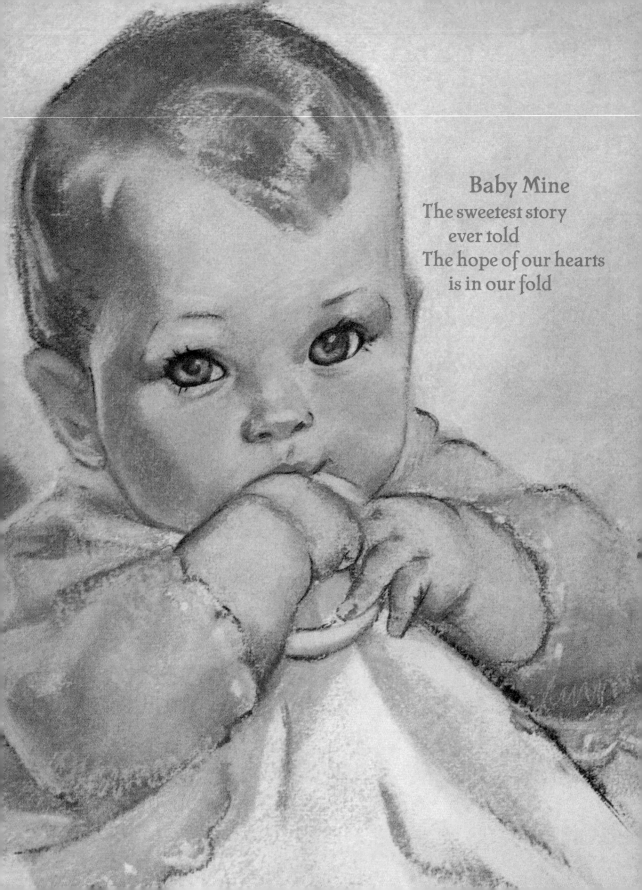

Baby Mine
The sweetest story
ever told
The hope of our hearts
is in our fold

Bronze Booties

Your parents or grandparents may have done it, and now it's your turn to preserve your baby's first shoes by having them bronzed or porcelainized. You can search online and find many companies who can do it for you, or you can follow these steps and do it yourself.

rag, denatured alcohol, wire, liquid bronze (bronze, copper, or gold powder—available at paint or hardware stores—mixed with spare varnish), camel hairbrush.

1. Clean shoes thoroughly with a damp rag to remove dirt and polish.
2. Rub shoes with a rag saturated in denatured alcohol and allow to dry.
3. Arrange the shoes and laces in the way you'd like them to be bronzed.
4. Poke a hole in the bottom of each shoe and loop a wire through it.
5. Prepare liquid bronze as directed.
6. Apply the bronze with a good camelhair brush. Apply two or three coats, painting the shoes inside and out. Clean the brush between coats.
7. Between coats, dry by hanging up the shoes by the wire loop.
8. When the shoes dry, check to see if more coats are needed. The finish should be even and glossy.

FIRST KEEPSAKE BOX A photo album isn't always enough to capture what life was like in year one. To preserve larger or bulkier items, create your own time capsule of sorts—a small trunk or large box with subsections that make it easy for you to organize items. If you already have a good idea about what you want to save, you'll be better prepared to store those items for a lifetime. Some things to keep in mind:

- Choose a storage container that will be sturdy enough to hold your keepsakes for twenty-five years or more.
- Include a detailed multimedia baby album that documents baby's birth and growth.
- Write your baby a letter to be opened at a later date or birthday.

- Make sure your keepsake container is large enough to store your baby's blanket, favorite stuffed animal or toy, first pair of shoes, first outfit, confirmation gown, and memory book.
- Consider smaller compartments or built in drawers that can hold smaller items such as your baby's pacifier, spoon, rattle, hospital bracelet, and lock of hair.
- Include special archival envelopes to protect paper documents such as the birth certificate, arrival announcements, letters from family and friends, and greeting cards.

KEEPSAKE JOURNAL There are so many beautiful baby journals available to commemorate the first few years of a child's life (*or make your own scrapbook, see page 213*). Choose one with ample space for photos, memorabilia, and written descriptions BEFORE your baby is born. If you become too overwhelmed in that that first sleep-deprived year to fill out the journal, simply jot down notes in pencil or on scraps of paper. Be sure to note when milestones occur as it is hard to recall exactly later on. There will be a day when you can lovingly pull your notes and photographs together into a journal for you and your child to enjoy.

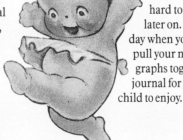

Smile Taking Pictures

If you're like most parents, you'll be bitten by the shutterbug the the moment you bring your baby home. This joy will last through toddler years and into childhood. You don't have to be a professional photographer to get the most out of picture taking, though. Start by having a camera nearby to capture candid moments and special photo ops.

How To Take Better Pictures

- Pay attention to light sources. Try to keep bright lights behind you. Use natural light whenever possible.
- Make sure your shadow doesn't appear in the frame.
- Photograph children at their own height.
- Don't wait for "the perfect moment." Take a series of pictures to show your child in action.
- Outdoor photos are best taken in early morning or late afternoon when natural light is softer.
- Use fill flash indoors or for close-up photos when shadows may be present.
- When indoors, avoid having your subject appear in front of a window.
- When taking pictures outdoors, avoid having your children face the sun, which would make them squint.
- Tell jokes or funny stories when you're trying to photograph your children to capture spontaneous laughter or quizzical looks.
- Have fun! If you're enjoying yourself, your subjects will enjoy themselves, too.
- When photographing two people of different heights, try to arrange the subjects with their faces close together.
- Allow your children to get comfortable having a camera around. They'll behave more naturally when you want to get that candid shot.
- Close-up shots are often more dramatic than pictures taken from far away. Remember, you don't have to include the subject's entire body in the picture.
- For great personality shots, try taking close-ups of your youngster's face that fill the frame.
- When you want to include the landscape in the frame of the picture, try to capture something in the foreground, your subject in the middle ground, and the landscape in the background. This can help show height difference, perspective, and distance.
- Experiment! Tilt the camera at different angles to capture a sense of playfulness.
- Try photographing the same subject several times and frame each shot differently. Compare the results and note the ones you like best so you'll remember that technique next time.
- Children often ham it up when they know you're taking their picture. Avoid phrases like "say cheese" if you want to see more natural expressions.
- Remember, your photos don't always have to document happy moments. Take photos of your children in all their various moods, or engrossed in some activity. Your photo album will reflect more of your children's personalities.
- Try to always avoid placing your subject in the center of the frame. Off-center pictures can be interesting.
- Keep on taking pictures! Taking more pictures improves your skill.

Consider making a Birthday Book of only birthday photos for each of your children. Or, create a large matted frame picture to hang on the wall with room for a birthday photo each year. Enjoy seeing the changes as years go by.

Going Digital

Digital cameras make it easy to take more pictures. You can view the picture immediately and determine if it's worth keeping. If you want to reproduce them on photo-quality paper, you can pick and choose which images to print, and save money from developing unwanted photos. Some online services make it easy to choose, share photos with family and loved ones around the world, and print photos at your convenience. Check out: *shutterfly.com*; *ofoto.com*; *Kodak.com/go/picturecenter*; or *pictures.aol.com*.

Organize by Theme

Simplify your album and strengthen what you want to communicate by focusing on a single theme.

✿ *Chronological highlights.* Let your album represent events in the course of a calendar year, a school year, or a particular time period.

✿ *Personal values.* Do your pictures reflect the values that are most dear to you or the subjects whose lives you're chronicling? Let values such as humor, integrity, compassion, honesty, sportsmanship, faith, health, or education drive the organization of your scrapbooks.

✿ *Birthdays.* Whether it's your daughter's eighth or your mother's eightieth, devote a single scrapbook to the celebration of the event.

✿ *Sports.* Do you have a little leaguer, gymnast, or soccer star in your midst? Showcase their season's best highs, lows, and action shots.

✿ *Vacation getaways.* Did you make a family trek to the mountains this winter for a ski and snowboard holiday? Or did your summer involve camping, canoeing, and horseback riding? Relive the best memories from your time away in a vacation-themed scrapbook.

✿ *Childhood home.* Share what home means to you in scrapbook pages that reflect your lifestyle, values, and taste. As our children grow quickly, our environments change. Capture images of home and family life that will serve as a poignant time capsule years from now.

✿ *Grandparents "mini" album.* Turn any scrapbook plan into an opportunity to make a similar album on a smaller scale with pictures and design elements that you don't plan on using in the larger album. Invite your children to participate in choosing photos and design elements for the mini album that they can present to their grandparents.

Scrapbook Supplies

❀ blank books or albums with plain, hard-stock pages ❀ regular and decorative-edge scissors ❀ colored markers ❀ acid-free materials ❀ double-sided tape ❀ glue stick ❀ photo corners ❀ die cuts ❀ rubber stamps ❀ ink pads ❀ craft punches ❀ stickers ❀ solid, colored, and designer papers ❀ glitter

Jazz It Up

Any scrapbook is more than a collection of photos. It's a way to convey ideas, share important events, and celebrate your creativity. Check out these design tips to bring your scrapbook pages to life:

Communicate with color. Use a color wheel to guide your selection of colors. It will take the guesswork out of combining colors that help you emphasize cheer, stability, calm, action, newness, power, sophistication, or quirkiness.

Think about backgrounds. Use strips of colored paper, borders, and frames to highlight your photos and give a more elegant look to your scrapbook pages.

Use fancy fonts to tell your story. Compare different fonts and notice how they can change the mood of what you're spelling out in words.

Script it. Scrapbook pages are like visual journals. Including handwritten elements; a simple script or fancy calligraphy can add style and individuality to your album.

Make it pop. Use 3-D elements such as bows, ribbons, sequins, corrugated papers, stitching, buttons, or layers of paper elements for an additional fun factor.

Photo Satisfaction

❀ Date and label photographs as soon as you get them developed.

❀ Until you can put them in a scrapbook, organize photos chronologically or according to a theme.

❀ Crop photos to bring out the best in them. Zero in on your subject, or reframe the picture to lead the viewer's eyes better.

❀ Assemble photos taken from different angles and vantage points that show variety and contrast.

  ❀ Create focal points that get your message across.

❀ Enlarge photos that you want to be the dominant image on your scrapbook page.

❀ Arrange pictures, text, and design elements on pages to naturally guide your viewer's eyes and "tell a story."

❀ Use pre-made frames or place a mat behind prominent photos to set them off from supporting photos.

❀ Combine several layout techniques for continual balance and flow throughout your scrapbook pages.

Putting Scrapbooking It Together

More than just photo album pages, the creative expression of designing scrapbooks is an increasingly popular way to preserve family memories. So where to begin? Looking at several stacks of newly developed photos can leave you feeling overwhelmed. Before sorting through the photos, think about what you want to preserve and why. Come up with a formula for your scrapbook before you start. What size do you want it to be? What style? Will there be a theme, such as your four-year-old's dance recital or your sixth-grader's soccer match? Or do you want your scrapbook to chronicle a year in your toddler's life? Knowing these answers ahead of time will make putting everything together quicker and easier.

Extra Extra

Beyond photographs, decorate your album with additional memorabilia from the events you wish to chronicle. Save newspaper clippings, letters from friends or relatives, ticket stubs, event programs, announcements, invitations, or trinkets that you can use as design elements on your scrapbook pages.

Things to Save

First lock of hair 🌹 First tooth 🌹 First shoes 🌹 First work of art 🌹 All teacher praise 🌹 Letters to/from Santa 🌹 Letters to/from the tooth fairy 🌹 Outstanding report cards 🌹 Family recipes (see *Family Recipe Book below*) 🌹 Postcards from friends and relatives 🌹 School photos (portraits and class pictures) 🌹 Programs from plays or music recitals 🌹 Favorite book 🌹 Year-end letters 🌹 Christening, confirmation, and communion certificates 🌹 Special toys 🌹 Musical instrument and sheet music 🌹 Videos of milestone events (christening, first meeting with grandparents, etc.) 🌹 First boarding pass (train, airline, bus) 🌹 Fabric from a favorite dress (either child's or mom's)

Keepsakes

One person's trash is another's treasure—or so the saying goes. Keepsakes are things we love, not because they are genuinely useful or valuable but because they lift our spirits and remind us of happy times. A blanket with tattered corners, a teddy bear with one eye missing, or a worn baseball mitt all are special to their owners alone. Let your keen eye for favorite things be your guide when deciding what to keep and what to toss.

SILHOUETTES There are few things sweeter than a child's profile. Ask your child to sit still on a chair facing sideways between a light source and a wall so that her face casts a shadow on a large piece of paper you have taped to the wall. Using a soft black pencil or a marker, trace your child's silhouette onto the paper. Next, place the outlined profile on a piece of black construction paper and carefully cut through both pieces of paper along the outline. Separate the papers, and you have a silhouette. You can mount your silhouette on a white background and frame it.

Family Recipe Book

Food and family—never was there a more perfect pair. What better way to preserve memories of wonderful family gatherings than in a family recipe book? Passing family recipes down to your children helps them connect to their heritage and family traditions, especially when the origins of the recipes are described. Attaching funny or meaningful stories associated with each recipe will help paint a full picture of family life, and jog memories when your children are ready to make use of their books. Collect recipes from members of your extended family for inclusion in the book.

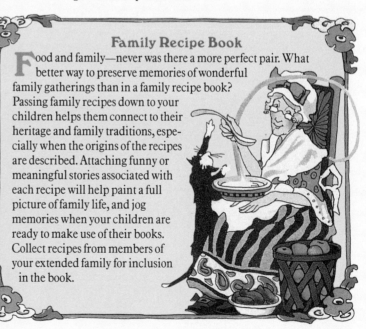

Organizing and Storing Keepsakes

Keepsakes are precious, even if only to you or your child. They are best enjoyed when well organized and carefully stored. There is certainly an art and science to saving your keepsakes for the ages. And unless you own a climate-controlled vault, you'll need some pointers on how best to store your precious belongings to keep them out of harm's way. Here are some organizational and storage tips:

- First, select categories for your keepsakes (e.g., birthdays, holidays, trips, school, etc.) or organize them chronologically. *Note: Keeping a running file for each child throughout the year can help you to easily organize the child's box at year's end.*
- Next, divide those categories into subcategories based on the medium of the keepsake, e.g., fabric, photographs, letters and cards, etc.
- Prepare each piece for storage. Letters should be unfolded, with the envelope placed behind. They should then be placed between acid-free archival papers. Do not staple or paperclip your letters. Fabric, dolls, and other textiles should be stored in a Mylar or muslin wrap. Try to avoid folding fabrics.
- Finally, store all keepsakes in archival-quality files or boxes. Two great resources for archival materials: Light Impressions (*lightimpressionsdirect.com*) and Exposures (*exposuresonline.com*).

amusement park, movie, or sporting event, a book report, a note from a secret admirer, the front page of the newspaper, a favorite magazine, a list of favorite songs, a toy, a page from a coloring book, a bulletin announcing an event your child attended, a party invitation, a shopping list, a drawing or picture of a favorite item your child can't bear to part with. Help your child decorate the capsule with lots of "KEEP OUT" signs and label it with your child's name and the date.

HANDPRINTS A baby's hands aren't the only ones worth casting, outlining, or stamping. It's fun to see your older child's hands grow. You can make castings using plaster-of-Paris molds. Or draw an outline around your child's hand on archival paper. Preschoolers love to participate in the finger-painting keepsake projects. Let them sign their art with a handprint.

TIME CAPSULES Less formal than a keepsake box, a time capsule contains whimsical items that create a snapshot in time. The idea is to fill the capsule with items that illustrate the times and then seal it until a later date—a twenty-first birthday, for example. The container can be anything from a homemade papier-mâché masterpiece to a poster tube or shoebox. Children love to brainstorm ideas for their capsules—a ticket stub from an

The Book Of Me

You could go out and buy the latest fill-in keepsake book for your child… or you could create your own. It doesn't have to be anything fancy—a spiral notebook will do the trick. Fill the notebook with questions to elicit both fun and serious responses that will help paint a picture of your child. The beginning portion can be a Mad-Libs-style story in which your child need just fill in her name, age, favorite color, favorite number, favorite food, best friends, favorite activities, and the like. Leave space for drawings and photos. It can be great fun to also include more open-ended questions tailor-made for your child's interests (e.g., Tap dancing makes me feel…). Encourage your child to decorate the cover and pages with drawings, photos, and magazine cutouts. Kids have so much fun with this project that they may ask you for another book next year!

If thou couldst know thine own sweetness,
O little one, perfect and sweet,
Thou wouldst be a child forever;
Completer whilst incomplete.

Francis Turner Palgrave

Dear Baby of Mine

Letters to Your Child

How many times have you wanted to share your thoughts and feelings about motherhood and your unique bond with your child to your son or daughter, only knowing that they're still too young to understand or appreciate what you'd like to say? Writing a letter to your child is one way to capture those sentiments as they come to mind and preserve them for future years. Choose to write one letter, or several over a period of time. As you pen your wishes for your growing baby, consider these ideas for that very special love letter.

✉ *During pregnancy, write a letter to your unborn child.* Share your experiences feeling your baby kick for the first time, seeing the ultrasound, learning the sex of your baby—or what it's like not to know. What are your hopes and dreams for your baby's future? What are your fears or concerns about parenthood? Include details about the foods you craved or special things you did to welcome your newborn home. Did you read stories or sing songs to your unborn baby? Consider adding something to the letter each month as you approach your delivery date.

✉ *Assemble a "Book of Me" from mom and dad's point of view.* Decide if your book should be a collection of letters from one year or from several. Write about developmental breakthroughs, such as learning to walk or cutting those choppers. Who were your son's first friends at the playground? When did your daughter start dance classes?

What are the things that tickle your child's fancy—favorite foods, games, or ways to wake up mom and dad on Sunday morning? Consider combining your letters with photographs in a scrapbook, using acid-free materials for best preservation.

✉ *Take time to write about what is most important to you.* If there is anything we can wish to pass down to our children, it is a set of values that we have gleaned from our own parents, family members, and community. Invite other relatives to contribute letters that impart virtues, wisdoms, and life lessons that will guide your child through life's path.

✉ *Create a collection of birthday letters.* Each year, write your child a letter that highlights the best and worst things that transpired. Whether it is your daughter's first bicycle ride without training wheels or the time your son broke his arm playing tackle football, record your hopes,

fears, and challenges of parenthood during those times. When your child finally passes into adulthood, you'll be able to bestow a birthday gift of eighteen letters for eighteen years.

✉ *Organize and store your letters.* If you're writing several letters, seal them in envelopes and label them appropriately: "Month six of my pregnancy," "On your tenth birthday," or "Grandma Millie's secrets for a long and happy life." Store the letters and artifacts you plan on presenting to your child in a box or chest that's in a cool and dry place. Look for archival quality materials at craft and stationery stores for the optimum preservation of your letters. When the time comes to share the letters with your child, your gift will be in the best possible condition and surely received with joy.

219

Once A Year Rituals

F rom that toothless grin to a mouth full of pearls, every year your little darling seems to show a lifetime's worth of changes. Birthdays and holidays are wonderful excuses to document and celebrate those changes. Create special rituals that your family can anticipate every year as ways to see how much they've grown in abilities or matured in thinking.

BIRTHDAY INTERVIEW

Record your child every year on her birthday from the time she can speak. When she is young, ask her simple questions to get her talking. How old are you? Are you having fun at the party? Did you like your presents? Which one was your favorite? What did you wish for when you blew out the candles? Every year, record her on her birthday. Ask similar questions and watch her development. By her sixth birthday, you won't have to ask the questions—she'll have her own story ready for you! This is a great way capture your child's growth in language and thought with great footage to balance out all the action shots.

FAVORITE THINGS As your child grows, so do your child's interests, hobbies, and activities. Each year, invite your child to draw up a list of favorites—books, movies, dreams, or ways to spend a Saturday afternoon. Incorporate your child's contributions into a photo journal or birthday scrapbook.

HOLIDAY ACTS Does your child love to ham it up in front of the camera? Does your son or daughter love to pick up the guitar or xylophone sticks and serenade you? Get out the tape or video recorder and document your rising stars singing, acting, or performing their favorite activities. Holidays are a great time for performances. Try staging a talent show before Thanksgiving dinner for your extended family or recording your children singing their favorite Christmas carols every year. Your recording can be as simple as taping their responses to what they are thankful for or describing what their favorite holiday present was.

GROWING INTO CLOTHES
Do you have a special dress that your daughter loves to play dress up in or see you wear? Does your son have a favorite shirt of dad's? Stage a modeling session each birthday (or for all your children on a holiday) and have your daughter wear mom's dress or your son wear dad's suit jacket and tie. Take snapshots each year of your children in those same outfits and watch the clothes miraculously seem to get smaller as your children get taller!

LITTLE THINGS Sometimes the day-to-day life occurrences that we don't give a second thought become precious memories to us later. Each year around your child's birthday, write a journal entry about the little routines, habits, customs, and traditions of your son or daughter this year. Was it the wearing baseball cap backwards year or the falling out of chair at dinner year? It could be a favorite word or expression your child discovered to describe everything, or a favorite food your child insisted on for practically every lunch.

WHAT PROGRESS! Every year your child's abilities and accomplishments grow. Last year's timid jump into the pool is this year's cannonball and next year's swan dive. What better way to record this childhood growth than with pictures, audio, and videotapes? Capture your child's progression of skills in activities like swimming, biking, skiing, or skating. End of the year recitals for dance and music are a must. You can also record something as simple as your child reading a book at the end of a school year.

Holiday Keepsakes

Family life is usually busy and full. Holidays, while filled with holiday to-do's, are usually a time when the family is together for a while. Holidays also mark the passing of time: "Another Christmas! Where has the year gone?" They are a good time to slow down and create memories to treasure. Here are a few holiday keepsake ideas:

NEW YEAR'S Even the youngest children can have New Year's resolutions. So what if three-year-old Little Henry resolves to be Spiderman or grow twelve inches this year? Keep a simple notebook that records each family member's resolutions every year. VALENTINE'S DAY Keep a box to store family valentines to each other. Young children are sure to bring home valentine creations from school. Your annual valentines to your children could include a list of things you love about your child: "because you always have peas on your nose; because you give nice hugs; because you do great somersaults..." THANKSGIVING Start a book of thanks. Ask each person: what will you give thanks for this year? How are you blessed?

Me and My Family

One of the most important gifts you can give your child is an understanding of their past. Where do they come from? Who are their ancestors? What are our family's traditions? Learning about your family history provides your child with a connection to his roots and knowledge of the forces that shaped his family's values. Nurture relationships between your children and older family members by encouraging them to discuss family history together. Children can record and illustrate stories that their grandparents tell about previous generations. There are also many tools available to help the project along from libraries, town halls, and now the Internet. Use the information to create a homemade book, scrapbook, mural, or illustrated document that can be treasured and passed on to future generations.

Grandmother Remembers

Another great way to learn about your family's history is to give something like *Grandmother Remembers: A Written Heirloom for My Grandchild* to your child's grandmother. This best-selling illustrated book provides questions for grandmother to answer that describe her life and experiences. Your child will get an intimate portrait of her grandmother who will share the wonderful memories of the past and dreams for the future with her.

Handprint Family Tree

paint (in assorted colors), paintbrush, paper plates, white cotton fabric (an old sheet works well), permanent marker, fabric glue, 12-inch-long strong stick or wooden dowel, long piece of string or ribbon

1. Paint a tree trunk with bare branches on the fabric.
2. Ask each of your children to pick out their favorite color from your selection of paints and spread a little of each color on the paper plates.
3. Working from biggest to the smallest hands, have each child dip his or her hands in their chosen paint and press them on the branches. Ask other family members—grandparents, aunts, uncles, etc.—to also get their hands dirty and make your family tree more complete.
4. Use a permanent marker to write names next to the handprints.
5. Children can paint birds, the sky, the sun, grass, and flowers to complete the scene. Let the artwork dry.
6. Fold over a few inches at the top of the fabric and glue the edge to the back to form a sleeve for your stick or dowel. When the glue is dry, slide the stick or dowel through the sleeve.
7. Tie the ribbon or string to each end of the stick to make a hanger for your masterpiece. Ask your children to find the perfect place to display your family banner.

Family Tree

notebooks, pencils, and large envelopes or plastic boxes (good for keeping the photographs, newspaper clippings, and documents you will collect)

1. The best place to start is with the family members your children know best—themselves! Help the children record their own full names, birthdays, and birthplaces using their birth certificates. Then they can record their immediate family: father, mother, brothers, and sisters.
2. From here you will move backward, one generation at a time. The children can interview cousins, aunts, and uncles, and grandparents. Encourage them to ask lots of questions and take plenty of notes. They should record marriage dates, nicknames, occupations, and interesting family stories. In the case of dead relatives, record where and when they died. Keep copies of all documentation.
3. Take your kids on an excursion to your local courthouse. They have birth, marriage, and death certificates there, and may have the information you need.
4. Your local library may keep old newspapers on microfilm. You can look in the birth and obituaries sections. The obituaries will usually list the surviving family members. Ask if they have census records for the city, too.

For those of you who want to get serious about searching out your ancestors, there are many resources available. Check online for free ancestry sources. The Social Security Death Index is also available for free online. It can give you some information and leads for those in the U.S. who were born after 1930. Another free website that is useful is *Rootsweb.com*.

5. If the person you are looking for was born after 1930, contact the Social Security office and request the records for that person. Their application forms will contain the date of birth, date of death, and names of their parents. When you finish compiling all of your historical data, you can create a chart to illustrate your family tree. There are software programs available to help the more technologically savvy family. Many programs aid in gathering information and create family tree printouts to display your findings. Try *Family Tree Maker*, Broderbund; *Family Trees Quick and Easy*, Individual Software; and *Generations Family Tree*, Broderbund.

chapter seven

The Best of Everything

A Reading-Friendly Environment

★ Make an event out of getting your child a library card and using it often.

★ Ask school and community librarians for reading lists for your child's age group.

★ Find out about your library's story time, summer reading programs, and other special events.

★ Encourage older siblings to read to younger ones.

★ Make books to read available at home that are tailored to your child's interests.

★ Keep an illustrated children's dictionary and an adult dictionary handy.

★ Make up stories together and illustrate them.

★ Use everyday outings (grocery shopping) and field trips (zoo) as opportunities to read.

★ Practice writing and penmanship with your child, as clear writing has a positive impact on learning to spell.

★ Visit a bookstore and browse with your child.

★ Check out audio books from your library for your child. This is good for reluctant readers.

★ Use books without words to spark imagination and creativity.

★ Play word games together (such as crossword puzzles; Boggle, Jr.; Scrabble; Hangman).

★ Make flashcards for vocabulary and practice spelling words together. (Flashcards are even great for babies and toddlers. Magnetic letters are fantastic for early readers.)

★ Read and write poetry together. (Suggested poets: Shel Silverstein, Arnold Adoff, Woody Guthrie, Valerie Worth.)

★ Encourage your child to keep a journal.

★ Promote letter writing to friends, family members, and pen pals.

★ Comic books, newspapers, magazines, poetry volumes, and biographies make for great reading, too. Support your child in finding different genres of material at the library.

★ Encourage kids, ages four to eight, to watch *Reading Rainbow* and *Between the Lions* (PBS).

Read! Read! Read! Books

*T*he popular baby and toddler book Read to Your Bunny *by Rosemary Wells advises, "Read to your bunny often. And...your bunny will read to you." Helping your child develop a love of reading one of the most important service you can perform as a parent. From the time your child is born, reading aloud together for twenty minutes or more every day lays the foundation for your child's reading, writing, speaking, listening, and relationship skills.*

When your child first starts reading, it is a fantastic and frustrating time. A sense of power and pride comes with each success, but getting stuck or having difficulty with comprehension can be debilitating. Remember that it's not the number of books your child plows through, but the time spent reading that counts most! Once your child is reading, your job as reading cheerleader doesn't end. Early, middle, and upper grade readers need to be immersed in a print-rich environment with continued encouragement to choose reading over television or video games. Make your home a reading-friendly environment. Happy reading to your family!

20 Books for Babies and Toddlers

Black on White and *White on Black* by Tana Hoban ▪
Bread and Jam for Frances by Russell Hoban and Lillian
Hoban ▪ *Brown Bear, Brown Bear, What Do You See?*
by Bill Martin, Jr. ▪ *Counting Kisses* by Karen Katz ▪
Freight Train by Donald Crews ▪ *Goodnight, Moon* by
Margaret Wise Brown, illustrated by Clement Hurd ▪
Guess How Much I Love You by Sam McBratney ▪
Harold and the Purple Crayon by Crockett Johnson ▪
Hop on Pop by Dr. Seuss ▪ *Hush!: A Thai Lullaby*
by Minfong Ho ▪ *Jamberry* by Bruce Degen ▪
The Little Engine That Could by Watty Piper ▪
Little Miss Spider by David Kirk ▪ *No, David!* by
David Shannon ▪ *Pat the Bunny* by Dorothy Kunhardt
So Big! by Dan Yaccarino ▪ *Sylvester and the
Magic Pebble* by William Steig ▪ *Ten, Nine, Eight* by
Molly Bang ▪ *Time for Bed* by Mem Fox, illustrated
by Jane Dyer ▪ *The Very Hungry Caterpillar*
by Eric Carle

The American Library
Association has two distinguished
awards: The Newberry Medal and The
Caldecott Medal. The Newbery Medal is awarded
annually to the author of the most distinguished con-
tribution to American literature for children. The
Caldecott Medal is awarded annually to the artist of
the most distinguished American picture book
for children. Go to *ala.org* for the lists of
winners from 1922 and 1938 to
the present.

Resources for Parents

Classics to Read Aloud to Your Children by William F.
Russell ▪ *Getting Beyond "I Like the Book": Creating
Space for Critical Literacy in K-6 Classrooms* by Vivian
Vasquez ▪ *The Read-Aloud Handbook*, 5th Ed.
by Jim Trelease ▪ *Reading Magic: Why Reading
Aloud to Our Children Will Change Their Lives
Forever* by Mem Fox

Websites

▪ *ala.org* (American Library Association)
▪ *slj.reviewsnews.com* (School Library Journal)

20 Books for Preschoolers

Are You My Mother? by P. D. Eastman ▪ *Blueberries for
Sal* by Robert McCloskey ▪ *Chicken Soup with Rice* by
Maurice Sendak ▪ *Chrysanthemum* by Kevin Henkes ▪
Corduroy by Don Freeman ▪ *Eloise* by Kay Thompson
Five Little Monkeys Jumping on the Bed by Eileen
Christelow ▪ *George and Martha* by James Marshall ▪
Green Eggs and Ham by Dr. Seuss ▪ *Harry the Dirty
Dog* by Gene Zion and Margaret Bloy Graham ▪
If You Give a Mouse a Cookie by Laura Joffe Numeroff
and Felicia Bond ▪ *JoJo's Flying Sidekick* by Brian
Pinkney ▪ *Mike Mulligan and His Steam Shovel*
by Virginia Lee Burton ▪ *The Mitten* by Jan Brett ▪
Officer Buckle and Gloria by Peggy Rathmann ▪
The Polar Express by Chris Van Allsburg ▪ *The Snowy
Day* by Ezra Jack Keats ▪ *Stellaluna* by Janell
Cannon ▪ *The Story of Ferdinand* by Munro Leaf,
illustrated by Robert Lawson ▪ *Where the Wild
Things Are* by Maurice Sendak

20 Books for Early Grade Readers

Amelia Bedelia by Peggy Parish ■ *Arthur* by Marc Brown ■ *Clifford the Big Red Dog* by Norman Bridwell ■ *Curious George* by H. A. Rey ■ *Frog and Toad Are Friends* by Arnold Lobel ■ *Good Night, Good Knight* by Shelley Moore Thomas ■ *Leo the Late Bloomer* by Robert Kraus ■ *Little Bear* by Elsa Holmelund Minarik and Maurice Sendak ■ *Madeline* by Ludwig Bemelmans ■ *The Magic School Bus* by Joanna Cole ■ *Millions of Cats* by Wanda Gag ■ *Miss Nelson Is Missing* by Harry G. Allard and James Marshall ■ *Stone Soup* by Marcia Brown ■ *The Story of Jumping Mouse* by John Steptoe ■ *Strega Nona* by Tomie De Paola ■ *Swimmy* by Leo Lionni ■ *Tar Beach* by Faith Ringgold *Tikki Tikki Tembo* retold by Arlene Mosel, illustrated by Blair Lent ■ *The Velveteen Rabbit* by Margery Williams ■ *Yoko* by Rosemary Wells

20 Books for Middle Grade Readers

Because of Winn Dixie by Kate DiCamillo ■ *Ben and Me: An Astonishing Life of Benjamin Franklin* by Robert Lawson ■ *Bud, Not Buddy* by Christopher Paul Curtis ■ *Charlotte's Web* by E. B. White ■ *The Cricket in Times Square* by George Selden ■ *The Giver* by Lois Lowry ■ *Harriet the Spy* by Louise Fitzhugh ■ *Holes* by Louis Sachar ■ *The Hundred Dresses* by Eleanor Estes ■ *Island of the Blue Dolphins* by Scott O'Dell ■ *Matilda* by Roald Dahl ■ *The Phantom Tollbooth* by Norton Juster ■ *Pippi Longstocking* by Astrid Lindgren ■ *Ramona Quimby, Age 8* by Beverly Cleary ■ *Sarah, Plain and Tall* by Patricia MacLachlan ■ *Tales of a Fourth Grade Nothing* by Judy Blume ■ *A Tree Grows in Brooklyn* by Betty Smith ■ *The Wind in the Willows* by Kenneth Grahame ■ *Winnie-the-Pooh* by A. A. Milne ■ *A Wrinkle in Time* by Madeleine L'Engle

Help! I'm Stuck!

Getting stuck on words is often discouraging. But it's important to let your child have a moment to work on figuring it out before you jump in to help—otherwise they may grow dependent on your help.

Read to Your Baby

Start with one or two well-selected books in the beginning. Something with bold black and white graphics or simple, sing-song text is good for tiny ones. Read every day. You will be amazed how soon your child will react when a familiar book is pulled out. Once your baby is hooked, try other books. A three-month-old child will show you what he likes by how long he sits still. Lay out a few book choices and your four-month-old child may reach for the one he wants you to read. He may prefer books with photographs of babies or familiar items. For harder-to-please babies, try pop-up or lift-the-flap books. I remember being grateful for my babies' love of books, especially in the pre-crawling days when it can be an effort to keep the little ones amused. There were days when each fifteen-minute session resting in bed with the little one and some books felt like a lifesaver.

20 Books for Upper Grade Readers

Alice in Wonderland by Lewis Carroll ■ *Anne of Green Gables* by L. M. Montgomery ■ *Bridge to Terabithia* by Katherine Paterson ■ *The Diary of a Young Girl* by Anne Frank ■ *Catherine Called Birdy* by Karen Cushman ■ *Hatchet* by Gary Paulsen ■ *Julie of the Wolves* by Jean Craighead George ■ *The Lion, the Witch and the Wardrobe* by C. S. Lewis ■ *Little Women* by Louisa May Alcott ■ *Maniac Magee* by Jerry Spinelli ■ *Missing May* by Cynthia Rylant ■ *National Velvet* by Enid Bagnold ■ *Out of the Dust* by Karen Hesse ■ *Roll of Thunder, Hear My Cry* by Mildred Taylor ■ *The Secret Garden* by Frances Hodgson Burnett ■ *Tuck Everlasting* by Natalie Babbitt ■ *The True Confessions of Charlotte Doyle* by Avi ■ *The View from Saturday* by E. L. Konigsburg ■ *Walk Two Moons* by Sharon Creech ■ *When Zachary Beaver Came to Town* by Kimberly Willis Holt

20 Magazines for Kids

American Girl (General Interest), *ages 9-14* ■ *Appleseeds* (Social Studies), *ages 8+* ■ *Ask* (Science), *ages 6-9* ■ *Cobblestone* (American History), *ages 9-14* ■ *Child Life* (General Interest), *ages 9-11* ■ *Click* (Reading), *ages 6-8* *Cricket* (Reading), *ages 9+* ■ *Creative Kids* (Reading/Writing/Art), *ages 5+* ■ *Highlights for Children* (Reading), *ages 2-12* ■ *Hopscotch for Girls* and *Boys' Quest* (Reading), *ages 6-12* ■ *Kids Discover Magazine* (Nature/Science), *ages 6+* ■ *Nick, Jr.* (Reading/Entertainment), *ages 2-6* ■ *National Geographic Kids* (Nature/Culture/Current Events), *ages 8-14* ■ *Chick-a-dee* (Reading), *ages 6-9* ■ *Ranger Rick* (Nature), *ages 7-13* ■ *Sports Illustrated for Kids* (Sports), *ages 8+* ■ *Stone Soup* (Reading/Writing), *ages 8-14* ■ *Time for Kids World Report edition* (Current Events), *ages 9-12* ■ *Word Dance* (Reading/Writing/Art), *ages 5-14* ■ *Zoobooks* (Reading/Nature), *ages 4-11*

10 Short Books (30 minutes or less)

Short audio selections by Weston Woods Studios and Live Oak Media are two of the best producers of young children's audio material.

Weston Woods

AGES 2-6 *Good Night, Gorilla* by Peggy Rathmann, performed by Anthony Edwards

AGES 4-8 *Click, Clack, Moo: Cows That Type* by Doreen Cronin, performed by Randy Travis; *How Do Dinosaurs Say Good Night?* by Jane Yolen; *Martin's Big Words: The Life of Dr. Martin Luther King, Jr.* by Doreen Rappaport, performed by Michael Clarke Duncan with music by Crystal Taliefero; *The Ugly Duckling* by Hans Christian Andersen, performed by Lynn Whitfield

AGES 9-12 *So You Want To Be President?* by Judith St. George, performed by Stockard Channing

Live Oak Media

AGES 4-8 *Joseph Had a Little Overcoat*, book and audio performance by Simms Taback; *Mama Don't Allow* by Thatcher Hurd, performed by Tom Chapin; *Mole Music* by David McPhail, performed by Jim Weiss; *Mufaro's Beautiful Daughters* by John Steptoe, performed by Robin Miles

20 Longer Titles

AGES 4+ *Where the Sidewalk Ends* poems and narration by Shel Silverstein; *Winnie-the-Pooh* by A. A. Milne, narrated by Charles Kuralt.

AGES 4-8 *The Just So Stories: And Other Tales* by Rudyard Kipling, narrated by Boris Karloff; *Little Bear Audio Collection* by Else Holmelund Minarik, performed by Sigourney Weaver; *Where the Wild Things Are, In the Night Kitchen, Outside Over There and Other Stories* by Maurice Sendak, performed by Tammy Grimes.

AGES 5+ *The Children's Museum of Los Angeles Presents The Wonderful Wizard of Oz: A Centennial Edition* by L. Frank Baum, performed by Robert Guillame, Phyllis Diller, et al.; *The Little Prince* by Antoine de Saint-Exupéry, performed by Richard Gere, Haley Joel Osment, et al.

AGES 7-11 *The Twits* by Roald Dahl, performed by Simon Callow; *Gone-Away Lake* by Elizabeth Enright, performed by Colleen Delany; *The Children's Shakespeare*, various narrators.

AGES 9-12 *The Tales of Uncle Remus: The Adventures of Brer Rabbit* by Joel Chandler Harris, performed by Julius Lester; *Fireside Tales: More Lessons from the Animal People*, book and performance by Dovie Thomason Sickles; *Harriet Tubman: Conductor on the Underground Railroad* by Ann Petry, performed by Peter Francis James; *Harry Potter and the Sorcerer's Stone* by J. K. Rowling, performed by Jim Dale; *Henry Huggins* by Beverly Cleary, performed by Neil Patrick Harris; *Island of the Blue Dolphins* by Scott O'Dell, performed by Tantoo Cardinal; *King Arthur and the Knights of the Round Table* by Benedict Flynn, performed by Sean Bean; *The Magician's Nephew*, part one of the Chronicles of Narnia series by C. S. Lewis, performed by Kenneth Branagh; *A Series of Unfortunate Events: The Bad Beginning* by Lemony Snicket, performed by Tim Curry ; *Sounder* by William H. Armstrong, performed by Avery Brooks.

Listen Here
Audio Books

Your local library is the best place to cull through a wide selection of great audio books. Audio books are fabulous for unsure readers to listen to as they follow along with the printed book. They are also superb on family road trips.

Shake, Rattle, & Roll Music

Even if you didn't grow up singing four-part harmonies around the piano with your family, you are still the most qualified and important music teacher your child will ever have. A parent's enthusiastic participation in a child's musical world is invaluable, from the reassuring lullaby you sing to your infant son (night after night) to the jump-rope songs you teach your eight-year-old daughter.

Hearing and touch are the initially developed senses. This means that sounds and tactile stimulation provide your baby with her first clues about the world around her. Babies are most receptive to—and actively seek out the sound of—human voices. In fact, your voice and heartbeat are the two most soothing sounds your baby knows. It is no wonder then, that a lullaby sung to a baby who is held near to his mother's heart relaxes him into a deep slumber.

Being surrounded by music is more than just soothing for your child—it's a wonderful tool to strengthen the mother-child bond— establishing a sense of security and closeness. It exercises both sides of the brain, and promotes listening, language, and coordination skills while nurturing imagination and creativity. And finally, music connects a child to his cultural roots and to those of others.

■ Make sure that music classes for very young children emphasize play and fun through imitation rather than cognitive skills and exacting lessons.
■ Make time for music in family life. This can be enriching for everyone, and is a great substitute for television and computer.
■ Keep tabs on which children's albums become Grammy nominees and winners.

10 Music-Themed Books by Age

AGES 3-7 *Baby Beluga* by Raffi, illustrated by Ashley Wolff; *Carnival of the Animal* by Saint-Saëns (Classical Music for Kids) book and CD, with commentary by Barry Carson Turner, illustrated by Sue Williams; *Down by the Bay* by Raffi, illustrated by Nadine Bernard Wescott; *Nora's Room* by Jessica Harper, illustrated by Lindsay Harper duPong; *Hip Cat* by Jonathan London, illustrated by Woodleigh Hubbard.

AGES 4-8 *Jazz Fly* by Matthew Gollub, illustrated by Karen Hanke; *Musical Instruments from A to Z* by Bobbie Kalman.

AGES 5-8 *Ella Fitzgerald: The Tale of the Vocal Virtuosa* by Andrea Davis Pinkney, illustrated by Brian Pinkney.

AGES 6-10 *Ah, Music!* by Aliki; *Sing Me a Story: The Metropolitan Opera's Book of Opera Stories for Children* by Jane Rosenberg, with an introduction by Luciano Pavarotti.

A Dozen Dream Collections

All Through the Night: Lullabies and Love Songs, Mae Robertson and Don Jackson (Lyric Partners) ■ *Baby's First Lullabies*, various classical composers (St. Clair Records) ■ *Dedicated to the One I Love*, Linda Ronstadt (Elektra) ■ *Lullabies for Little Dreamers*, Emmylou Harris et al. (Rhino Records) ■ *Lullaby: A Collection*, various artists (Music for Little People) ■ *Mellow My Baby: Soothing Songs and Lullabies*, Sherry Goffin Kondor (Sugar Beats) ■ *Mother Earth Lullaby*, various artists (Ellipsis Arts) ■ *On a Starry Night*, various artists (Windham Hill Records) ■ *Oyasumi-Goodnight: Japanese Lullabies and Restful Melodies*, various artists (Koto World) ■ *Pillow Full of Wishes*, Cathy Fink and Marcy Marxer (Rounder Records Group) ■ *Planet Sleeps*, various artists (Sony Wonder) ■ *The Rock-a-Bye Collection, Vol. 1*, Tanya Goodman Sykes (Someday Baby)

30 Playtime Albums by Age

AGES 0-2 *Baby Time Series: Play Time* (Peter Pan Records).

AGES 0-6 *Baby Beluga*, Raffi (Rounder); *Good Morning Guitar*, Ray Penney (Applewild Recordings); *Singable Songs for the Very Young*, Raffi (Rounder); *Songs for Learning*, various artists (Twin Sisters Productions); *What Kind of Cat Are You?*, Billy Jonas (Bang a Bucket).

AGES 2-5 *Elmo and the Orchestra* (Sony Wonder Audio); *Elmopalooza!*, various artists (Sony Wonder Audio); *The Gift of Make-Believe*, Ginger Sands (Laughing Sun). *Toddlers Sing Rock 'n' Roll* (Music for Little People); *Waltzing with Fireflies*, Elizabeth McMahon (Rosie Rhubarb Records); *Woody's Roundup Featuring Riders in the Sky*, Riders in the Sky (Walt Disney Records).

AGES 3-8 *1000 Pennies*, Norman Foote (Shoebox Music); *All Wound Up!*, Cathy Fink and Marcy Marxer, with Brave Combo (Rounder Select); *Can Cockatoos Count by Twos?*, Hap Palmer (Hap-Pal Music, Inc.); *Doctor Looney's Remedy*, Parachute Express (Trio Lane Records); *Goin' Wild*, Banana Slug String Band (Slug Music); *InFINity*, Trout Fishing In America (Trout Records).

AGES 6-12 *African Playground and Latin Playground*, various artists (Putumayo World Music); *All Aboard!*, John Denver (Sony Wonder Records); *Beethoven's Wig: Sing Along Symphonies* (Rounder Records); *Big Wide Grin*, Keb Mo (Sony Wonder Records); *Brown Girl in the Ring: A World Music Collection*, various artists (Music for Little People); *Celebration of America*, various artists (Music for Little People); *Around the World and Back Again*, Tom Chapin (Sony Wonder Records).

ALL AGES *Bigger than Yourself*, John McCutcheon (Rounder Kids Records); *Daddy-O Daddy!: Rare Family Songs of Woody Guthrie* (Rounder Records); *Inside Out*, Jessica Harper (Rounder Records); *Shake Sugaree*, Taj Mahal (Music for Little People); *This Land Is Your Land*, Woody and Arlo Guthrie (Rounder Records).

21 Song Games for Babies and Toddlers

Use the following songs to teach your infant or toddler about language, counting, animal sounds, weather, emotions, body parts, clapping, pantomime, and general movement.

I'm a Little Teapot (pantomime)

Itsy Bitsy Spider (pantomime)

Where Is Thumbkin? (pantomime)

Pat-a-Cake (clapping)

Pease Porridge (clapping)

Bunny Hop (exercise)

Row, Row, Row Your Boat (exercise)

The Wheels on the Bus (exercise)

Head, Shoulders, Knees, and Toes (body parts)

The Hokey Pokey (body parts)

If You're Happy and You Know It (emotions)

Alouette (French/body parts)

Frère Jacques (French)

Die Blümelein, sie schlafen (German)

La Caña (Spanish)

Five Little Monkeys (counting)

This Old Man (counting)

It's Raining; It's Pouring (weather)

Rain, Rain, Go Away (weather)

Old MacDonald Had a Farm (animals)

Alphabet Song (pre-language)

Music Games for Big Kids

Older children love words, rhyming, mimicking sounds and patterns, nonsense songs, suspense songs, playing instruments, and learning dance steps. Try some of these games and activities with your "big kids":

Ring Around the Rosy

Jack-in-the-Box, Hand-Jive

Do Your Ears Hang Low?

Skip to My Lou

London Bridge

Musical chairs

Statue/Freeze (children stop and start movement and dance with the music)

Dance with props such as scarves, ribbons, jingle-bell bracelets, batons, mirrors, etc.

Fill-in-the-blank songs (e.g. Mary Had a Little _____)

Whistling contests (children repeat a tune by whistling)

Square dancing

10 Music-Themed Videos by Age

AGES 0-3 *Baby Einstein Series: Baby Bach, Baby Beethoven, and Baby Mozart* (2000), Julie Aigner-Clark (Buena Vista Home Video); *Baby Songs* (1987), Hap Palmer (Golden Book Video).

AGES 0-6 *Kidsongs Series: Baby Animal Songs* and *I'd Like to Teach the World to Sing* (2002), (Image Entertainment, Inc.).

AGES 3-8 *The Orchestra* (1969), Peter Ustinov (Facets Video); *Tubby the Tuba* (1977, Allied Artists Entertainment Group).

AGES 6-12 *The Composer's Specials: Bach, Strauss, Bizet, Handel, Liszt, and Rossini* (2000, Hal Leonard Corporation); *Beethoven Lives Upstairs* (1992, Naxos); *Schoolhouse Rock!: The Ultimate Collector's Edition, 1973-1985* (2002, Buena Vista Home Entertainment); *Free To Be You and Me* (1974).

ALL AGES *Marlo Thomas and Friends* (Hen's Tooth Video); *Singing for Freedom* (1995); *Sweet Honey in the Rock* (Music for Little People).

10 Classic Lullabies to Sing to Your Child

All Through the Night

Hush, Little Baby

Kum-Bah-Yah

Brahms's Lullaby ("Lullaby and good night...")

Over the Rainbow

Rock-a-Bye, Baby

Sleep, Baby, Sleep

Sweet and Low

Twinkle, Twinkle Little Star

When You Wish upon a Star

Great Ideas

- Choose a favorite lullaby to sing to your child each night—or create one of your own that includes your child's name.
- Start a musical dialogue with your baby. You might be surprised that given the space for a response, your baby will joyfully fill in the gaps.
- Create your own bedtime or playtime compilations for your children from music in your collection.
- Find out about children's programming on your local radio stations.
- Attend live age-appropriate musical concerts with your children.
- Record your child singing or making sound effects. Children love to hear the sound of their own voices.
- Personalize songs whenever possible. Children, especially toddlers, delight in hearing their names in a song.
- Dance with your child.
- Take a music class with your child.
- Take musical tapes in the car for a family sing-along.
- Make a game of selecting a familiar song and intentionally make a mistake while singing it. Your child will love to correct you.
- Introduce many kinds of music to your child.
- Make everyday activities fun by adding music (e.g., dance your way to bed, or sing the dinner menu).

Off the Beaten Path

These ten kid-friendly albums rock the cradle, providing the perfect solution when you just can't bring yourself to play little Luke's Raffi CD for the 147th time.

Greasy Kid Stuff: Songs from Inside the Radio, Various Artists (Confidential Recordings) ■ *No!*, They Might Be Giants (Rounder) ■ *Ants in My Pants!*, Gunnar Madsen (G-Spot) ■ *For the Kids*, various artists (Nettwerk Records) ■ *For Our Children*, Sting et al. (Rhino Records) ■ *Great Big Sun and Yellow Bus*, Justin Roberts ■ *Night Time!*, Dan Zanes and Friends (Festival Five) ■ *Not Dogs... Too Simple (A Tale of Two Kitties)*, various artists (Casino Music) ■ *Not Just for Kids*, David Grisman and Jerry Garcia (Acoustic Disc) ■ *Songs from a Parent to a Child*, Art Garfunkel (Sony Wonder Records).

10 Fun Film Soundtracks

Chitty Chitty Bang Bang (1968), Richard M. and Robert B. Sherman (Rykodisc)

Follow That Bird (1985), Jim Henson's Muppets and the Sesame Street cast (RCA)

Jungle Book (1967), Richard M. and Robert B. Sherman (Walt Disney Records)

The Lion King (1994), Elton John and Tim Rice (Walt Disney Records)

Mary Poppins (1964), Richard M. and Robert B. Sherman (Walt Disney Records)

Singin' in the Rain (1952), Nacio Herb Brown and Arthur Freed (Rhino Records)

Snow White and the Seven Dwarfs (1937), Frank Churchill and Leigh Harline (Walt Disney Records)

The Sound of Music (1965), Richard Rodgers and Oscar Hammerstein II (RCA)

Willy Wonka and the Chocolate Factory (1971), Leslie Bricusse and Anthony Newley (Paramount Pictures Records)

The Wizard of Oz (1939), Harold Arlen and E. Y. Harburg (Rhino Records)

Movies Get Your Popcorn Here!

What could be better than snuggling up with your kids on a cold, rainy day with some popcorn and a great family film? But choosing a film that is original, creative, and suitable for your kids is not easy. You are the watchdog for what your child sees. Most parents are willing to monitor their child's viewing carefully; but they don't know where to start. Here are ideas, information and lots of recommendations.

GREAT IDEAS

Here are some ideas about how to be involved in what your children are watching, from selecting to viewing the material.

☆ Before choosing a film, get recommendations from other parents you trust.

☆ Try to preview the film first, if possible.

☆ Remember that film ratings are not always reliable.

☆ Seek out international kids films and animation to expose your child to different cultures and languages.

☆ Ask librarians and educators for advice about films that are appropriate for your child's age and stage of development.

☆ Discuss films together during or after viewing.

☆ Prepare or review themes related to a movie you watch with your child by organizing learning activities.

☆ Be aware that movie theaters can have their own policies on how they wish to follow the MPAA ratings (for example… *anyone can buy a ticket to a PG-13 movie*).

☆ Call the local movie theater for more specific information and guidelines on age-appropriateness for a particular film.

☆ Check your local library for short subjects that can include early reader books made into videos.

☆ Role model through your own behavior. If your child knows that you watch rough films, they will not be able to take your rules for them very seriously.

☆ Encourage children to read the book that a film is based on.

☆ Even if you've screened the film your children are watching, try to be there to answer questions.

☆ Keep tabs on those films that are winning Academy Awards in the animation categories.

☆ Beware of different age appropriateness within the same series.

Off the Beaten Path

Don't overlook the wonderful selection of international children's films. Some of the very best children's films are created outside of the United States, including those by Hayao Miyazaki (Japan) and Nick Park (United Kingdom). Here is a select list of their best films for kids:

Miyazaki: *Castle in the Sky* (1986), *My Neighbor, Totoro* (1988), *Kiki's Delivery Service* (1989)

Park: *Creature Comforts* (1990), *A Grand Day Out* (1991), *The Wrong Trousers* (1993), *A Close Shave* (1995), *Chicken Run* (2000)

Best Bedtime Videos

Goodnight Moon and Other Sleepytime Tales (2000) HBO Studios

Little Bear: Goodnight Little Bear (1998) Paramount Studio

Nighty Night (2000) Parade

12 Series Recommendations

AGES 0-3 *Baby Einstein* (Buena Vista Home Video); *So Smart!* (Baby School Company); *Brainy Baby* (Brainy Baby)

AGES 2-5 *Little Bear* (Paramount Home Video); *Maisy* (Universal Studios); *Richard Scarry* (Sony Wonder); Sesame Street (Sony Wonder)

AGES 3-6 *The Berenstain Bears* (Columbia TriStar),

AGES 3-9 *Zoboomafoo* (PBS Home Video)

AGES 4-8 *Magic School Bus* (A Vision)

AGES 5-14 *Getting to Know the World's Greatest Artists* (Kiki & Associates)

AGES 7-14 Owl/TV Series 1-6 (Owl Television, Inc.)

Teaching Tools

AGES 0-18 MONTHS *Baby See 'N Sign* (2001) Karen Kronz Faber

AGES 6-36 MONTHS *Talking Hands: A Sign Language Video for Children* (2000) Small Fry Productions

AGES 0-4 *Baby-Know-It-All: Lil' Bloomer* (2001) Tapeworm; *Baby-Know-It-All: Smartypants* (2001) Tapeworm

AGES 1-3 *It's Potty Time* (1990) Learning Through Entertainment; *Once Upon a Potty for Him/Her* (1990) Barron's Educational

AGES 2-4 *All By Myself "Getting Dressed," vol. 1* (2002) Ladybug Productions

AGES 2-5 *Blue's Clues: All Kinds of Signs* (2001) Paramount

AGES 3-8 *All By Myself "Taking Care of My Pet," vol.2* (2002) Ladybug Productions

10 Videos for Babies and Toddlers

AGES 0-1 *My Grandbaby and Me* (2003) My Baby and Me Exercise

AGES 0-3 *Child Smart: Your Tiny Jungle Tot* (2002) Warner Home Video

AGES 2-4 *Blue's Clues: ABC's and 123's* (1998) Paramount Video

AGES 2-5 *The Adventures of Curious George* (2001) United American Video; *Dr. Seuss: Dr. Seuss' ABC* (1991) Sony Wonder; *George and Martha* (2000) Sony Wonder; *Spot: Spot Goes to the Farm* (1993) Disney Studios

AGES 2-6 *Maggie and the Ferocious Beast: Adventures in Nowhere Land* (2003), Columbia Tristar Home Video; *Thomas & Friends: Salty's Secret & Other Thomas Adventures* (2002) Anchor Bay Entertainment;

AGES 2-8 *Winnie the Pooh and Tigger Too* (1974) Disney Studios

Babies begin to show sustained interest in television at about fourteen months. Limited exposure to high quality programs can be enjoyable and rewarding for toddlers.

Top 10 Christmas Classics for Families

A Charlie Brown Christmas (1965) Paramount Studios
A Christmas Carol (1951) United Home Video
A Christmas Story (1983) Warner Studios
How the Grinch Stole Christmas (1966) Warner Studios
It's a Wonderful Life (1947) Republic Studios
Miracle on 34th Street (1947) Twentieth Century Fox
A Muppet's Christmas Carol (1992) Disney Home Video
Rudolph the Red-Nosed Reindeer (1964) Sony Music (Video)
Santa Claus Is Comin' to Town (1970) Sony Music (Video)
The Year without a Santa Claus (1974) Warner Studios

Unreliable Ratings

Since 1968, the Motion Picture Association of America (MPAA) has been assigning ratings to films—G, PG, PG-13, R, and NC-17—as part of a voluntary rating system. But these ratings often lack sufficient information for parents to make good choices about which films contain offensive material. Selecting age-appropriate films for your children can, therefore, be dicey business. Even G movies—though devoid of violence, sex, drugs, swearing, and crude comments—can still be at odds with a family's values. So what is a parent to do? Critics, Inc., a company based out of Cincinnati, vows to make your life easier by giving you "Movie Ratings that Really Work" at kids-in-mind.com. For a nominal fee, you can tap into their database of parent reviews and see what a film is rated using what the company touts as "objective, non-critical assessments." You can also try *Film Values/ Family Values: A Parent's Guide* by H. Arthur Tanssig, Ph.D or *familyvalues.com*.

Top 10 Animated Features

Charlotte's Web (1973) Paramount Studios
Chicken Run (2000) Universal Studios
Finding Nemo (2003) Disney/Pixar
The Iron Giant (1999) Warner Home Video
James and the Giant Peach (1996)
Buena Vista Home Video
The Lion King (1994) Buena Vista Home Video
Snow White and the Seven Dwarfs (1937)
Buena Vista Home Video
Spirited Away (2002) Buena Vista Home Video
Toy Story (1995) Buena Vista Home Video
Toy Story II (1999) Buena Vista Home Video

10 Family Classics

AGES 4+ *Willy Wonka and the Chocolate Factory* (1971) Warner Home Video

AGES 5+ *The Adventures of Robin Hood* (1938) Warner Home Video; *National Velvet* (1944) Warner Studios; *The Red Balloon* (1956) Vision Home Entertainment

AGES 5-12 *Chitty Chitty Bang Bang* (1971) MGM/United Artists

AGES 5-15 *Mary Poppins* (1964) Walt Disney Home Video

AGES 8+ *Duck Soup* (1933) Image Entertainment; *The Sound of Music* (1965) Fox Home Entertainment; *To Kill a Mockingbird* (1962) Universal Studios; *The Wizard of Oz* (1939) Warner Studios

10 Destined-to-Become Family Classics

AGES 2-8 *The Adventures of Milo and Otis* (1989) Columbia TriStar Studios

AGES 5+ *Babe* (1995) Universal Studios; *Stuart Little* (1999) Columbia TriStar Studios

AGES 6+ *The Way Home* (2002) Paramount Home Video

AGES 8+ *The Adventures of Barron Munchausen* (1989) Columbia TriStar Studios; *Back to the Future* (1985) Universal Studios; *The Black Stallion* (1979) MGM/United Artists Studios; *The Princess Bride* (1987) MGM/United Artists Studios; *E. T.: The Extra-Terrestrial* (1982) Universal Studios; *The Secret of Roan Inish* (1995) Columbia TriStar Studios

Babes in Toyland Toys

Toys and childhood go hand-in-hand. A snuggly stuffed animal helps your littlest one feel secure in the crib. Mastering a shape sorter is a big event in your toddler's world! Your preschooler's first puppet show is home movie material. You are bowled over when your third grader beats you at Scrabble (well... Scrabble, Jr.). Milestones all. Shouldn't the toys you choose be worthy of their starring role in your child's life? Here's help in searching out the good ones.

Be sure to check for toy recalls through the Consumer Product Safety Commission (CPSC) at: *cpsc.gov*.

Five Important Toy Buying Tips

1 *Think Fun!* Perhaps the most important factor in toy buying is your child's interests. The toy should be fun and stimulating for your child. Parents naturally gravitate toward toys that promise accelerated development. Remember, however, that a child rarely learns from toys that aren't fun!

2 *Age Appropriateness:* By and large, product labels are remarkably accurate when pinpointing the suitable age range for toys. This age range covers both issues of keeping the child's interests and safety.

3 *Variety Is the Spice of Life:* A good mix of make-believe toys, art and crafts supplies, construction toys, musical toys, and toys that promote fine and gross motor skill development will help keep your child's interest while expanding their growth. The best toys

also offer multiple uses that will spark your child's creativity.

4 *Safety First:* Check product labels to see if it meets safety requirements. Also, check the toy to make sure there are no broken parts, leaking batteries, sharp edges, or small parts that might be swallowed. Make sure the toy is durable enough for the child. When your child is playing with it, make certain that it is used as intended. If parental supervision is required, provide it or don't get the toy. Toys for little ones should be of the appropriate size and have non-toxic finishes. Eyes on stuffed animals should be sewn on, and there should be no ribbons or strings longer than twelve inches.

5 *The Price Must Be Right:* The price should match the product. With all the choices in toys, you can afford to be picky and get your money's worth.

Your house can be filled to the brim with toys, toys, and more toys and your nine-month-old child is more interested in playing with your cell phone. In the first year, babies progress so rapidly that something that catches their fancy in the morning is tossed aside by evening. A dozen or so well-chosen pieces purchased over the first year can be plenty. Your pre-toddler is more interested in their favorite "toy"—you.

Toy Chest

Toy boxes and chests are rarely safe for children. They are loaded with hazards such as lids that can slam down, sharp corners and edges, splinters, and, locking latches. Better bets for toy storage and organization are open bins, low toy shelves, or an open wicker hamper.

Best Bets for Babies

Babies love toys that stimulate the senses. The best toys at this age make gentle and pleasing sounds, have soft and varied textures, and are decorated with appealing graphic patterns. Baby-safe mirrors, rattles, mobiles, musical toys, and activity gyms are all great first toys for infants. Look for toys that help develop hand-eye coordination, hone gross and fine motor skills, teach about cause and effect, help a baby discover colors and shapes, encourage exploration of spatial relationships, and promote social and language development.

0-7 MONTHS Kick and Play Bouncer by Fisher-Price; Toy Bar by Children on the Go (fits Graco car seats)

3-18 MONTHS Soft Busy Blocks by Earlyears

4-12 MONTHS Ultrasaucer Activity Center by Evenflo

6 MONTHS + Piro Teether/Rattle by Haba; Soft Blocks by Galt Toys, Squish Classic by Pappa Geppetto's Toys

AGES 0-1 Nursery Verse Mobile and Baby Bed Bugs Mobile by North American Bear Company; Learning Patterns Changing Sensations Mobile by Fisher-Price, Animal Sounds Pals by The First Years; Lyrical Lion by Sassy; Flatso Farm by North American Bear Company; PlayAbout Kingdom by Little Tikes; Bell Rattle by BRIO Discovery Toys, Gymini Super Deluxe Lights & Music 3-D Activity Gym by Tiny Love

AGES 0-2 Me in the Mirror by Sassy, Rattle and Teether Gift Set (six toys) by Sassy; Teether Babies (It's a teether, rattle, and toy in one!) by Munchkin

AGES 0-3 Gymfinity by Today's Kids; Whoozit! (Rattle/Mirror/Textures/Squeaks/Crinkles) by Manhattan Toy; Music Box Bunny/Lamb/Bear/Dog by Käthe Kruse

Top Toys for Toddlers

Toddlers live to play! In fact, play is the primary way that a toddler learns about his/her world. It is their equivalent to work. Toddlers play detective with all new objects; climb on anything and everything they can; love to play, hear, and dance to music; stack and knock down blocks; create art; and engage in pretend play. Some great toys for this age are push and pull toys, riding toys, balls, blocks, crayons, finger paints, musical toys, dexterity toys, toy dishes, pretend food, play houses and dolls, stuffed animals, toy phones, toy cars, puppets, and puzzles.

9 MONTHS + Discover Sounds (Play Store, Kitchen, or Workshop) by Little Tikes

18 MONTHS + Play Car Set by Travel Town; Squeak E. Mouse Gets Dressed by Earlyears; Pound-a-Ball by Small World Toys

AGES 1-2 Sounds on the Farm by Puzzliblilties; Large Farm Jumbo Knob Puzzle by Lights, Camera, Interaction!; Musical Bear Pull-Toy by Eden; Busy Park Playground by Battat/*Parent's* Magazine

AGES 1-3 Jester Jack-in-the-Box by Schylling; Flip 'n' Play Table by Chicco; Marble Train (*Note: marbles cannot be removed*) by KidStation; Ryan's Room Push Along Block Cart by Small World Toys; Things I Know Tot Tower by eeBoo; My First Lunchbox and My First Toolbox Toy by Kids II; Plush Stacking Toy: Shep by Haba; Charlton Baby Driver 2 Trike

AGES 1-4 Chiccoland Treehouse by Chicco; Cosmosphere by Hands on Toys

Pretend Play

AGES 2-7 Aquini Drink 'n' Wet Baby by Gotz Dolls; It's 2 Cute Ryan's Room (dollhouse) by Small World Toys

AGES 3-6 Jolly Dolly by Zapf Creations; Small Miracles: Let's Pretend Careers Costumes by Learning Curve International

AGES 3-7 Madeline Poseable Doll by Eden

AGES 3-12 FeltKids, FeltHouse, and Story Pieces Collection, Learning Curve International; Puppet Theater by Folkmanis

AGES 4-8 Theatre Stories by Lego, ages 4-8

AGES 6-10 Bendos Camper by Kid Galaxy, ages 6-10

ALL AGES Folkmanis Puppets (pets and bugs are big!)

Arts and Crafts/Creativity Toys

AGES 3-5 My First Desk by Alex

AGES 4-8 Color Workshop Blopens Magic Color Change Kit by P&M Products USA; Lite Brite Cube by Hasbro

AGES 6-10 Gee-Perz! Great Projects to Share by S&S Worldwide; Clip Crafts by Basic Fun

AGES 8-12 Crayola Crayon Maker by Binney & Smith

Resources for Parents

Dr. Toy's Smart Play: How to Raise a Child with a High P.Q. by Stevanne Auerbach, Dr. Toy ■ *Earth Friendly Toys: How to Make Fabulous Toys and Games from Reusable Objects* by George Pfiffners Sons ■ *Oppenheim Toy Portfolio, 2003: The Best Toys, Books, Videos, Music, and Software for Kids*, Stephanie Oppenheim, et al. ■ *Toys, Play, and Child Development* by Jeffrey H. Goldstein

Construction Toys

AGES 0-3 Cubee Tunnels by PAKA Preschool Products

AGES 2+ Bob the Builder Play-Doh Playset by Hasbro; Bob the Builder Clock Tower by Lego

AGES 3+ Airport, Parking Garage, or Tree House by Brio; Lego Explore: Lego Systems Traffic City: Mountain Action Figure 8 Set by Brio; Thomas & Friends Conductor's Figure 8 Set by Learning Curve

AGES 3-5 Name Train by Maple Landmark Woodcraft; Thomas & Friends Down by the Docks Train Set by Learning Curve International

AGES 3-10 Geomag by Plastwood Corporation

AGES 4-8 3186-Airport by Playmobil

AGES 5-10 Atollo Sa120 Building Kit by Atollo Systems; Mega Tube Traxx by Battat

AGES 6+ Monorail Start Set by Rokenbok

AGES 8-10 Kids Workshop EZ Build Projects by Action Products International

AGES 8-13 Air-Musement Park by Discovery Toys

Musical Toys

Music toys are a hit with any age group. Instruments tend to be more popular than sound equipment or kits.

AGES 6 MONTHS-2 Octotunes by Lamaze

AGES 0-6 Mozart Magic Cube and Sing with Me Mozart Magic Cube by Munchkin

AGES 2-5 Squeeze Me Music Soft Piano by Rising Stars Toys

AGES 2-7 Maestro Music Blocks by Neurosmith

AGES 3-6 Sing Along Microphone by LeapFrog

AGES 3-8 Musini by Neurosmith

AGES 4-7 Tuff Stuff Stereo CD Player by KIDdesigns, Inc.

AGES 6-13 Radio DJ by Wild Planet

Puzzles and Games

AGES 2+ Block Puzzles by Magic Sound Blocks

AGES 3-5 Honey Bee Tree by International Playthings; Clifford the Big Red Dog Wooden Shape Sorter, Scholastic Entertainment

AGES 4-12 Scramble Squares Puzzles by b. dazzle

10 Toys that Teach

AGES 4-12 Young Scientists Club Science Kits Curriculum by Young Scientists Club

AGES 5-7 Talking Clever Clock and Workbook by Learning Resources; Wraps (e.g. Kindergarten Early Words) by Klutz

AGES 5-8 Knights of Knowledge by Vtech Electronics

AGES 6-12 Playstages Theater Set by Playstages Incorporated

AGES 7+ LeapPad Pro by LeapFrog

AGES 8-13 Digital Blue QX3 Microscope by Intel; GeoSafari USA Search by Educational Insights; Electronic Snap Circuit by Elenco Electronics

AGES 10-12 Zome DNA Kit by Zometool

20 Fun Board Games

AGES 3-6 Candy Land by Milton Bradley; Cariboo by Cranium; Chutes and Ladders by Milton Bradley; My First Amazing Game Board Book by Innovative Kids; The Original Memory Game by Milton Bradley

AGES 4-7 Fun-in-a-Box: The Dr. Seuss Matching Game by University Games

AGES 4-12 LEGO Creator Deluxe Game by Warren Industries; Lewis and Clark Bingo by Lucy Hammett Games

AGES 5+ Checkers; Chess; Dominoes

AGES 5-10 Scrabble, Jr. by Hasbro; There's a Growly in the Garden by Family Pastimes; RohSzamBo by Lolo Company

AGES 5-12 Seven Horses of the Redfly Sacred Circle by Redfly; The Touch Game by Anthony Innovations

AGES 7-12 Proverbial Wisdom, Jr. by Proverbial Wisdom; Gobblet by Blue Orange Game

AGES 8-12 I Spy Rhyme-A-Thon Game by Briarpatch

AGES 10-12 Time's Up by R&R Games

20 Low-tech Toys that Score High Marks

What is it about some low-tech toys that make them perennial favorites? In today's hugely competitive toy market, standing the test of time speaks volumes about a toy. Though most kids love the bells and whistles of the latest toys, some find them over stimulating. It's good for them to take time with puzzles, playing cards, and low-tech toys. The following classic toys make the list of old standbys:

Bubble Pipe	LEGOS
Dollhouse	Lincoln Logs
Erector Set	Marbles
Etch-A-Sketch	Mr. & Mrs. Potato Head
Frisbee	Play Doh
Gyroscope	Silly Putty
Hula Hoop	Slinky
Jacks	Tinkertoys
Jump Rope	Top
Kaleidoscope	Yo-Yo

Mysteries Unveiled

Does navigating the vast sea of children's game and educational software titles leave you feeling in over your head? Don't despair. Here are tips and titles to help you make the right choices in fun, educational, age appropriate software for your kids.

Art

AGES 3+ *KaleidoDraw*, Protazone, Inc.

AGES 3-6 *Blue's Art Time Activities*, Humongous Entertainment

AGES 4+ *Kid Pix Deluxe 3rd Edition*, Broderbund; *Krazy Art Room*, GuruForce, Inc.; *Flying Colors v.2.11*, Magic Mouse Productions

AGES 8+ *HyperStudio 4*, Knowledge Adventure

Tips for Choosing Children's Software

Make sure your child is ready. Most children under the age of 2 don't derive much benefit from computer play—they fair better with tangible toys and direct interaction with others. ▪ *Match the software to your child's interests.* Fun and learning go hand-in-hand , especially for younger kids. Your children will get more out of something that piques their interest than software that meets your educational expectations. ▪ *Research the programs before you buy.* Use recommendations from other parents, lists like ours, and reviews on parenting websites (*see page 250*). Also, check the Entertainment Software Ratings Board (ESRB) rating for the software you are buying on the box or at *esrb.org* to gauge the age appropriateness of the product. ▪ *Select games with multiplayer options.* This will cut down the amount of time your child is isolated while at the computer. ▪ *Recognizable characters don't guarantee quality.* Resist the temptation to buy a software title based on the licensed characters you see on the box. Not all licensed software programs live up to their book, TV, or movie predecessors. ▪ *Beware of out-of-date technology.* Check the copyright date of the game before you buy. If it is more than two years old, it may be eons behind the current technology.

Foreign Langues

AGES 4+ *Muzzy: The BBC Language Course*, DVD edition in French, Early Advantage, LLC

AGES 6-10 *Kids! Spanish*, Syracuse Language Systems; *KidSpeak 10-in-1* (Chinese, Spanish, French, Portuguese, Japanese, German, Italian, Hebrew, Indonesian, and Korean) Language Learning, Transparent Language

General Interest Learning Games

AGES 2-5 *Peanuts: Where's the Blanket Charlie Brown?*, Tivola Publishing; *Fisher-Price Little People Discovery Airport*, Knowledge Adventure; *LEGO Preschool: My Style*, CD Access International; *Bob the Builder: Bob Builds a Park*, THQ; *Educator's Choice Numbers and Letters Excelerator*, TOPICS Entertainment

AGES 3-6 *Preschool Excelerator*, TOPICS Entertainment; *Putt Putt Travels Through Time*, Atari; *Blue's Clues Play Time*, Humongous Entertainment; *Wizmo's Workshop: The Dragons of Frozzbokk*, Infogames

AGES 4+ *Piglet's Big Games*, Disney Interactive

AGES 5-7 *Dr. Seuss's ABC*, The Learning Company

AGES 6-10 *Powerpuff Girls Mojo Jojo's Clone Zone*, Riverdeep/The Learning Company

History and Geography

AGES 6-10 *The Oregon Trail*, 5th Edition, The Learning Company

AGES 8-12 *Where in the World is Carmen Sandiego?*, Riverdeep/The Learning Company

Logic

AGES 3-6 *Curious George Downtown Adventure*, Knowledge Adventure; *Ollo and the Sunny Valley Fair*, Hulabee Entertainment

AGES 5-8 *StarFlyers: Alien Space Chase*, Riverdeep/The Learning Company; *StarFlyers: Royal Jewel Rescue*, Riverdeep/The Learning Company

AGES 5-10 *I Spy Series*, Scholastic New Media, *Moop and Dreadly: The Treasure on Bing Bong Island*, Plaid Banana Entertainment

AGES 7+ *Hoyle Puzzle Games 2003*, Vivendi; *SPY Fox: Operation Ozone*, Humongous Entertainment

AGES 8+ *ClueFinders Series*, Riverdeep/The Learning Company; *Learn to Play Chess with Fritz and Chesster*, Tivola Electronic Publishing, Inc.

Math

AGES 5+ *The Quarter Mile Math, Levels 1, 2, and 3*, Barnum Software

AGES 5-6 *Math 1*, School Zone Interactive

AGES 6-8 *Math 2 and Math 3: Time, Money, & Fractions*, School Zone Interactive

AGES 6-10 *Mia's Math Adventure: Just in Time!*, TOPICS Entertainment; *GeoSafari Knowledge Pads: Addition & Subtraction*, Beginning Math, Educational Insights; *On-Track: Multiplication & Division 3-4*, School Zone Interactive

AGES 8-12 *Math Arena*, Sunburst Communications

Music

AGES 4+ *Mozart's Magic Flute the Music Game*, Music Games International; *Tchaikovsky's Nutcracker the Music Game*, Music Games International

AGES 6+ *Dolphin Don's Music School*, Dolphin Don

Set a limit on the total amount of "screen time" your kids spend per day. This time should cover television, computers, and movies combined. Two hours is a good target, especially for young children.

Reading & Writing

AGES 3-6 *Zoboomafoo Animal Alphabet*, Brighter Child Interactive; *Curious George Reading and Phonics*, Knowledge Adventure

AGES 4-8 *FlashAction Phonics Made Easy*, School Zone Interactive, *Help Me 2 Learn Phonics 1a-Vowel Sounds*, Help Me 2 Learn Company; *Help Me 2 Learn Phonics 2b-Consonant Sounds*, Help Me 2 Learn Company

AGES 5-12 *Educator's Choice Language Excelerator*, TOPICS Entertainment

AGES 6-10 *The Little Prince*, Viva Media; *Mia's Reading Adventure: The Search for Grandma's Remedy*, TOPICS Entertainment

AGES 8-15 *Journal Zone* (web-based writing journal tool), Logo Computer Systems, Inc.

Reference

AGES 5+ *Internet EZKidWeb* (web page maker), KidWeb LLC

AGES 10+ *World Book Multimedia Encyclopedia, 2003*, World Book

Science

AGES 4-8 *Millie Meter's Nutrition Adventure*, Viva Media

AGES 6-10 *Mia's Science Adventure: Romaine's New Hat*, TOPICS Entertainment, *Starry Night Backyard 4.X*, Space Software

Sports

AGES 5+ *Tiger Woods PGA Tour 2003*, Electronic Arts; *Backyard Baseball*, Infogrames; *Backyard Football*, Infogames; *Backyard Soccer*, Infogames

Resources for Parents

Complete Sourcebook on Children's Interactive Media, 2002, Volume 10 by Warren Buckleitner ■ *Media Violence and Children: A Complete Guide for Parents and Professionals* by Douglas Gentile ■ *Young Kids and Computers: A Parent's Survival Guide, First Edition* by Ellen L. Wolock. ■ *childrenssoftware.com* ■ *smartkidssoftware.com*

The Internet Websites for Kids & Mom

There are zillions of sites in the vastness of cyberspace, and we've plowed through them all (well, almost) to bring you the best of the best. The most popular and useful sites on the Web are chock-full of information and fun for the kids, and parenting help and hints for mom. Kids can get homework help, do an interactive science experiment, or follow weekly news stories from young reporters. Busy moms can gather the information they need in a pinch or simply get a recipe for tonight's dinner. So here are the outstanding sites—the ones that are safe, educational, and entertaining for the whole family-to explore and enjoy.

Art

KINDER ART For a more hands-on approach, check out the ideas on the Kinder Art website. They provide endless creative ideas for everything from how to make edible clay to beautiful crackle-painted drawings. A perfect website to encourage your budding Monet. *kinderart.com*

NGA KIDS The National Gallery of Art in Washington, D.C. has a great website for children that will help them explore works of art in fun, interactive ways. Learn about sculpture or painting and make some of your own art online. *nga.gov/kids*

Cooking & Food

ALL RECIPES Billing itself as a "worldwide community cookbook," All Recipes contains ranked and reviewed recipes and meal ideas in almost every cuisine imaginable. Use the Nutri-Planner with your children to plan healthy and delicious meals the whole family will love. *allrecipes.com*

EPICURIOUS Cooking is a great skill to share with your children. Don't be afraid—making a great meal together is as easy as reading a recipe. Epicurious is loaded with delicious ideas, some more complex than others, and you will never be at a loss for dinner ideas again. *epicurious.com*

Family Games & Fun

IKNOWTHAT Filled with educational tools and games, this site is as entertaining for younger kids as it is for their parents. Check out interactive games that will help your kids learn about math, science, art, and engineering—she'll have so much fun playing around that your child won't even realize she's learning. *iknowthat.com*

THEPUZZLEFACTORY When you have a long rainy day ahead of you, show your kids this site. It's full of jigsaw puzzles, memory games, and even online coloring books for younger children. *thepuzzlefactory.com*

History

THE HISTORY CHANNEL The cable network also sponsors an online classroom section containing educational exhibits to help your kids learn more about important historical figures and events. *historychannel.com/classroom/classroom.html*

NATIONAL GEOGRAPHIC The website connected with this renowned magazine offers a kids' section, homework help, and lots of useful historical interactive features. Take a trip through the Underground Railroad and make

Top Parenting Websites

As a new parent, it's great to have online resources to turn to when you need a little objective advice, other parents' thoughts on a new toy, or an inventive educational activity for your little one. Turn to these top sites on the Web for new ideas, treasured traditions, and fun family projects.

babycenter.com
childfun.com
familyeducation.com
forparentsbyparents.com
iparenting.com, momtomom.com
npin.com (National Parent Information Network)
parenthoodweb.com
parents.com
parentsoup.com
parentsplace.com
practicalparent.org
positiveparenting.com
theparentreport.com

your way to freedom, or experience the panic of the Salem Witch trials. *nationalgeographic.com/homework/*

NATIONAL MUSEUM OF AMERICAN HISTORY Here you can explore fascinating historical exhibits online and learn more about the events that shaped our nation's history. View the virtual exhibits and discover everything from the plight of the Japanese in American internment camps, to the history of the flag, to the advent of the American conservation movement. *americanhistory.si.edu/*

News

SCHOLASTIC NEWS This is a fantastic kid-oriented news website that presents timely current events issues, special in-depth reports, entertainment, and sports—all aimed at the pre-teen set. *teacher.scholastic.com/scholastic-news/index.asp*

TIME FOR KIDS Your weekly source of news and information now has an online counterpart for your kids. There are pertinent news stories, research tools, and even articles by Time's kid reporters. *timeforkids.com*

Science and Math

COOLMATH4KIDS Bright colors and animated graphics will keep your kids interested while they brush up on their math skills. Be sure to check out the Lemonade Stand, and watch as your children use their number knowledge to become business tycoons. *coolmath4kids.com*

EXPLORE SCIENCE This is an excellent interactive website with fantastic animated experiments and cool problems to solve that will get your kids excited about science and math. *explorescience.com*

EXTREME SCIENCE Here you and your child can explore the ex-tremes of nature, weather, time, and space on this interactive site. Want to know what the biggest bug is? What makes up a tornado? How the space station works? You'll find it here! *extreme-science.com*

Search Engines

ASK JEEVES FOR KIDS The benefit of this search engine is that it lets you phrase your search in the form of a question, for example "Why is the sky blue?" Jeeves will get back to you with possible answers to your questions, and you can click on the links to learn more. Ask Jeeves also boasts easy-to-use Study Tools, such as an online dictionary, thesaurus, and almanac. *ajkids.com*

LYCOS ZONE In addition to being a great kid-friendly search engine, Lycos Zone offers homework help, book information, attention-grabbing graphics, and fun games. *lycoszone.lycos.com*

YAHOOLIGANS This website is just for kids, packed with all the information they need: homework help, games, interesting facts, and tons of fun and safe downloads. *yahooligans.com*

Sports

THE OLYMPICS If your child wants to learn more about the next Olympic games, log on to this website and check out the plans. Kids can learn all about the sports included in both the summer and winter games, along with qualifying events and bios of their favorite athletes. *olympics.com*

Serious Internet explorers can arm themselves with Net Mom's Internet Kids and Family Yellow Pages, *by Polly Jean Armour. It lists hundreds of family-friendly websites that are educational, fun, and worth visiting with children.*

Family Magazines

For those who would rather flip through a magazine than surf the Web, try these top publications:

- ***American Baby; Baby Years; Child; Parenting; Parents*** For information on pregnancy, health, family finance, style and parenting advice, these magazines offer a monthly dose of knowledge moms need.
- ***Family Fun*** With an emphasis on activities, crafts, party planning, and travel, it offers tons of creative ideas to share with your family.
- ***Martha Stewart Kids*** and ***Martha Stewart Baby*** Martha Stewart is putting her touches on family life with her beautifully designed magazines, offering family-oriented style, crafts, recipes, and advice.
- ***Scholastic Parent and Child*** An educationally focused magazine, Scholastic Parent and Child presents ways to make learning enjoyable for you and your kids.
- ***Working Mother*** This magazine targets the millions of women trying to balance their professional and home lives.

This book is dedicated to my mother and my husband. It is through their love, care, and support of me and my little ones that my life is blessed and filled with work and family.

Special thanks to Sara Baysinger, a dedicated and talented perfectionist who worked tirelessly on her text while one-year-old Zachary slept; and to Wendy Wax, who saved our schedule by delivering her text quickly and brilliantly while three-year-old Jonah was at preschool. —A.W.

Published in 2004 by Welcome Books®, an imprint of Welcome Enterprises, Inc.
6 West 18th Street, New York, NY 10011 · (212) 989-3200; Fax (212) 989-3205
www.welcomebooks.biz

Publisher: Lena Tabori   *Project Director:* Alice Wong   *Designers:* Timothy Shaner and Christopher Measom
Text Contributors: Sara Baysinger, Bethany Cassin Beckerlegge, Kristen Behrens, Megan Elias, Monique Petersen, Sasha Perl-Raver, Wendy Wax, and Alice Wong   *Project Assistants:* Walaimas Cherdmethawut, Nicholas Liu, and Lawrence Chesler

Distributed to the trade in the U.S. and Canada by Andrews McMeel Distribution Services
Order Department and Customer Service toll-free: (800) 943-9839; Orders-only fax: (800) 943-9831

Library of Congress Cataloging-in-Publication Data on file.

ISBN 1-932183-00-0

Printed in Hong Kong

FIRST EDITION

1 3 5 7 9 10 8 6 4 2

ILLUSTRATION CREDITS Cover: Charlotte Becker; p. 1, 21, 63, 84, 196, 197B, 209A, 212, 213A, 222A: C. M. Burd; p. 2, 142: L. Clarkson; p. 3: Edna Cooke; p. 7, 106: Kate Greenaway; p. 16: Torre Bevaus; p. 18, 49: Lucile Patterson; p. 13: Agnes Richardson; p. 22, 25, 52: Vernon Thomas; p. 26A: Beatrice Mallet; p. 27B, 60A, 132, 134, 164A, 181, 192, 197A, 226, 232: Jessie Willcox Smith; p. 28: S. G. Hulme Beaman; p. 30: G. F. Christie; p. 32: Alice Beach Winter; p. 33B, 200B, 217A: Frances Brundage; p. 35, 58A, 206A, 209B: Rose O'Neill; p. 38: Maud Tausey Fangel; p. 41A: A. Bertigla; p. 50: B. Cory Kilvert; p. 51: Adina Sand; p. 57, 100, 141A, 216A, 229: Pauli Ebner; p. 68: Cyril Cowell; p. 72: Maxfield Parrish; p. 73: G. G. Drayton; p. 75, 111, 173: Maud Humphrey; p. 77, 115A: Maginel Wright Barney; p. 78A, 86, 154: E. Curtis; p. 80: E. Kreidolf; p. 80A, 227: Anne Anderson; p. 87: Frank Hart; p. 95: Gaffron; p. 104: Robert E. Lee; p. 107A: C. Allen Gilbert; p. 123A: Pippo; p. 123B, 184, 201: Miriam Story Hurford; p. 124: Howard Butler; p. 126, 177A, 222B: Janet Laura Scott; p. 127, 225: A. Parkhurst; p. 129B: R. F. Outeault; p. 130: Neuf A. Rien; p. 133A: Armande Martin; p. 136A, 162B, 164, 180B, 193C, 200A: Ellen H. Clapsaddle; p. 137: Katharine Gassaway; p. 139: Harrison Cady; p. 140: Win Pleniger; p. 141B: Oliver Herford; p. 148: Rachel Robinson Elmer; p. 151: Hazel Frazee; p. 157, 198B: Margaret Evans Price; p. 158: Herbert Paus; p. 161A: Edith A. Cubitt; p. 163A: Louis Fancher; p. 168: Edith S. Truman; p. 171: Forrest W. Orr; p. 174: B. Butler; p. 178, 188: Raphael Kirchner; p. 179: Robert Lawson; p. 182B: E. Dorothy Rees; p. 194C: M. G. Hays; p. 195: L. M. Glackens; p. 199B: Dorothy Henderson; p. 202A: Elizabeth Cadie; p. 202C: Alice Bolam Preston; p 207: Dorothy Hope Smith; p. 208: H. Hoecher; p. 213B: Ethel Delvees; p. 217B: Albertine Randall Wheelay; p. 230: Russell Sambrook; p. 234: Rowell; p. 243: Frances Tipron Hunter; p. 256: Lawson Wood